PUBLICATIONS OF THE UNIVERSITY OF
MANCHESTER

No. CCLXXV

THEOLOGICAL SERIES No. V

THE ORIGIN AND SIGNIFICANCE OF
THE NEW TESTAMENT BAPTISM

Published by the University of Manchester at The University Press
(H. M. McKechnie, M.A., Secretary), 8–10 Wright Street, Manchester 1 5

THE
ORIGIN AND SIGNIFICANCE
OF THE
NEW TESTAMENT BAPTISM

BY

H. G. MARSH, M.A., B.D.

MANCHESTER UNIVERSITY PRESS

1941

TO THE MEMORY OF

MY MOTHER,

WHO BROUGHT ME IN CHILDHOOD TO RECEIVE THE
SACRAMENT OF BAPTISM,
AND TAUGHT ME BY HER LIFE ITS TRUE SIGNIFICANCE

CONTENTS

PREFACE

THIS book is offered as a small contribution to the study of a rite which, with certain notable exceptions, is observed in all parts of the Christian Church. Yet there is little doubt that among the least understood parts of our Faith must be included the doctrine of the first sacrament. Some modern scholars indeed regard the rite as a relic of paganism which the natural conservatism of religion has preserved in the twentieth century. The pastoral experience of the writer compels the admission that the actions of many who seek baptism for themselves or for their children resemble more a tribute to superstition than the seeking of a Christian experience.

The history of the early Church shows that baptism held an important place in the missionary work of the apostolic age. This sacrament was given a prominence by the first apostles and evangelists which implied not only that they believed the recipient obtained something of real value, but even something which was essential to the full Christian life. The how and why may be matters of controversy; the New Testament states the fact of the call to baptism. In the light of this teaching we do well to ask ourselves the reason of this attitude. Have modern ignorance, indifference and neglect blinded us to the meaning of a doctrine which held such a position in the eyes of those who proclaimed the Gospel of their Master that they classed it with faith and repentance as among " the first principles of Christ " ?

It will be obvious to all who consult the short bibliography, at the end, that no attempt has been made to give a comprehensive list of writings on the subject. Indeed, the writer makes no claim to be able to furnish such a list. At a time when strict economy of space was needed it was felt that the most useful contribution in the matter of bibliography was to give not merely a selected list of books and articles dealing specifically with New Testament baptism and the problems connected with it, but out of many books read to include only those which seemed to contribute something distinctive to the subject. The author regrets that present war conditions have prevented him from securing a copy of *Die Taufe im neuen Testament*, by W. Koch, 1921 which, if read, would probably have been included in the list. Other books dealing with various matters arising out of the discussion are referred to in the notes.

One personal note must be added. I cannot close this foreword without acknowledging my indebtedness to many friends. Among these I must mention by name the Rev. G. G. Hornby, M.A., B.D., who kindly consented to read through the proof, and the Rev. Wilbert F. Howard, M.A., D.D., of Handsworth College, Birmingham, whose encouragement, counsel and help have meant so much at this time.

H. G. MARSH.

MANCHESTER, 1940.

CHAPTER I

INTRODUCTION

THE modern critical study of Christian doctrine has resulted in a serious challenge to the attitude which for many centuries was the only one adopted by the vast majority of those who considered the subject. It is no longer possible to take for granted a belief in the uniqueness of the Christian teaching, or even that Judaism was the faith in which many of its doctrines found their origin. The challenge has come mainly from the side of Comparative Religion. This has emphasized the similarity of early Christian thought to that of contemporary ethnic, and especially oriental, cults.[1] While there has been a reaction against the extreme views of some of the exponents of the theory of borrowing, mainly in regard to the excessive claims made for the influence of the mysteries,[2] it is still true to say that many scholars

[1] The literature on the subject is so enormous that it is impossible here to do anything more than refer to works which may serve as an introduction to the study. Such are : A. D. Nock, " Early Gentile Christianity and its Hellenistic Background ", in *Essays on the Trinity and the Incarnation*, edited by A. E. J. Rawlinson, 1928 ; A. Schweitzer, *Paul and His Interpreters*, E.T., 1912, chap. vii ; E. Hatch, *The Influence of Greek Ideas and Usages upon the Christian Church*, 1890 ; S. Angus, *The Mystery Religions and Christianity*, which contains an excellent bibliography to date, 1925 ; R. Reitzenstein, *Die hellenistischen Mysterienreligionen*, 3rd ed., 1927 ; P. Wendland, *Die hellenistisch-römische Kultur in ihren Beziehungen zu Judentum und Christentum*, 2nd ed., 1912.

[2] So far as the mystery cults are concerned the failure to connect with the early Christian sacraments is admitted by

believe that the tracing of the origin of early Christian sacramentalism to non-Christian and non-Jewish sources must be included as one of the assured results of modern critical studies of contemporary religious faiths.

This belief is based not merely on the recognition of striking pagan resemblances to the Christian rites, but also on the fact that there are grave difficulties in the way of the assumption that this part of Christian teaching was developed from Judaism. The late F. C. Burkitt [1] expressed the judgment of many scholars when he wrote : " The Christian sacraments are certainly not part of the inheritance taken from Judaism. They are not derived from the Temple worship, nor, except in minor details, from the services of the Synagogue."

Reitzenstein himself in regard to the Lord's Supper (*Die h.M.*, 3rd ed., p. 81). But the case for baptism is little better. The passage from the papyrus letter of the second century, which appeared to offer a sure proof of the early connection of the ideas of baptism and salvation in the mysteries has been subjected to a criticism which is very damaging from this point of view. The argument built upon the presumed meaning of βαπτιζώμεθα has been shown to be very doubtful. See H. A. A. Kennedy, *St. Paul and the Mystery Religions*, 1913, p. 231 f. Even Reitzenstein, who pointed out the importance of this passage in the second edition of *Die h.M.* (1920), pp. 85 f., abandoned the argument in the third edition (1927), p. 207. Tertullian makes reference to the rites of Isis, Mithras, and the Apollinarian and Eleusinian games (*De Baptismo*, v), but if the bath of purification is similar to that described by Apuleius (*Metamorphoses*, xi. 23) it would appear to have little connection with the Christian rite of baptism. It is also difficult to accept the process of reasoning by which the Dionysian or Orphic initiatory rites are connected with the baptismal symbolism of the early Christian communities, as R. Eisler supposes (*Orpheus the Fisher*, p. 69). The fact that in some of these rites there are points of resemblance to Christian practices should not blind us to the essential differences.

[1] *Legacy of Israel*, 1928, p. 71. Equally emphatic is H. J. D. Astley, article on " Primitive Sacramentalism ", *The Modern Churchman*, XVI, no. 6, Oct. 1926 ; also K. Lake, *Earlier Epistles of St. Paul*, 1911, p. 215.

The denial of a Jewish origin for Christian sacramentalism certainly serves one very useful purpose. It reminds us that many of the ideas which we were accustomed to regard as unique in Christianity or, at the most, shared with the earlier faith of Judaism, were common to contemporary pagan faiths. Christianity grew and flourished in an environment which was able to give a favourable reception to its teaching because much that it contained found an echo in the heathen world in which the apostles preached their gospel.[1] This fact should cause little surprise. Human needs and hopes are very similar among all races of mankind, and so are the means by which men have sought to meet and answer these same needs and hopes.

In attempting to reconstruct the early Church teaching we must recognize from the first one serious difficulty. The actual evidence with which we have to deal is often tantalizingly meagre, and at times almost non-existent. This paucity of material has led many scholars into an attitude of pessimism in regard to results. We have Harnack's summing up of the position : " The origin of a series of the most important Christian customs and ideas is involved in an obscurity which in all probability will never be cleared up. Though one part of these ideas may be pointed out in the epistles of Paul, yet the question must frequently remain unanswered, whether he found them in existence or formed them independently, and accordingly the other question, whether they are exclusively indebted to the activity of Paul for their spread and naturalization in Christendom. What was the original conception of baptism ? Did Paul develop independently his own conception ? What significance had it in the following period ? When and where did baptism in the name of the Father, Son and Holy Spirit arise, and how did it make its way in Christendom ? In what way were views about the saving value of Christ's death developed

[1] See the evidence of A. D. Nock, *op. cit.*, pp. 111–20.

3

alongside of Paul's system ? . . . When were baptism and the Lord's Supper grouped together ? " [1]

In seeking to avoid the pessimism suggested by this paragraph there is a danger that the available evidence may be studied in too subjective a mood, and inferences drawn which depend for their support more on the personal predilections of the student than on the solid proofs afforded by the documents studied. This temptation is very great in dealing with questions which concern matters of faith. Thus there is the difficult task of trying to steer between the Scylla of solutions, whose chief merit lies in the fact that they are congenial to the finder rather than in their truth, and the Charybdis of negations, in which in despair the seeker abandons all attempts at an answer on the ground of insufficient evidence, and neglects to consider the modicum of truth, however small, which this evidence despite its scantiness may suggest.

In discussing the origin of the Christian sacraments it is impossible to ignore the similarities found in pagan cults. But while the possibility of heathen influences may be accepted our search for origins must not begin abroad in the cults which reveal only a few resemblances and connections with Christianity. It should commence nearer home. We cannot allow ourselves to forget that Judaism was the cradle in which the infant faith was placed by Providence, and it is most natural to begin there in our search for evidence. We may admit the striking likeness of some Christian rites to acts performed in mystery cults, but a mere outward similarity is not a definite proof of connection. Is there anything in Judaism which can offer a possible explanation of the sacramental teaching, or does the philosophical basis of the more ancient faith present a difficulty which closes the door against any search in that direction ?

First of all it should be recognized that much of the evidence against the Jewish origin of the sacraments has

[1] A. Harnack, *History of Dogma*, E.T., 1894, I, pp. 132-3.

been negative rather than positive in character. This is due mainly to the fact that we have had little reliable information of the conditions of Judaism in the period when the Gospel was being preached as a new message in the world. In recent years a closer study of rabbinic and other Jewish literature has enabled us to feel that despite the paucity of the evidence we are not without some definite proofs of certain Jewish antecedents of the Christian sacraments.[1]

Before considering these it is necessary to refer to an argument of which much use has been made in discounting the Jewish origin—that the conception of sacrament is foreign to Jewish thought. The difficulty which is presented by Jewish methods of thinking is not to be avoided, but it must not be exaggerated. Gavin points out that the failure to discover the theory does not justify us in denying the fact. It is possible to allow that the sacramental phraseology and definitions belong to " an un-Jewish environment " and indeed are " congenial to the world of nascent Gentile Christianity " and yet to realize that there are strong arguments for maintaining the position that " the essential germinal principles of a sacramental outlook on the universe were not only tolerated by Judaism, but even lay intimately at its centre ".[2]

While Judaism had a kind of practical dualism in its teaching about demons and angels, the evil impulse and the good, it had no dualistic philosophy in the Hellenistic sense of a distinction between material and spiritual. Judaism never accepted, as did some other faiths, the idea that the visible material world was evil in its origin and nature. God was its Creator, and He " saw that it was good ". The Jew also believed and taught that it was possible to use material means in the furtherance of closer relationship between man and the unseen God. Thus

[1] F. Gavin, *The Jewish Antecedents of the Christian Sacraments*, 1928. I. Abrahams, *Studies*, I, 1917.
[2] F. Gavin, *op. cit.*, pp. 22 ff.

Jesus, who had been trained in a Jewish environment, touched a sympathetic chord in the minds of His hearers when He linked together in His teaching the visible world and the spiritual and invisible realities. The parable of the lilies of the field carried conviction to men and women accustomed to connect God with the world He had made. It is no exaggeration to say that the relationship of Jesus to nature took on a sacramental character. In this Jesus may be regarded as bringing to expression ideas which were in complete harmony with the thought of His people. We may indeed affirm with confidence that the Jewish philosophical position does not reject sacramental conceptions. It allows for the consideration of any facts which may be brought forward from Jewish practice in support of the idea that the sacrament of Christian baptism finds its roots in the faith in which, speaking from the human standpoint, Jesus learned the truths of God.

It is not within the purview of the present study to discuss the general philosophic position in regard to sacramentalism. The main desire is to get to the facts relating to the early history of the Christian sacrament of baptism and the doctrine connected with them. But, as a preliminary to this, it is necessary to prove that the path, so far as it relates to any approach to Judaism, is not blocked already by hindering philosophic conceptions. This starting-point is of great importance since, while it is easy to recognize a similarity in Christian and Hellenistic ways of thinking, the contrast between Judaism and much of the teaching of the early Church has been more readily assumed than it has been proved.

The ideas of holiness and cleanness, and their corresponding negatives, held a very prominent place in Hebrew religious beliefs. Much of this thought may be regarded as a survival from the beliefs of primitive Semitic religion, or at least suggestive of close affinity with it, but some of the laws represent a more advanced stage. They must

6

have come from a protest of the higher religion of Israel against heathenism.[1] Later religious developments in the history of Israel are noteworthy for the increasing emphasis on the distinction between true and false ideas in worship, and the attempt to exclude all forms of adoration other than that of Yahweh. The effort to preserve the religion from pagan contamination, so noticeable in the post-exilic period, became still more marked in the years following the Maccabean deliverance. A witness to this is found in the literature of the period which reveals an increased sensitiveness to the uncleanness of the Gentiles. There can be traced through Ezra, Daniel, the books of the Apocrypha and the Pseudepigrapha a growing spirit of exclusiveness. It was inevitable that this attitude should find expression in the legislation, and Gavin calls attention to such legislative acts dating from about 150 B.C. to the fall of Jerusalem, A.D. 70.[2]

This emphasis on the distinction between the Jew and the Gentile was reflected not only in the laws but also in the greater attention paid to the religious acts which marked the passage of the convert from heathenism to Judaism.[3] The rites were three in number: circumcision, sacrifice and baptism. While there is no doubt about the early prevalence of the first and second, there has been much discussion whether baptism had been adopted in the period immediately preceding the birth of Christ. We have indisputable evidence of the employment of the tebilah, or bath of purity for proselytes, from the first century of the Christian era. Regarding the earlier period we have no conclusive proof. But we believe that

[1] A. S. Peake, *HDB*, IV, p. 827a.

[2] F. Gavin, *op. cit.*, *Lecture II*. An interesting reference to this exclusive attitude is found in Gal. ii. 15, where Paul recalls his early Pharisaic position, which regarded Gentile and sinner as words that were almost synonymous: " We may be Jews by birth and not Gentile sinners " (Moffatt).

[3] J. Juster, *Les Juifs dans l'Empire Romain*, 1914, I, p. 255, n. 1.

B

the arguments advanced in favour of the existence of such a rite at that time bring an evidence that is cumulative in its effect, and make us feel fairly sure that proselyte baptism was practised before the days of Jesus Christ.

We would mention first of all the probability of such a rite. The Hebrew religion had always stressed the use of water as a means of cleansing from ceremonial uncleanness.[1] Foreign lands as well as their peoples were unclean in a ritual sense. Every Jew who had become ritually unclean was required to undergo some rite of purification before being allowed to take part in the acts of worship.[2] It is not surprising, therefore, to find that a similar rite of cleansing was expected from a Gentile before he could be permitted to share the privileges of the Jewish religious and social life.

Certain faiths appeal to certain types of mind, and the strong monotheism of Judaism caused it to have considerable influence and win many converts among other nations. But it was not only a sincere religious conviction that led men to seek admission into Judaism. It is possible that at some periods social and economic reasons were even more potent than those of religion in securing converts. There seems little doubt that many sought the status of proselyte from motives similar to those which in modern times prompt foreigners to seek naturlisation in the country in which they live. These secular motives probably operated most powerfully in those

[1] E.g. Exod. xxix. 4, a preliminary to the consecration of the priests ; Lev. xvi. 4, a preparation for the Day of Atonement. Perhaps more significant are the prophetic references which give the idea an ethical implication : Isa. i. 16 ; Ezek. xxxvi. 24 ff. ; Zech. xiii. 1 ; cf. *Fragments of a Zadokite Work*, I, 17 ; *AP*, II, p. 802. In Numb. xix. 18 we have the use of טבל in connection with water purification. As a technical term for cleansing from ritual impurity the word belongs to later Judaism. Judith performs her tebilah, or ritual washing, at the fountain (*Judith* xii. 7).

[2] Numb. xix. ; cf. xxxi. 19–24 ; Lev. xiv. 8 ; xv. ; Exod. xxix. 4 ; xxx. 17–20.

crises of the Jewish national life when the lax relationships between Jews and strangers were frowned upon, and attempts were made to introduce more stringent regulations. Gentiles who had enjoyed through the laxity considerable social and commercial relationships with Jews suddenly found themselves deprived of these by the strictness with which the laws of uncleanness were enforced. In the great national movement under the Maccabees we find an attempt to enforce the ritual laws in order to secure purity of religion and race. Although there is no proof of the existence of the tebilah at the time of the Maccabean revival one may surmise that it was at such a period that the question of proselyte baptism would become urgent.

The actual date of the tebilah is unknown. There is proof that it existed at the close of the first century A.D., and this leaves us with a choice of three periods for its commencement. It must have originated before Christian baptism, at the same time as this rite, or immediately after it. The second or third choices can be ruled out as most unlikely in view of one important fact—the hostility of the Jews to Christianity. The eagerness of the Jews in disavowing any connection with the Christians—of which the scene at Ephesus described in the Acts [1] provides an excellent illustration—makes it scarcely credible that the leaders of the Jewish faith should have adopted a rite which, through its extensive use in the Christian Church, must have led inevitably to a confusion regarding the two faiths in the minds of the authorities. It is even less likely that this rite was borrowed from Christianity.

We come now to the more positive arguments. The first concerns a statement of Epictetus, the celebrated Stoic philosopher, who belonged to the latter half of the first century A.D. He discusses the question of Greeks who are called—or call themselves—Jews, Syrians, or

[1] Acts xix. 33.

Egyptians, on the ground that they have accepted the religious customs of one of these peoples. According to the statement of Epictetus the distinguishing feature of Judaism is baptism. To quote his words : " Whenever we see a man wavering, we are accustomed to say : ' He is not a Jew but pretends to be one.' But when he accepts the experience of the baptized and chosen, then he is in name and reality a Jew. So we also are pseudo-baptists, in name, Jews, but in fact ", etc.[1] The obvious interpretation of this passage is that which sees in it a recognition of baptism as the special rite used for converts to Judaism.

In the *Mishnah*[2] there is recorded an account of a debate on proselyte baptism between the two schools of Hillel and Shammai. It would seem that this took place at a time when the worship in the Temple was still being maintained. There is a probability that the argument is ' merely scholastic ", as the Jewish scholar Abrahams

[1] *Dissert. Epictet.* ii. 9, Arrian. There is an interesting discussion of the meaning of this passage by Reitzenstein, who denies the early origin of the tebilah (*Die Vorgeschichte der christlichen Taufe*, 1929, pp. 232-3). He suggests that τὸ πάθος τὸ τοῦ βεβαμμένου καὶ ᾑρημένου refers to a sect of ascetics and has no connection with the rite of the proselytes. This interpretation, he thinks, is supported by the use of the term " pseudo-baptists " (παραβαπτισταί) and also by the words in which Josephus refers to the title given to John ὁ ἐπικαλούμενος βαπτιστής (*Antiq.*, xviii, 5, 2), which he understands as implying that Josephus connected him with this sect. In maintaining a late date for proselyte baptism Reitzenstein appears to ignore the Rabbinic testimony. See *TWNT*, I, p. 533 and note 31.

[2] Pesahim, viii, 8. Eduy., v, 2. " The School of Shammai say : If a man became a proselyte on the day before Passover, he may immerse himself and consume his Passover-offering in the evening " (*The Mishnah*, trans. H. Danby, 1933, p. 148). Edersheim thought this passage was a proof that at that time—previous to Christ—the baptism of proselytes was customary. He admitted that " the case supposed by the School of Shammai would, however, have been impossible, since, according to Rabbinic directions, a certain time must have elapsed between circumcision and baptism " (*Jesus the Messiah*, II, 1901, p. 747).

maintained.[1]   But the very possibility of such a scholastic debate supports the conclusion that it had to do with a rite which had had a fairly long existence.   For his own belief in the early origin of the tebilah Abrahams attached more importance to the statement in the Palestinian Talmud in which Rabbi Eleazar ben Jacob recorded the conversion of some Roman soldiers to Judaism.[2]   The date of this incident is uncertain ; A.D. 67 has been suggested.

Not one of these statements is absolutely convincing evidence for an early existence of the tebilah.   Taken together they have a certain cumulative effect which supports the contention that the tebilah had its origin in the pre-Christian era.   Further than this we cannot go with our present knowledge.   The origin of the rite is hidden in obscurity.[3]   But it should be recognized that the obscurity is due in all probability to the fact that the tebilah was a natural development from the laws of uncleanness, and in its early stages would not suggest or be felt to suggest any innovation from the usual Levitical laws relating to purification.   Some have seen a reference to the baptism of proselytes in the *Sybilline Oracles*, IV, line 165 : " wash your whole bodies in ever-running rivers ".   But the late date of this book renders the quotation of little value in helping to determine the time of the origin of proselyte baptism.[4]

[1] *Studies*, I, p. 36 f.

[2] T. J. Pesahim, viii. 8.   According to Rabbi Eleazar ben Jacob, these soldiers, after being circumcised on the 14th Nisan, underwent the tebilah on this day and partook of the Paschal lamb in the evening.   Abrahams thought that we must place the incident in the latter half of the first century.   He pointed out that Graetz put it in the year A.D. 67.

[3] This was felt even by our Jewish authorities.   As Gavin says : " When the authorities of the Talmud have to do with this Mishna, their recorded opinions show how the clue to the origin and significance of the rite lay outside their ken " (*op. cit.*, p. 31).

[4] A. Plummer, who quoted it, admitted the lateness (*HDB*, I, p. 239).   R. H. Charles placed it about A.D. 80, and moreover thought that the lustration referred to, as in III, 594,

The absence of any mention of the tebilah in the earlier period is no decisive argument for its late origin. The early laws of uncleanness could easily allow such a rite, and if it was not felt to be an innovation there would be little reason for any special reference to it. There are many references to the laws of uncleanness, and proselyte baptism would be regarded as the application of these laws to Gentiles, the rite being accepted as the obvious purificatory act preliminary to the sacrifice in the Temple. It was when the sacrifices in the Temple were no longer possible that the tebilah might be expected to assume a greater prominence.[1] Its significance would be recognized more clearly when the rite was no longer the way to Temple worship but an end in itself. Abrahams has made the helpful suggestion that it was the application of proselyte baptism to women which contributed most to its increased importance. After the destruction of the Temple the tebilah became the sole initiatory rite for women proselytes, and since these formed the more numerous section of proselytes, baptism would tend to be regarded by the outside world as the more important if not the only rite. It must not be forgotten also that Gentile peoples were familiar with the idea of ritual purifications by water and would be quick to appreciate its value.[2]

was that of the Essenes (*AP*, II, pp. 373, 396). For a further discussion of proselyte baptism see Schürer, *GJV*, III, 4th ed., 1909, pp. 181 ff.; W. Brandt, *Die jüdischen Baptismen*, 1910.

[1] " Though there is no probability that baptism without circumcision was ever adopted by the Palestinian Jews as sufficient for the initiation of proselytes, there is some evidence that baptism, or washing with a religious significance, was emphasised in the Diaspora. It may have been sometimes regarded as sufficient to admit a Gentile as a proselyte, or at least, if followed by a virtuous life, to secure his salvation in the Age to come " (*JLBC*, I, p. 342).

[2] Jewish washings, in common with many Gentile ablutions, have reference only to ritual uncleanness, as is shown by a study of the Mishnah tractate Mikwaoth. See H. Danby, *The Mishnah*, pp. 732–45.

INTRODUCTION

Whatever difficulty we may have in arriving at any decision in regard to the tebilah for the period immediately preceding the birth of Christianity—and it must be borne in mind that our trouble is due as much to the paucity of contemporary Jewish literature as to the lack of evidence in such literature—its importance from the first century onwards is soon realised. Apart from the many references we have detailed accounts of the ceremony.[1] A consideration of these presents us with many striking resemblances to the details of the early Christian rite. A comparison may be made by setting side by side the regulations of the *Mishnah* with the details of Christian baptism supplied by the *Didache*.[2] The meaning of this similarity is of importance in studying the relationship of the two rites. But this similarity is of minor importance compared with the fact—attested by the Gospel writers— that the origin of Christianity was closely associated with the mission of a Jewish teacher, whose work was distinguished by a water rite that Jesus Himself accepted. It is in the study of the baptism offered by John that we may find a valuable contribution to the question of the origin of its Christian counterpart.[3]

[1] These are provided by the tractate on Proselytes (Gerim) and the Tannaitic memoir in the tractate on Levirate Marriages (Yebamoth) of the Babylonian Talmud. Gavin assigns these documents to the second or third centuries A.D. For discussion, see Gavin, *op. cit.*, pp. 31 ff.

[2] F. Gavin, *op. cit.*, p. 42 ; *EBi*, 1914, p. 473. Special value may be attached to this comparison when one bears in mind the anti-Jewish tone of the *Didache*.

[3] There has been much argument as to the relationship of the Christian baptism with that of John. Foakes-Jackson thinks there is probably no direct connection (*JLBC*, I, p. 343). M. Goguel has emphasised the differences between the two (*Au Seuil de l'Évangile Jean-Baptiste*, 1928, pp. 39 ff.). J. Weiss, who thought that proselyte baptism was the prototype of the Christian rite, and yet found a difficulty in the fact that Jews like Paul were baptised, wrote : " It is difficult to assume that this was a reactionary generalization of proselyte baptism. In that case we have to assume a permanent influence of the

baptism of John. This, however, had a somewhat different meaning than did proselyte baptism, for it was administered to Jews living under the Law, and could not thus be taken in the strict sense of being a purification after demoniacal defilement (*The History of Primitive Christianity*, E.T., 1937, II, p. 631). Among those who have contended for a connection between the Johannine and Christian rites are: Rendtorff, *Die Taufe im Urchristentum im Lichte der neueren Forschungen*, 1905, p. 45 ; A. Seeberg, *Die Taufe im neuen Testament*, p. 18 ; E. v. Dobschütz, *Probleme des apostolischen Zeitalters*, 1904, pp. 47 f. Any study of the relationships of the Johannine and Christian baptisms must take into account the problem whether our descriptions of John's rite in the Gospels are too much influenced by Christian conceptions to offer any safe guidance. See Heitmüller, *Im Namen Jesu*, 1903, pp. 272 ff.

CHAPTER II

THE JOHANNINE RITE

THE main and—apart from the brief reference in Josephus—the only primary authority for our knowledge of the life and work of John the Baptist is the New Testament.[1] Even here there is no mention of John outside the Gospels and the Acts of the Apostles. A close study of these references shows, as might be expected, a similarity in the accounts given in the Synoptic Gospels, both in regard to the character and also the actions of John. We may say further that the Acts repeats the

[1] Some have thought that valuable information might be gathered from a study of the literature of the Mandæans. Much has been made of the theory that this ancient sect originated with the direct spiritual descendants of John the Baptist. Despite the arguments of its supporters (R. Bultmann, *Eucharisterion*, 2 Teil, N.T., 1923, pp. 1–26; *ZNTW*, XXIV, 1925, pp. 100–46; R. Reitzenstein, *Die Vorgeschichte der christlichen Taufe*, 1929) the objections brought against them leave the impression that the theory is untenable. It seems most likely that this sect arose considerably later than New Testament times, and its adoption of John the Baptist as its prophet probably dated from the period of the rise of Mohammedanism. W. Brandt made the suggestion that the introduction of the name of the Baptist into their baptismal formula was perhaps the result of the lesson constantly impressed by Roman Catholic missionaries during the 17th century, that their baptism was only the baptism of John mentioned in Acts xviii. 25, xix. 3 (*ERE*, VIII, p. 391). Whatever the origin of the Mandæans, a study of their history is of no value for our purpose. F. C. Burkitt summed up the present critical position : " Mandaism may be interesting in itself, but it is useless to go to it as a key to unlock the mysteries of early Christian development " (*JTS*, April, 1928, pp. 225–35). See E. S. Drower, *The Mandæans of Iraq and Iran*, 1937; A. Loisy,

tradition of the Synoptic Gospels. It includes also some references to disciples of John in incidents which naturally are not found in the Synoptic writings since they occurred after the period covered by these Gospels. In the Fourth Gospel the writer presents us with information differing considerably from that found in the other New Testament books. There are indications which lend colour to the belief that the author is not concerned merely to give an historical portrait of John but, as in other parts of his book, is theologising and using the figure of John as a foil for his picture of Jesus. Yet although the tendency writing in this Gospel is obvious the recognition of the fact need not imply that we feel the matter it contains lacks historicity. It calls rather for a careful examination of the incidents and their interpretation. As is the case with other parts of this book, it is possible that the very differences from the story of the Synoptic Gospels may be due to the employment of different sources and because of this it may offer a valuable contribution to a study of the history of John.[1]

The Synoptic Gospels themselves give us no impartial objective picture of the life of the Baptist. This is natural when we consider the object of these writings. No ancient authors accepted the modern theory of complete detachment in the writing of history, and the

Le Mandéisme et les Origines chrétiennes, 1934 ; M. Goguel, Jean-Baptiste, pp. 113–35 ; H. Odeberg, Die mandäische Religionsanschauung, 1930 ; W. F. Howard, The Fourth Gospel in Recent Criticism and Interpretation, 1931, pp. 24, 92 ff. ; W. F. Howard, " The Fourth Gospel and Mandæan Gnosticism ", London Quarterly Review, Jan. 1927 ; Articles in ZNTW, by E. Peterson, " Bemerkungen zur mandäischen Literatur ", XXV, 1926, pp. 236 ff. ; " Urchristentum und Mandäismus ", XXVII, 1928, pp. 55 ff. ; by M. Lidzbarski, " Mandäische Fragen ", XXVI, 1927, pp. 70 ff. ; " Alter und Heimat der mandäischen Religion ", XXVII, 1928, pp. 321 ff.

[1] The work of M. Goguel, Jean-Baptiste, furnishes a striking illustration of the important information which may be gathered from a study of the Fourth Gospel.

supreme interest of the writers of the Gospels was the
story of Jesus, who, they claimed, was the Son of God.
The place of John was decided by the relationship of
himself and his work to that claim. One may go even
further and agree with the statement of a modern com-
mentator that there is in the first three Gospels " a pro-
gressive tendency in the Christian tradition to draw the
Baptist, as it were, more fully within the circle of the
Christian movement, and to represent him, more and
more exclusively, as having been consciously a forerunner and herald of Jesus Christ ".[1] But although most
of the New Testament references bear witness to this
tendency, and in the Fourth Gospel we see the extreme
position, the danger of exaggeration must be avoided.
As far as the Gospel of Mark is concerned one feels that
there is little justification for the sweeping statement of
Loisy that " tous les passages du Nouveau Testament où
il est parlé de Jean sont dominés par une préoccupation
commune, qui est d'exploiter ou simplement de neutra-
liser, pour l'avantage du christianisme, Jean et les
souvenirs ou idées qui s'attachaient à son nom ".[2]
Such a conclusion fails to explain some of the most
important facts. Among these we must include Mark's
account of the baptism of Jesus, which has a special
significance in view of the treatment of the subject in the
other Synoptic writings.[3] Later apocryphal Gospels
and other early Church writings attest the difficulties
which this narrative was felt to create. We have too the

[1] A. E. J. Rawlinson, *St. Mark. Westminster Commentary*,
1925, p. 8.

[2] *Le Mandéisme et les Origines chrétiennes*, 1934, p. 45.

[3] Mark i. 9–11. Matthew (iii. 13–17) makes the incident
the occasion for John's recognition of his need of baptism by
Jesus, while the perfunctory manner in which Luke (iii. 21, 22)
deals with it called forth the remark of Plummer (*St. Luke,
ICC*, s.v.) : " It is remarkable that this, which seems to us to
be the main fact, should be expressed thus incidentally by
a participle." The Fourth Gospel omits the story.

detailed account of the incidents leading up to the martyrdom of John, which reveal an interest in the subject apart from that which concerns merely John's relations with Jesus. That the latter was the chief concern is natural ; but the way in which the points of difference as well as those of agreement are narrated is not without significance. Indeed, some have read into the references to disagreement a greater importance, and, on the principle that the writers would endeavour to soften as far as possible the notes of discord, have argued that these passages [1] are evidence of a keen rivalry existing in the early days of Christianity between the disciples of John and the followers of Jesus.[2]

Much or little can be read into these statements according to the personal inclination of the reader. But without more definite historical evidence there would seem to be little support for the extravagant claims based upon them. By themselves these references merely prove a disinclination among the disciples of John, and probably even of John himself, to accept unquestioningly the claims of Jesus. This was a quite natural development, and indeed almost inevitable unless we assume some miraculous intervention of Providence to obviate such human difficulties. It is a feature of Mark's Gospel that there is no attempt to cover up unpleasant facts. From it we learn that even the mother of Jesus did not always understand His ways, and this is true also of the disciples.[3] That

[1] Matth. ix. 14 f. ; xi. 2 ff. ; Mark ii. 18 ; Luke v. 33 ; vii. 18 ; John i. 6 f. ; iii. 23 ff. ; iv. 1, 2. The references to John's disciples in the Acts probably denote Christians belonging to the earliest period, who had received the original form of Christian baptism, which was very similar to that of John. See H. Lietzmann, *The Beginnings of the Christian Church*, E.T., 1937, pp. 80, 81.

[2] M. Goguel, *op. cit.*, pp. 293–4 ; M. Dibelius, *Die urchristliche Überlieferung von Johannes der Taufer*, pp. 13 ff.

[3] Mark iii. 21, 31, 35 ; viii. 33 ; x. 26, 32, 38, etc. In considering the Gospels as historical documents it is satisfactory

a certain amount of rivalry should develop between the disciples of John and of Jesus was to be expected. One can appreciate the contention of Lietzmann that the subordination of the Forerunner to Jesus in the Fourth Gospel is so expressed because the author was acquainted with churches of John's followers.[1] Much stress has been laid upon passages in the Acts which relate to Apollos and the men of Ephesus (xviii. 24 ff. ; xix. 1–7). These have been quoted in support of a polemical interpretation of the Johannine references in the Fourth Gospel since it has been pointed out that this Gospel is supposed to have originated in Ephesus. But such arguments do not warrant the theory of a general conflict between rival bodies, which must surely have left a deeper impression on both the writings and history of the Church.

While the apologetic purpose of the passages in the Fourth Gospel must be admitted, it should be recognized that this is true of the Gospel as a whole and not merely of those references relating to John. The incidents in the Acts are capable of other explanations which will be discussed later. Concerning the relations of the two bands of disciples it is difficult to imagine that there could be any lengthy conflict. The merging of the Johannine movement in that of Jesus was a natural process. John never claimed to be the founder of a new party. His whole work was preparatory for someone greater. One of the most authentic parts of his message is surely that, recorded by all four Gospels, in which he is declared to be the voice of one crying in the wilderness calling men to prepare for the coming of the Lord. This attitude is in direct contrast with the tremendous claim made by Jesus, and later by His disciples for Him. Nowhere in the New Testament is there any mention of

to recognize this inclusion of incidents that might be regarded as disadvantageous for the purpose of the story, which was to present Jesus as the Son of God.

[1] H. Lietzmann, *op. cit.*, p. 303.

a counter-claim by the disciples of John for their master,[1] although the silence of the New Testament in regard to any counter-claim does not mean that there was no such expression. But while a few men may have used extravagant words about John the mass of his followers must have been under no illusion concerning his true position. For those followers of John who refused to accept the Messianic claim of Jesus there was an alternative, but it was not the ascription of this title to their master. It was —to use John's own phrase to Jesus—to look for another (Matth. xi. 3 ; Luke vii. 19). From its very nature there was no permanency about the position of the disciples of John, and those who, according to the author of the Fourth Gospel, guided by the Baptist himself (i. 35–7), left him to become disciples of Jesus, were but carrying to its logical conclusion the teaching of their former master.

In considering the character and work of the Baptist it is important to compare the accounts given in the three Synoptic writings. It should be noted that in each the passage from Isaiah xl. 3, serves as an introduction, and that Mark precedes this by a quotation from Malachi iii. 1. This latter quotation is not found in the parallel passages of Luke and Matthew, but the writers of these books are familiar with its application to the mission of John, for they use it later when giving Christ's own description of the work of the Baptist (Matth. xi. 10 ; Luke vii. 27). The Fourth Gospel also applies the passage from Isaiah xl. to the ministry of the Forerunner, but makes the words a part of John's own message to the people in explaining

[1] Support for the belief that there was a counter-claim has been found by some in the words of the Fourth evangelist : " He was not the light, but came that he might bear witness of the light. There was the true light " (i. 8, 9). *The Clementine Recognitions* contain passages (I, liv, lx) in which the writer affirms that some of John's disciples proclaimed their own master as the Christ. It is probable, however, that the number of these disciples was insignificant.

his position to those who sought to know the purpose and character of his work.

Mark i. 4–8	*Matthew* iii. 1–12	*Luke* iii. 2–17
John came, who baptized *(ὁ βαπτίζων)*[1] in the wild e r n e s s, a n d preached the baptism of repentance unto remission of sins *(κηρύσσων βάπτισμα μετανοίας εἰς ἄφεσιν ἁμαρτιῶν)*. And there went out unto him all the country of Judæa, and all they of Jerusalem ; and they were baptized of him in the river Jordan, confessing their sins. And John was clothed with camel's hair, and had a leathern girdle about his loins, and did eat locusts and wild honey. And he	In those days cometh John the Baptist *(παραγίνεται Ἰωάννης ὁ βαπτιστὴς)*. . . saying Repent ye ; for the kingdom of heaven is at hand. . . . And they were baptized of him in the river Jordan, confessing their sins . . . he said unto them . . . I indeed baptize you with water unto repentance ; but He that cometh after me . . . He shall baptize you with the Holy Ghost and with fire *(ἐγὼ μὲν ὑμᾶς βαπτίζω ἐν ὕδατι εἰς μετάνοιαν . . . αὐτὸς ὑμᾶς βαπτίσει ἐν πνεύματι ἁγίῳ καὶ πυρί)*.	. . . the word of God came unto John the son of Zacharias in the wilderness. And he came into all the region round about Jordan preaching the baptism of repentance unto remission of sins *(καὶ ἦλθεν εἰς πᾶσαν τὴν περίχωρον τοῦ Ἰορδάνου κηρύσσων βάπτισμα μετανοίας εἰς ἄφεσιν ἁμαρτιῶν)*. . . . He said therefore to the multitudes that went out to be baptized of him *(τοῖς ἐκπορευομένοις ὄχλοις βαπτισθῆναι ὑπ' αὐτοῦ)*. . . . And as the people were in expectation . . . John answered,

---

[1] There is a difference of text in Mark i. 4. T. K. Cheyne (*EBi*, 1914, p. 2499 note) maintained that it was very improbable that ὁ βαπτίζων was a synonym for ὁ βαπτιστής. He thought that " the article slipped in through the influence of the familiar phrase ". H. B. Swete (*The Gospel according to St. Mark*, 3rd ed., 1909, p. 3, note) accepted the synonymic use and treated the participle as a substantival use without reference to time (cf. Matth. xxvii. 40 ; Gal. i. 23). The usage is repeated in vi. 14, 24, the latter instance being followed immediately by the usual noun βαπτιστής. Moulton, who discussed this as an example of the timeless present participle, believed that the phrase was less of a technical term than the noun, but otherwise was synonymous (*Grammar of N.T. Greek*, I, p. 127).

Mark i. 4–8	*Matthew* iii. 1–12	*Luke* iii. 2–17
preached saying, There cometh after me He that is mightier than I, the latchet of Whose shoes I am not worthy to stoop down and unloose. I baptized you with water; but He shall baptize you with the Holy Ghost (*ἐγώ ἐβάπτισα ὑμᾶς ὕδατι αὐτὸς δὲ βαπτίσει ὑμᾶς πνεύματι ἁγίῳ*).[1]		saying unto them all, I indeed baptize you with water (*ἐγὼ μὲν ὕδατι βαπτίζω ὑμᾶς*) . . . He shall baptize you with the Holy Ghost and with fire (*αὐτὸς ὑμᾶς βαπτίσει ἐν πνεύματι ἁγίῳ καὶ πυρί*).

Certain words and phrases occur in slightly different forms in all the accounts. First, there is the name. Matthew has " John the Baptist " ; Mark gives " John the Baptizer ", and the words in Luke are more explicit, " John the son of Zacharias ". The second important point concerns the characterisation of the Forerunner's work and message. In Matthew this reads : " Repent ye ; for the kingdom of heaven is at hand . . . and they were baptized of him in the river Jordan confessing their sins." The account in Mark is : " John came who baptized in the wilderness and preached the baptism of repentance unto remission of sins . . . and they were baptized of him in the river Jordan, confessing their

---

[1] Swete thought that some distinction was implied in Mark's use of the dative alone when compared with the employment of *ἐν* in the parallel passages. But evidence derived from a study of the Greek of this period suggests that it is unlikely that any real difference was intended. See Moulton, *op. cit.*, I, p. 104. In support of this we may note that while Mark has simply the dative, and Matthew and John the preposition also, in Luke and the Acts we find *ὕδατι* . . . *ἐν πνεύματι ἁγίῳ*. It is possible that the variation in Luke and Acts may be due in part to a certain stereotyping of the formula *ἐν πνεύματι ἁγίῳ*.

sins." Luke says: "He came . . . preaching the
baptism of repentance unto remission of sins."

The last parallel to be noted is John's own estimate of
his baptism. In Matthew this is given as: "I indeed
baptize you with water unto repentance . . . He shall
baptize you with Holy Spirit and fire"; in Mark:
"I baptized you with water, but He shall baptize you
with the Holy Spirit", while in Luke the words are:
"I indeed baptize you with water . . . He shall baptize
you with Holy Spirit and fire." This characterization of
John's baptism is repeated three times in the Acts of the
Apostles (i. 5; xi. 16; xix. 4). In the Fourth Gospel,
John the Baptist replies to those who seek his credentials
in words very similar to those mentioned, "I baptize with
water", but he does not follow this directly by a reference
to the Spirit baptism of his Successor. He adds instead
a confession of his own inferiority (i. 26, 27). That the
thought of Spirit baptism is in his mind, however, is
shown by the fact that in verse 33 of the same chapter
he refers again to his own water baptism and follows
immediately with a mention of the Spirit baptism (i. 33).

A study of these references in the Gospels and the Acts
enables us to get a fairly definite outline of the Forerunner's mission. His baptism may be regarded as
distinguished by five characteristics:

1. It had an eschatological value and was conceived as
preparatory to the coming Messianic Age (Mark i. 7).
This is the tenor of the Old Testament quotations which
the Synoptic writers use as an introduction to the description of the Baptist's work. There is a likelihood that the
introductory passages from the prophecies were given
not merely because they expressed the popular opinion
of John, but also because they were actual quotations
from the message of John when he sought to explain his
function to the people. This is definitely asserted in the
Fourth Gospel (i. 23). But whatever reason led to the
inclusion of the prophetic quotations their presence serves

to keep before us the significance of the prophetic background of the new teacher.

The summary of John's preaching is given by the writer of the first Gospel in words identical with those which he uses afterwards to describe the message of Jesus : " Repent ye, for the kingdom of Heaven is at hand." [1] No other New Testament writer states this so directly. The proclamation of the coming Kingdom was no new teaching. Although the actual phrase " the kingdom of God " is not found in the Old Testament the utterances of later prophets such as Isaiah (xxiv.–xxvii.), Joel, Zechariah, Obadiah (verses 16–21) and Malachi testify to the prevalence of the conception. Even more prominently does it appear in the considerable amount of apocalyptic writings which came into existence before the close of the pre-Christian era, and of which one, Daniel, is found even in the canon of the Old Testament.

These apocalyptic writings have great value as witnesses to the thought and aspirations of the time in which they were written, but the quality of the literature is very uneven. It touches both the highest and lowest levels in style, prophetic inspiration, insight and thought. Yet the books furnish an invaluable knowledge of Jewish religious and political ideals in that period which saw the beginnings of Christianity, for they were written during the three hundred years which extended from the closing half of the third century B.C. to the days before the fall of Jerusalem.[2] It is necessary to lay emphasis on the

[1] See note A at the end of the chapter.

[2] " From 200 B.C. to 70 A.D. the religious and political ideals that really shaped the history of Judaism found their expression in this literature " (R. H. Charles, *EBi*, p. 215). Although modern critical opinion might demand some qualification of this statement, there is no doubt about the influence of this literature among the people from whom John and Jesus came. R. Otto has argued that the *Book of Enoch* had a great part in moulding the thought of Jesus (*The Kingdom of God and the Son of Man*, E.T., 1938).

witness of the apocalyptic writings to the prevalence of belief in the coming of the Messianic Kingdom, since the question has been raised whether this conception actually formed a part of the message of the Baptist. Whatever the content of John's preaching we may say—if the apocalyptic writings offer any guide to the popular beliefs—that he spoke to a people who were familiar with the thought of a coming Kingdom of God.

Those who deny the presence in John's message of any statement concerning the coming Kingdom hold that he uttered a call to repentance in view of an imminent judgment. They explain the words of Matthew iii. 2 by declaring that they are an assimilation to the description of the message of Jesus in iv. 17. Whether we allow or reject the possibility of editorial interpolation in securing this similarity of content in the preaching of John and Jesus it is a fact that all the writers of the New Testament who deal with the work of John accepted the idea of a close relationship between the teaching of the two.[1]

It would be a tremendous help in defining the message of John if we could gauge accurately his assumed role. What was his position, and who did he claim to be ? [2] The answer to these questions would render much clearer the whole meaning of his teaching and his rite. He has been called a forerunner. The title is suggested by the description of his work and words ; [3] but a clearer definition is required. Of whom was John the forerunner ? What position did he assign to his successor ? The answers are not so easy as a merely superficial investiga-

[1] Matth. iii. 14 ; xi. 2 ; xvii. 13 ; Mark i. 14 ; vi. 16 ; Luke vii. 19. Goguel maintains that Jesus was a disciple of John at the first (*op. cit.*, pp. 235–57). In commenting on certain parts of Christ's teaching Goguel says : " Tout cela qui vient de Jean-Baptiste ne constitue pas l'Évangile mais en est un élément essentiel " (p. 255).

[2] See note B at the end of the chapter.

[3] Matth. iii. 3 ; Mark i. 3 ; Luke iii. 4 ; vii. 27. Cf. Mal. iii. 1 ; iv. 5 ; Mark ix. 13 ; Matth. xvii. 12, 13.

tion might imply. We have to reckon with the fact that the Gospel accounts themselves appear at times to be contradictory. Also we learn from them that popular opinion of the time was far from unanimous in its belief concerning him.

Probably our main difficulty in defining the position of John is caused by our ignorance of the eschatological belief which he held. In part too we are handicapped by our incomplete knowledge of the belief of Jesus Himself. These beliefs must be studied against a confused and confusing background. Jewish eschatology of the period offered no fixed uniform programme, but only a medley of ideas the extravagant nature of which is a tribute to the unlimited imaginations of the people who conceived them. From a temporal kingdom to an everlasting kingdom, from a Messianic era to a personal Messiah, sometimes conceived as human sometimes as divine—all gradations of thought are to be found in the apocalyptic literature. Even the teaching of one book was not necessarily uniform. It is interesting, for example, to note the different conceptions revealed in Daniel vii. 1–14, compared with those of xii. 1–3.[1] Environment and individual experience probably had as much to do with belief as did inherited tradition. One might say that the creed varied according to the mind of the thinker and his individual experience of life. This statement may be linked with the words of Schweitzer that "the Hasmonean Kingdom created the conditions necessary for the reintroduction of the Davidic Messiah into Eschatology", and also his argument that the belief held by Jesus suggests a certain synthesis of the Danielic and the prophetic eschatologies.[2] A striking witness to the prevalence of these different eschatological conceptions in the Christian

[1] See Paul Volz, *Die Eschatologie der jüdischen Gemeinde im neutestamentlichen Zeitalter, nach den Quellen der rabbinischen apokalyptischen und apokryphen Literatur*, 1934, p. 11.

[2] *SMP*, E.T., p. 78.

as well as the pre-Christian period is provided by the letters of Paul to the Thessalonians, which show the apocalyptic side of Paul's theology and also the interest displayed by his converts in such discussions.

Whatever the actual form of John's belief and the position that he assumed, there is no doubt that he regarded himself, and must be regarded, as the herald of a new age, summoning men to repentance and proclaiming a coming judgment. Whether he adopted the role of Elijah, or some other preacher of righteousness, the dress worn by the Baptist, his food, and the whole tenor of his message were in keeping with the attitude of one who, although describing himself as a " voice ", regarded his work as belonging to the prophetic order. It is illuminating to compare the Gospel descriptions of John with such passages as I Kings xix. 13 ; II Kings i. 8, and Zechariah xiii. 1. Jesus and the multitude differed in their appreciation of the position of John, but there is recorded a complete agreement in regard to one fact—that he was a prophet (Matth. xxi. 26 ; Luke xx. 6). We must bear in mind too the quotations from the prophetic writings, which were associated with John, and which, as already hinted, probably were echoes of his preaching. They may indeed have formed an important part of his actual message. Is it fanciful to believe that in Luke's phrase " the word of God came unto John the son of Zacharias in the wilderness " (iii. 2) we have the recollection of the very declaration of the Baptist, in which, after the manner of an Old Testament prophet, he announced his ministry? [1]   It was in the spirit of

---

[1] Luke iii. 2. It is true that the Septuagint expression is usually different, with πρός instead of ἐπί and Κυρίου for Θεοῦ. There is, however, a remarkable similarity in the words which introduce the call of Jeremiah in the Septuagint : τὸ ῥῆμα τοῦ θεοῦ ὃ ἐγένετο ἐπὶ Ἱερεμίαν τὸν τοῦ Χελκίου (" The word of God which came to Jeremias the son of Chelcias ", i. 1).   In Luke iii. 2 we have ἐγένετο ῥῆμα Θεοῦ ἐπὶ Ἰωάννην τὸν Ζαχαρίου υἱόν : " The word of God came unto John the son of

a prophet that John placed in the forefront the demand for moral reform, and made it the sine qua non for those who, perhaps trusting in the efficacy of a merely ritual act, sought to obtain his baptism (Luke iii. 7 ff. ; cf. Jer. ii. 22, 35 ; xiv. 12).

Probably an additional proof of the eschatological significance of John's baptism may be found in his description of the Messianic baptism as being " with fire " ; for his own rite must be regarded as anticipatory of the Messianic. The words " with fire " are absent from Mark's account but occur in both the remaining Synoptic writings. The baptism which was practised in the Christian Church and which was claimed to be based on Dominical authority appears to have little in common with a rite of judgment, yet the Christians accepted this passage and regarded it as pointing to their own usage.[1] The interpretation is beset with difficulties. That these difficulties did not originate with modern commentators but were felt even by those who gave us the New Testament itself is shown by the story of the Day of Pentecost given in Acts ii. The familiar but curious picture of the " tongues of fire " in the Pentecostal outpouring of the Holy Spirit was the form in which the author believed there came the fulfilment of the words of John.

An obvious interpretation of the reference to fire is that which has found in it a close association with the idea of a judgment on man's sin, similar to that contained in John's own preaching. C. A. Briggs attempted a reconstruction

Zacharias." In any case, one could have understood the change from Κυρίου to Θεοῦ. Κύριος was regarded as a special title of Jesus in the early Church and the author of the Acts, probably Luke himself, has the phrase τὸ ῥῆμα τοῦ Κυρίου applied to the words of the risen Christ (xi. 16).

[1] M. Goguel says of the account in Mark (i. 8) : " Mark has mutilated the text of the source, and has substituted the baptism of the Spirit, that is to say, Christian baptism, for the baptism of the Messianic Judgment " (*The Life of Jesus*, E.T., 1933, p. 267 note).

of a possible original Aramaic discourse of John in support
of this interpretation, which he translated :

I indeed baptize you with water ;
But He that is mightier than I cometh after me ;
Whose shoes I am unworthy to untie ;
He will baptize you with fire.
Whose fan is in His hand,
Thoroughly to cleanse His threshing floor ;
And to gather the wheat into His garner ;
But the chaff He will burn up with unquenchable fire.[1]

It will be noted that there is no reference to " Holy
Spirit ", since Briggs held that the original Aramaic
referred to fire alone and contained no mention of the
Holy Spirit. If we accept the sentence as given in
Matthew (iii. 11) and Luke (iii. 16) the natural meaning
of the whole is found by taking together the words " with
Holy Spirit and with fire " and assuming that only one
type of baptism is intended. We should understand fire
to be a purifying agent after the manner suggested by the
message of the prophet Malachi iii. 2, 3.

In the Lewisian Syriac of Matthew iii. 11, the sentence
reads : " he shall baptize you with fire and with Holy
Spirit ". Here the order is reversed, and perhaps the
implication that there was some uncertainty about the
actual form of words may lend some support to Briggs'
suggestion that the original Aramaic referred to fire alone.[2]

[1] C. A. Briggs, *The Messiah of the Gospels*, 1894, p. 67. He
adds : " The Baptist connects the baptism with fire and the
judgment of fire without discrimination in time, just as the
Old Testament prophets were accustomed to do " (p. 68).

[2] C. A. Briggs, *op. cit.*, p. 67. The contrast between fire
and water is certainly more natural than that of water and
Spirit, as several critics have pointed out. But it is not necessary
to accept the interpretation that John wished to make a contrast.
Christian baptism took the outward form of a water rite also,
and those who practised it quoted these words as witness to
the fact that it brought also an experience of the Spirit (Acts

If this latter were correct the reference must have been to the fire of judgment.

2. It was a water baptism. This fact is stated very definitely by John himself, who points out that his sucessor's baptism would have the distinguishing feature of being " with Holy Spirit ". The descriptions given in the Gospels leave us with the impression that the meaning and value of the Johannine rite was determined in part by its relationship to the later Spirit baptism. It has

---

xi. 16 ; xix. 1–7). This would imply that Spirit baptism did not supersede but was supplementary to water baptism. If we accept the words " He shall baptize you with Holy Spirit and with fire ", it is possible to interpret the " you " as including both the repentant and the unrepentant. Then the meaning would be that one should receive baptism by the Spirit and the other should be punished by fire. (See T. Zahn, *Das Evangelium des Matthäus*, p. 40.) In support of this rendering it may be noted that the passages which follow in both Matthew and Luke make reference to the separation of the good from the evil : " Whose fan is in His hand, thoroughly to cleanse His threshing floor, and to gather the wheat into His garner ; but the chaff He will burn up with unquenchable fire." There is, however, another interpretation which keeps the meaning of " you " as a reference to both classes, the penitent and the impenitent, and makes also the experience of Spirit and fire common to both. But whereas in the case of the repentant the winnowing power of the Spirit becomes an agent of cleansing, to the unrepentant it becomes a wind of judgment. Similarly the fire becomes for the wicked penal and not cleansing. Abrahams thought that in the phrase " baptism by fire " we had two Old Testament ideas combined : fire is poured out, and it is used as a purifying and punitive agent (*Studies*, I, p. 44). Spirit has been understood also under its common translation as wind. Fire and wind have a natural connection in a winnowing process, the wicked being regarded as the chaff separated for the burning. Eisler thinks that the Baptist had in mind Psalm i. 4. He recalls many other references to the wind of judgment in the Old Testament (*The Messiah Jesus*, E.T., pp. 275–6). In the description of the Pentecostal outpouring in Acts ii. there is a very obvious attempt to combine the two ideas of Spirit and fire baptisms. The effect is grotesque, but it testifies to the difficulty of finding a satisfactory solution.

been affirmed that the " emphatic contrast " between the water rite of John and the spiritual baptism of the new era points to the immersion in the Jordan as a symbol and seal rather than as a sacrament.[1] The main strength of this argument lies in the word " contrast ". Is such interpretation valid ? Have we any sure ground for holding that John wished to point out a contrast between the two rites ? Ought we not to regard his words as implying that the later rite of his successor was supplementary to his own ? A. Schweitzer argues against any attempt to minimize the value of the Johannine baptism and declares that it was not " a provisional, merely symbolic act, merely pointing forward to that true baptism ".[2] He thinks that John gave it a special significance which placed it in " a causal connection " with the Spirit baptism. To quote his own words : John " promises those whom he baptizes that, in consequence of what he has now done with a view to their repentance, they have received an initiatory consecration, which at the coming outpouring of the Spirit will qualify them to receive the Spirit ". This, or a similar conception, would alone allow any real or permanent value to the Johannine act. But from the narrative of Acts xix. 1–7 it is evident that the author of the book did not accept such a view, since in verse 5 he records another baptism which was necessary for those who had received only the Johannine rite. If the writer of this book and the author of the third Gospel are one and the same person, as many believe, the interpretation of Luke iii. 16 must be such as to harmonize with this meaning. Of course the possibility must be admitted that the writer may have misunderstood the meaning that John himself gave to the rite. Moreover, some recognise conflicting conceptions as to the nature

---

[1] S. Angus, *The Religious Quests of the Græco-Roman World*, 1929, pp. 148 ff. See also W. Morgan, *The Religion and Theology of Paul*, 1917, pp. 205–9.

[2] *SMP*, p. 230.

of Spirit baptism in the Acts, and the difficulties should warn us against an easy dogmatism.

In estimating the value of the Johannine baptism one must never lose sight of its Jewish background. Like every true Jew, John would be well grounded in the knowledge of Levitical purification, and his interest would be more intense if, as Luke states, his father was a priest. Yet the ethical note suggests that his rite was indebted more to the idea of moral cleansing which is to the fore in the message of the prophets than to the ceremonial purifications of the Temple code. This must not be taken as implying that the prophets taught the necessity of any outward ritual for moral cleansing. As one writer says: " neither in the Old Testament nor in Jewish writings is there any evidence that purificatory washings were thought of as removing moral stains ".[1] The prophets were outspoken against mere formalism. But in the prophetic message itself we find the ritual act employed as a symbol,[2] and it is not difficult to understand how John, the last of the prophets, could use a rite of purification at a time when purifications were playing an important part in the life of the nation.[3]

One needs only to recall the Old Testament practices to realise the unmistakably Jewish character of John's rite. There is no need to go outside Jewish thought in seeking its origin. The same also may be said of the Spirit baptism which John declared would be the gift of his successor. The connection of water cleansing and the gift of the Spirit is found in Ezekiel xxxvi. 25–7. " Then

---

[1] W. Morgan, *op. cit.*, p. 208.

[2] Morgan quotes Isa. i. 16 ; Ezek. xxxvi. 25 ; Zech. xiii. 1 ; Ps. li. 7. He adds : " It was probably in attachment with the prophets that John the Baptist gave to the rite itself, so far as we know for the first time, a moral significance " (*op. cit.*, p. 209).

[3] As an indication of this we may recall the purificatory ritual of the Essenes and the Pharisees, and also that of private indi- dividuals like Banus, mentioned by Josephus.

I will pour clean water over you, cleansing you from all impieties and purifying you from all your idols ; I will give you a new nature, and I will put a new spirit into you, I will take away your hard nature and give you a nature that can be touched ; I will put my own spirit within you, I will make you live by my laws, and you shall obey and observe my orders " (Moffatt). It is probable that considerable importance should be attached to this passage. It has been regarded as providing a clue to John's preaching of a future Spirit baptism.[1]

Nowhere in the New Testament records of John do we find any mention of a claim to a special efficacy in the baptism associated with his name. But from the prominence of the rite in his work—to which his own name bears witness—it is evident that it was not an act to be lightly esteemed. Some have thought that the language used by the Forerunner in Matthew iii. 7, 8 (cf. Luke iii. 7, 8), indicates the care with which he sought to prevent unworthy candidates from sharing the privileges conferred by baptism. This is possible, but it is difficult to gauge the exact nature of these privileges. Nevertheless, one feels that there is little ground for the contention that John's baptism possessed a " magical dunamis " which provided " a charm against the menace of the eschatological order ".[2] Nor is it possible to accept without more definite proof the claim that the rite operated " magically and ritualistically to wash away sinful matter ".

Apparently the chief reason for such statements is the

[1] K. Lake, *ERE*, II, p. 381. Abrahams has quoted other illustrations in support of the connection with Jewish thought. He affirmed that there was " no ground for the emphatic statement of Dr. S. Krauss (*Jewish Encyc.*, ii, 499) that ' the only conception of baptism at variance with Jewish ideas is displayed in the declaration of John that the one who would come after him would not baptize with water but with the Holy Ghost ' " (*Studies*, I, 1917, p. 43).

[2] R. Otto, *The Kingdom of God and the Son of Man*, E.T., 1938, p. 80.

fact that John was an ascetic. R. Otto, whose view we have quoted, held that " ascetic and magical soteriological practices belong closely together ".[1] This, however, is by no means a universal law. It is probable also that too much emphasis has been placed on John's ascetic practices.[2] The value of such ascetic practices depends upon their importance in the eyes of the ascetic himself. There is nothing in the teaching of John, as we know it, which can be quoted in support of the belief that he attached any special importance to asceticism. It is true that we have words of Jesus in which he distinguished between His own attitude to life and the asceticism of John (Matthew xi. 18 ff. ; Luke vii. 33 ff.). But the language of Jesus does not imply that John demanded ascetic practices from his followers as the sine qua non of righteousness. It was a comparison of the personal attitudes of two teachers in approaching a task common to both. The suggestion conveyed by the speech of Jesus is that neither method had any real value in itself except as a means to an end. " Wisdom is justified by her works." These are the words of Jesus, not John, yet we cannot imagine their use if in the preaching and doctrine of John the ascetic ideal had assumed a supreme importance. Moreover, from the intimate knowledge of John's work which Jesus possessed,[3] would He have regarded as parallel to His own method the activity of one who linked together ascetic and magical soteriological practices that culminated in a rite of pure magic ? This question has a special relevance in view of the well-known attitude of the Master to outward ritual. When we con-

[1] R. Otto, *op. cit.*, p. 77.

[2] It is interesting to note that Abrahams, who believed that John was connected with the Essenes, felt that he was able to make a wider appeal than the Essenes because he relaxed some of the Essenic stringency (*Studies, I*, p. 34).

[3] This is generally accepted by critics. Goguel goes so far as to argue that at the beginning of His career Jesus was a disciple of John (*Jean-Baptiste*, pp. 235-57).

sider too the character of the Baptist we may ask—does this emphasis on the material act harmonize with the high moral note in John's preaching ?

Surely the truth is that there is absolutely nothing in the Baptist's message which gives any undue exaltation of ascetic ideals. His habits, garb and food are the language of symbolism, not asceticism. They can be understood best in the light of the Forerunner's prophetic character and the message by which he called men to repentance. Fasting is definitely linked with confession of sin in Joel ii. 12.[1] But the significance of the act is to be found in its symbolic character, for the truly prophetic attitude is shown in Jeremiah xiv. 12, where it is regarded as possessing no value when divorced from right conduct. Fasting became very common in post-exilic times, and the value placed upon it was that of a meritorious work, not that of a means of magical power. Any special significance attributed by John to the act of fasting must surely have revealed itself in his message. John's disciples are said to have fasted (Mark ii. 18 ; Matth. ix. 14 ; Luke v. 33), but the same statement makes mention of the fasting of the Pharisees, and leaves the impression that so far from there being anything exceptional in such action the real surprise was caused by the neglect of the disciples of Jesus to observe a custom which perhaps the known previously close association of Jesus and John suggested would be honoured. Such a custom was fairly common among religious sects.[2] Among indi-

[1] The children of Israel fasted in their act of repentance in the time of Nehemiah (ix. 1). Fasting had its place in the Day of Atonement (Lev. xvi. 31).

[2] Abrahams pointed out that fasting could be regarded as a form of mourning, supplication, penitence or communion. In discussing the significance of Pharisaic fasting he gave quotations to show the spiritual conception underlying it. His conclusion should be noted : " It is manifestly unjust to charge with ritualism fasts on which such homilies were a regular feature " (*Studies*, I, pp. 121–8).

viduals too it had a recognized spiritual value. Jesus, who was no ascetic, fasted (Matth. iv. 2 ; Mark i. 12, 13 ; Luke iv. 2) and foresaw the coming of a time when, because of their condition, His own disciples would fast (Mark ii. 20). The apostle Paul showed an attitude very similar to his Master when dealing with matters of ritual and custom, but he too fasted (Acts xiii. 2, 3). Josephus makes no mention of any ascetic traits in his description of the teaching and character of John. The significance of this can be recognized best when we recall that ascetic practices held a special interest for the Jewish historian.[1] He called attention to the Johannine practice of baptism, but stated that the teaching of the Baptist was that the rite had value only as an outward purification following an inward purification of the soul by righteousness.

Yet it must be understood that the recognition of the Johannine baptism as symbolic and devoid of any magical power does not imply that it had no value in itself. No symbol was without some inherent value in ancient thought, and it did actually imply a closer connection with the action symbolized than the modern mind would accept. The full significance of baptism must be discussed after a consideration of its distinguishing features.

Why was the Jordan used for baptism by John ? It has been stated that the river was not regarded as pure enough to be used for sacred purposes.[2] But Abrahams (*Studies*, I, p. 33), maintained that the ban applied

---

[1] *Vita*, sect. 2 ; *Antiq.*, XVIII, i, 3, 5.

[2] T. K. Cheyne (*EBi*, 2499) has a reference to the statement of Neubauer (*Geographie du Talmud*, 1868, p. 31) that according to the Mishnah the waters of the Jordan were not pure enough for sacred uses. The passage is found in Tohoroth, Parah. viii. 10 : " The waters of the Jordan and the Yarmuk are invalid because they are mixed waters. They are deemed mixed waters whereof the one is valid and the other invalid, and they mingle together ; if both are valid and they mingle together they remain valid. R. Judah declares them invalid " (*The Mishnah*, translated by H. Danby, p. 707). R. Reitzenstein employs the idea

only to one ceremony—that of the Red Heifer—
and that " no rabbi ever dreamed of pronouncing the
Jordan unfit for the rite of baptism ". The prominence
of the Jordan in the accounts of the work of John makes
one feel that some positive reason lay behind the
activity depicted there. To take the simplest explanation
first—one might say that a study of the geography of the
Holy Land furnishes an adequate cause. There are few
streams worthy of note in Palestine and the Jordan easily
takes pride of place. It is possible that its very name is
an appellative rather than a proper noun, and it might be
translated " ford " or " watering-place ". [1] The prominence of this river in Hebrew history needs little emphasis.
In Ezekiel's vision (xlvii.) the river of life in its mission
of healing ran towards the Jordan and the Dead Sea.[2]
Elisha directed the Syrian general to the Israelite Jordan
that he might obtain his cleansing from leprosy, and the
protest of Naaman extolling the merits of the Syrian rivers
is noteworthy. It was quite natural too that a Jew, whose
mind was steeped in Old Testament knowledge, should
think of the Jordan—the river through which Israel passed
to the Promised Land—as a very suitable place for the
performance of a purificatory rite. There may have been
also an individual preference due to reasons of which we
are ignorant. Perhaps we might include the possibility
that it gained an additional attractiveness in the eyes of
John from the fact of its close association with the lives

of the supposed impurity as an argument against the contention
that the Johannine and Christian baptisms were connected with
the tebilah (*Die Vorgeschichte der christliche Taufe*, p. 227).

[1] *EBi*, pp. 2575 ff. ; *HDB*, II, p. 756. Probably we have such
a use in Job xl. 23 ; see Job, *Century Bible*, by A. S. Peake, s.v.

[2] Eisler thinks that John found a sanction for his action in
the prophecies of Ezekiel. His belief is that the Baptist connected xxxvi. 16, 25, 26, 31—described by him as " funda-
mental " for the doctrine—with xlvii. 1–9, in which is fore-
shadowed a healing of the waters of the Jordan and the Dead
Sea (*The Messiah Jesus*, p. 271 f.).

of both Elijah and Elisha. John could not be unaware of the opinion of the multitude which connected him with Elijah. In recalling too the story of Naaman we must remember that his experience in the Jordan not only cleansed him from leprosy but converted him to a belief in Yahweh.

John had the prophet's poetic imagination as well as the prophetic garb, and it can be understood readily how he might feel that there was no fitter place for his work than the bank of the Jordan.[1] This statement must not be interpreted as implying that John would regard baptism in the Jordan alone as valid. We would remind ourselves that the account given by Josephus makes no mention of the Jordan, or indeed of any river, in connection with John's ministry.[2] There is also nothing in the words of his message given in the Gospels to lend support to the belief that he regarded any special river or place as essential to his baptism. The tradition preserved in John i. 28 ; iii. 23, suggests an absence of any restriction [3] and, in considering this tradition of the Fourth Gospel, it may be remarked that Goguel considers that the writer of this book probably possessed better and more complete information than the authors of the Synoptic Gospels on the relationship of Jesus and John. From this point of view it is interesting to recall that the Fourth Gospel gives the impression that Jesus also began His ministry in the region of the Jordan.[4]

---

[1] F. J. Badcock has suggested that John baptized on " the further side of Jordan " (John i. 28 ; iii. 26 ; x. 40) in order to compel those who wished to receive his baptism to put themselves outside the holy land and so assimilate themselves to those who had not yet entered on the promises which were to be theirs on receiving baptism and recrossing the Jordan (*The Interpreter*, 1917, XIII, pp. 155–60).

[2] W. Brandt, *Die jüdischen Baptismen*, p. 74.

[3] Goguel, *op. cit.*, p. 83.

[4] Sanday seems to accept this. *HDB*, II, p. 612. Cf. Mark i. 14 ; Matth. iv. 12.

3. It was a baptism of repentance.[1] There was a moral quality associated with John's baptism which distinguished it both from the proselyte's tebilah and from other Jewish ceremonial washings based, as these were, on the conception of ritual uncleanness. It is of the utmost importance, in assessing the value of the Johannine rite, to note that John's message reported in the Gospels had nothing to say about the efficacy of baptism. The only mention of the rite in his preaching occurs when the Forerunner distinguishes between the Spirit baptism of his Successor and his own act. But from his language to those who came to seek baptism John made it clear that a preliminary condition was that they should " bring forth fruit worthy of repentance ". This call for repentance is the outstanding feature of his message. There were many who were looking forward to the new era heralded by John, but now it was brought home to them with all the force of a great moral truth that they who would be partakers in the privileges of the new Israel must fit themselves by a sincere repentance. This emphasis on repentance bears the marks of originality of a truly inspired mind. The Old Testament in which John found the proof texts of his mission furnished him with little direct help. Likely passages are Ezekiel xiv. 6, and xviii. 30, but these have no reference to the Messianic Kingdom. Nevertheless, the distinction which Ezekiel draws between the destinies of those who repent and those who refuse, offers a limited parallel and foreshadows the expression of individualism so prominent in John's message. In his call to his people John affirmed that the fate of his hearers would depend on their individual spiritual condition and not on their racial status.[2] Perhaps the thought of John was debtor also to Ezekiel xxxvi. 25–7, which links together purification, a

---

[1] For water as a symbol of repentance, see I. Abrahams, *Studies*, I, pp. 39 ff.

[2] Matth. iii. 8, 9 ; Luke iii. 8.

D

new heart—which may testify repentance—and the gift of God's Spirit. The New Testament, apart from the writings of Luke, has little to say about repentance ; yet from a study of the Acts we gather the impression that the subject occupied a prominent place in the preaching of the early Christian missionaries. Certainly this prominence is not to be explained by any influence of the Gentile world of thought with which Christianity might have come into contact. It has been claimed that Pharisaic eschatology of the first century connected the Messianic Age with repentance, but it is not possible to say how much John owed to this.[1]

A study of the language used to describe this Johannine baptism is important. Matthew has simply εἰς μετάνοιαν (iii. 11). Some have maintained that this cannot be a correct expression. If repentance were the sole object of the rite there would seem to be little point in the demand, which Matthew himself as well as the other Gospel writers mentions, for a previous confession of sins.[2] The texts of Mark and Luke read βάπτισμα μετανοίας εἰς ἄφεσιν ἁμαρτιῶν. This also is difficult. What is the meaning of εἰς ἄφεσιν ἁμαρτιῶν ? It is very improbable that

[1] Abrahams admits that there was a difference between the Pharisaic formula, " Repent *and* the Kingdom is at hand ", and the Johannine, " Repent *for* the Kingdom is at hand ". In the message of John the attitude of his hearers had no effect on the coming of the Kingdom, but only on their relationship to it (*op. cit.*, I, p. 34). See also C. G. Montefiore, *Jewish Quarterly Review*, XVI, Jan. 1904, pp. 209–57. For the use of μετάνοια in the Hellenistic world, see E. Norden, *Agnostos Theos*, 1913, pp. 1 34–40.

[2] H. B. Swete, *St. Mark*, pp. 4 ff., maintains that the baptism of John was strictly εἰς μετάνοιαν. It was εἰς ἄφεσιν only in an anticipatory sense (Matth. iii. 11 ; Acts xix. 3). Ἄφεσις belongs properly to the Messianic Kingdom (Mark ii. 5 ff.). It is interesting to study the discussion in Tertullian (*De Baptismo*, x) in which he seeks to show that John's baptism was for repentance alone and not for forgiveness. The argument bears witness to the difficulty felt by early commentators.

John affirmed that his baptism conferred actual forgiveness of sins. The Jews challenged the claim of Jesus to forgive sins, and it is most unlikely that they would have allowed such an affirmation by John to pass without any opposition. Moreover this assumption seems to be contradicted wholly by the fact that, according to the Gospel narrative, even the Pharisees and the Sadducees came to share the new baptism (Matth. iii. 7). It is difficult also to imagine that the Synoptic writers accepted the view that this baptism brought forgiveness. The prerogative of saving from sin belonged to Jesus (Matth. i. 21). It was Jesus too who claimed to bring the fulfilment of " the acceptable year of the Lord " (Luke iv. 19, 21), which has been connected with the year of release ($\dot{\epsilon}\nu\iota\alpha\nu\tau\dot{o}\varsigma$ $\dot{\alpha}\varphi\acute{\epsilon}\sigma\epsilon\omega\varsigma$) of Leviticus xxv. 10, described by Swete as " the archetype of an era of spiritual remission ".[1] Nowhere do we find any hint of John claiming any special virtue for his baptism save as the outward sign of an inward repentance. When Jesus came to be baptized John is reported in Matthew's Gospel as saying : " I have need to be baptized of thee ". Here was the recognition of the moral or spiritual superiority of Jesus, but the words seem inappropriate for a man who—according to some critics—felt that he had sole control of a magical sin-cleansing rite which he offered to worthy candidates.

It seems more in harmony with the facts to believe that the main purpose of John's baptism was to give by an outward act the assurance to the candidate for baptism that his " metanoia " had brought forgiveness of sins. This " metanoia " was revealed first by the candidate bringing " fruit worthy of repentance ", and in the second

[1] H. B. Swete, *St. Mark*, p. 4. In view of what we believe to be a close connection between John's baptism and the Jewish tebilah it should be noted that the latter was never regarded as ensuring sinlessness. This was reserved for the Messianic Age. See Abrahams, *op. cit.*, p. 42.

place by the very act of seeking baptism, which was an open confession of his need. Why such a rite was used is a question which probably finds its answer in a consideration of the prophetic interpretation of the ancient purificatory ritual. It was the outward symbol of an inward experience. The phrase " a baptism of repentance for the remission of sins " should be read in the light of the usage in Luke i. 77, where John's mission is foretold. His work was " to give knowledge of salvation unto his people in the remission of their sins ".[1] We should regard the last phrase as a definition of the salvation which is mentioned. The whole of John's message must be interpreted from the point of view of the Messianic expectation and his belief in the coming Kingdom of God.[2]

It must not be overlooked that Jesus also and His disciples spoke of the Kingdom and associated with it the preaching of repentance unto remission of sins (Luke xxiv. 47 ; Acts ii. 38). Had the words when used by John any difference of meaning from that implied in the teaching of the early Church ? One must consider also the probability that in part there has been an assimilation of the message of John to that of Jesus. But both shared a belief in a coming Kingdom. This expectation furnishes the key to an understanding of John's work. It was because of this that men were ready to accept his demands. It was the sense of an imminent divine event which made him a preacher of judgment and caused his insistence on the urgent need of repentance for sins.

There is an interpretation of the words " unto remission of sins " which understands them to mean " to the renunciation (' sending away ' by man, not remission by

[1] A. Plummer, *St. Luke*, *I.C.C.*, 1901, pp. 42–3. A discussion on some early Church interpretations is found in *HDB*, I, p. 240.
[2] See note A at the end of this chapter.

God) of sins ".[1] This is possible, but the more natural sense is that which regards the words as expressing the divine response to the human " metanoia ". A part of our difficulty in interpretation is due perhaps to the unsuitable English word which is used to translate " metanoia ". The word " repentance " confuses the thought which the Greek and Aramaic express very aptly. In " repentance " we have the associations of the Latin " poenitentia ", and the kindred idea of penance so familiar to students of Church doctrine.[2] The translation gives a quite inaccurate rendering of the Greek " metanoia " and distorts the message of John. The Greek word denotes a change of mind, and implies a transformation of the inner life witnessed to by a change in the outward life. Thus in the work of John the rite of baptism could be accepted as an outward expression which attested the reality of an inward change. It is very probable that the word used by John was the Aramaic " tubhu " (Heb. " shubu ") " return ", and this has been translated by the Greek " metanoia ".[3] The idea is a familiar one in the Old Testament prophecies. One need only recall the words of Isaiah xliv. 22 : " Return unto me ; for I have redeemed thee," or the even more familiar passage of lv. 7, where the Septuagint has both ἐπιστραφήτω (Let him return) and ὅτι ἐπὶ πολὺ ἀφήσει τὰς ἁμαρτίας ὑμῶν (for he shall abundantly pardon your sins).[4] The exhortation of Peter in Acts iii. 19 reminds us of the Old Testament language : " Repent ye therefore and turn again " μετανοήσατε οὖν καὶ ἐπιστρέψατε. A different turn of phrase occurs in Acts v. 31 and Luke xxiv. 47. The εἰς is replaced by καί " repentance . . . and

[1] A. C. Deane, " The Ministry of John the Baptist ", *Expositor*, VIII, xiii, 1917, pp. 420–31.

[2] Lactantius substituted for " poenitentia " the word " resipiscentia " as a translation of " metanoia " (*Div. Inst.*, vi. 24).

[3] F. C. Burkitt, *Christian Beginnings*, 1924, p. 20.

[4] See also Jer. iii. 1 ; iv. 1 ; xviii. 11, etc.

remission ", but although the sense is slightly different, no importance should be attached to the alteration. While the two conceptions are placed side by side there is no attempt to dissociate them. In recognising that the Old Testament passages furnish a background to John's language and its underlying conceptions we must recognize also that the deeper meaning of " metanoia " is found first in Christianity.[1] Moreover, even the word itself is by no means common in pre-Christian Jewish writings.[2]

4. John's baptism was demanded of all. This is the inference we must draw from the descriptions in the Gospels, although it is nowhere explicitly stated. There is one exception. According to the account given in Matthew, the Baptist hesitated to apply his rite to Jesus on the ground of the position of Jesus and his own unfitness to offer Him baptism.[3] But the insistence of Jesus on the performance of the rite in order that he might " fulfil all righteousness " lends support to the belief that it was demanded universally. The Gospel narrative leaves us with the impression that John's preaching proclaimed that every member of his race had apostatized from God. All men needed to repent and all must undergo the rite which stamped them as members of the new Israel.

[1] Moulton and Milligan, *The Vocabulary of the Greek Testament*, s.v., *ERE*, X, pp. 731–3.

[2] Swete (*St. Mark*, p. 4) has pointed out that μετάνοια in the Septuagint is nearly restricted to the non-canonical books, Proverbs (1), *Wisdom* (3), *Sirach* (3). Ἄφεσις, although frequent, occurs nowhere in the Greek Old Testament in the sense of forgiveness. A. Deissmann (*Bible Studies*, E.T., 2nd ed. 1909, pp. 98 ff.) has shown from the papyri that ἄφεσις was used as a technical term in irrigation. It is possible that the phrase " baptism of repentance to the remission of sins " conveyed a shade of meaning to the disciples which has escaped us.

[3] No hint of any hesitation is found in the accounts of Mark and Luke. The description of the latter is very brief and matter of fact. From the narratives of both one might assume that they regarded the baptism as natural in view of its own significance and that of the mission of Jesus.

44

The idea that the whole chosen race had backslidden was not new. A brief study of the prophetic writings is sufficient to enable us to realize this truth.[1] Men of deep thought and religious convictions found little to encourage the belief in a spiritual remnant. In his letter to the Romans the apostle Paul makes effective use of a quotation from Psalm xiv. 1–3 in support of his contention that the guilt of man was universal (iii. 10–12). Outside the pages of Scripture there is an excellent illustration of the way in which a Jew could come to regard his fellow-countrymen as unclean. This is found in a statement of Josephus concerning Eleazar and the Sicarii. These are said to have regarded all Jews who had submitted to the Romans as in no way differing from foreigners (*BJ*, VII, 8, 1). That John demanded an acceptation by all of his rite was the natural result of his belief in a national apostasy and in the significance of his baptism.

5. Like the tebilah, John's baptism does not appear to have been repeated. In this respect it contrasts with the frequent washings of the Essenes and the usual ritual lustrations of Judaism.

An attempt has been made to connect John with the Essenes. I. Abrahams, following Graetz, argued that John was an Essene. He thought that the Baptist made a wider appeal by not enforcing the strict Essenic rules in regard to communism, residence in separate colonies and asceticism, but he maintained that it was quite untenable to attempt to dissociate him altogether from Essenism. For support of this position Abrahams appealed to the witness of Josephus. He believed that the Jewish historian meant to identify John with the Essenes, and in proof of this he called attention to the similarity of the terminology which Josephus employed in describing both.[2] H. J. Holtzmann also recognized the fact that John's baptism in its sacramental character

[1] Isa. lxiv. 6 ; Jer. xxiii. 9 ff. ; Ezek. iii. 7, etc.
[2] *Studies*, I, 1917, p. 34.

reminds one of the Essenic washings.[1] But Holtzmann admitted that there were also considerable differences, especially the non-repetition of the Johannine rite in contrast with the habitual lustrations of Essenism, and the fact that the Essenic acts were ritual and performed against a background of Levitical and Nazaritic ideas, whereas John's baptism of repentance had a high moral quality and must be understood in the light of his pro-clamation of the coming Judgment. When every allow-ance is made for the points of contact of John and the Essenes one is constrained to acknowledge that whatever the similarities, the differences are so vital that it is impossible to believe that there was any real connection. Not only were the two baptisms essentially different but, as M. Goguel points out, " none of the characteristic features of the life of the Essenes, such as the worship of angels, or the prayer at sunrise, are adopted by John, and his costume differed as far as it is possible to imagine from the white robe of the Essenes ".[2] Goguel also doubts whether Essenic teaching could account for the emphasis on the Messianic Judgment in the preaching of John.

The generally accepted belief that John's baptism was performed only once is of great importance in helping us to form an estimate of its real meaning. Jewish purifications were applied frequently, and their habitual nature was a recognition that even the most devout Jew would need their service on occasions to cleanse himself from ritual impurity. Forgetting for the moment the moral con-notation of the Johannine rite we are compelled to recog-nize that its single application implied the conferring of a status which need not be—one might almost say, ought not to be—lost. In that it was demanded of all it must have been something which marked off those who had

[1] H. J. Holtzmann, *Lehrbuch der neutestamentlichen Theologie*, 2 Auf., 1911, I, pp. 171 ff.
[2] *Life of Jesus*, E.T., 1933, pp. 268-9.

received it from the rest of their fellows. Yet there is no evidence that those who received the new status formed themselves into a community after the manner of the early Christians. On the contrary, the inference to be drawn from such a passage as Luke vii. 29 f. is that the men who were baptized had resumed their places in the ordinary national life, although preserving the changed outlook and the way of life symbolized by their baptism.

However, some have argued that John's followers became a distinct society, and there has been an attempt to explain the apologetic tone of the Fourth Gospel by the theory of a continuing Baptist community, whose teaching and existence the early Church was obliged to combat. Reference has been made already to this theory of conflict. M. Goguel finds not only traces of opposition in the Gospels, but believes that we have even in the New Testament remains of a literature belonging to the Baptist party, and also evidence for the existence of such a body in the writings of the early Fathers.[1] Despite the skill with which the French scholar argues the case one feels that it requires much stronger proof before acceptation; and from our present knowledge we may say that the known historical records offer little trace of the existence of a continuing body of Johannine disciples, with an organization similar to that of the early Christians. It is very probable that a certain amount of missionary work was carried on by adherents of John who did not accept Jesus as the fulfilment of their master's proclamation of the " Coming One ". Such work would go on side by side with the work of the early disciples (John iv. 1). But it is most likely that these men acted as individuals. Without organization their work would cease, in all probability, with themselves. It has been pointed out already that John's own conception of the temporary

---

[1] *Jean-Baptiste*, pp. 45, 63, 74, 76, 104 ff. The attempt to prove a connection with the Mandæans has failed. See note 1, p. 15.

nature of his work would not have encouraged the growth of an organization centring in himself or his teaching. A preparatory community was possible in the sense of a body of men looking for the promised Successor, yet its absorption in the company of those who followed John's acknowledged Successor was inevitable. Much depends on the credibility of the Gospel statements concerning John's public recognition of Jesus. In John x. 41 there is a suggestion that the men who had heard John tested the reality of the claim of Jesus against the words spoken by the forerunner. Disciples of John are mentioned in all the Gospels,[1] but with the exception of John iv. 1, it is very probable that the word should be understood—as in the case of the disciples of Jesus—with reference to the close personal associates and not the mass of his followers.

The description of the characteristics of the Johannine baptism has been derived from the narratives of the four Gospels. We come now to a consideration of the question of their trustworthiness in this matter. Nowhere is there any suggestion of deliberate falsification, yet we are obliged to take into account the possibility that the description may have been assimilated to the better known rite of the Christian Church.[2] Thus, allowing for certain modifications regarding the eschatological value, each of the five characteristics already mentioned belongs equally to Christian baptism. It must be admitted that we have no certainty in this matter, except that which is derived from the value of our Gospels as historical documents and the recognition that while different documents lie behind these there is no hint of any contradictory statements regarding the nature of John's rite. But a more serious difficulty is created by the fact that Josephus, who is the only primary authority for the work of John outside the New Testament, appears to give an interpretation of

---

[1] Matth. ix. 14; xiv. 12; Mark ii. 18; Luke v. 33; vii. 18, 19; xi. 1; John i. 35; iii. 25; iv. 1.

[2] M. Goguel, *op. cit.*, p. 290.

his baptism quite different from that suggested by the descriptions in the Gospels. The words of Josephus imply that the rite was regarded merely as an act of ablution with no spiritual value in itself although it followed a spiritual transformation. To quote : " John . . . commanded the Jews to cultivate virtue, both justice in relation to one another and piety in relation to God, and so to come together through baptism ($\beta\alpha\pi\tau\iota\sigma\mu\tilde{\omega}$ $\sigma\upsilon\nu\iota\acute{\epsilon}\nu\alpha\iota$) for baptism would be acceptable to Him, if they used it not for expiating certain sins, but as a purification of the body after the soul had been thoroughly cleansed already by righteousness." [1] It is obvious that this statement suggests a very serious difference from that given in the Gospels, according to the usual interpretation of the latter. The authenticity of the Josephus passage has been questioned ; but it is impossible to accept the denial without strong proofs. These are not forthcoming. On the other hand, the arguments of Abrahams in favour of its genuineness would appear conclusive. He draws attention to the terminology, which it is very difficult to explain if we allow that this is a Christian interpolation. One would expect also a Christian interpolator to have brought the passage into closer accord with the Gospels. Most significant of all is the silence of this disputed passage concerning any connection between John and Jesus. Abrahams thinks this last fact of such importance that he adds : " This, of itself, is almost enough to authenticate the passage." [2]

[1] *Antiq.*, XVIII, 5, 2. R. Eisler has denied the genuineness of the passage, and has argued that the true statement is contained in a non-Greek version (Slavonic) which he quotes : " This man baptized the Jews for the forgiveness of sins " (*The Messiah Jesus*, E.T., 1931, pp. 246 ff.). M. Goguel thinks that Josephus toned down the message of John (*Jean-Baptiste*, pp. 17–19). Schürer regarded the passage as suspect (*GJV*, 4th ed., 1901, I, p. 438, note 24). The authenticity, however, is generally accepted ; this Goguel himself recognizes (*op. cit.*, p. 19, note).

[2] *Op. cit.*, pp. 30 ff.

If we accept the genuineness of the passage we must face up to the question of its meaning. There are several possibilities.

It may be a wrong view due to deliberate misinterpretation. We believe that Josephus was quite capable of such action, but the absence of any known motive makes it unlikely. There is also the possibility of sincere misunderstanding on the part of the Jewish historian, although the probability is lessened when we remember the personal interest of Josephus in the ritual and actions of characters similar to John. A very suggestive argument was put forward by Abrahams, who believed that the words of the Jewish historian probably preserve for us the exact nature of John's baptism. He thought that Josephus introduced the description in the form in which we have it with the deliberate purpose of dissociating it from the Christian rite since it was " scarcely credible that Josephus was ignorant of the Christian baptism which was ' for the remission of sins ' ".

While it is impossible to be dogmatic on the question in view of the meagreness of our information, we would suggest that there is a solution which would allow us to accept the statement of Josephus as a straightforward account of John's baptism free from any anti-Christian bias, and one which in no way conflicted with the Gospel accounts, apart from a slight error due to a pardonable misunderstanding. In the first place it should be noted that the words used by Josephus to sum up the ethical and spiritual teaching of John—" to cultivate virtue, both justice in relation to one another and piety in relation to God "—are an excellent summary of the Baptist's message as presented in the Gospels. According to this John pleaded for repentance before God, and demanded fruit worthy of repentance, becoming more precise in his demands when he came up against definite categories of men such as publicans and soldiers. It must be admitted that the historian makes no mention of the apocalyptic element in the message, whereas this is a prominent feature in the account of the Gospels. But the absence can be understood. This essentially Jewish aspect of John's preaching would evoke little interest in the majority of the readers of Josephus. On the other hand, any stress on the Messianic content of the message might have left an unfavourable impression on the minds of the official and governing classes. No writer understood better than Josephus the art of omission and also the best method of making his writing appeal to his readers.

When we consider the likelihood of the correctness of the account of John's rite we must remember that Josephus professed a special interest in ascetic and purificatory rites,[1] and for this reason is most likely to have made an effort to understand the nature of the work of John. In making this plea for a higher estimate of the historical value and genuineness of the description in Josephus, one cannot forbear from expressing the opinion that much of the scepticism concerning the genuineness of the passage, and the doubt as to the truth of its words, has arisen owing to the prevalence and persistency of the belief, based on what we believe to be a misinterpretation of the Gospel story, that John's baptism possessed some wonder-working efficacy. This belief, which, in some quarters, has caused it to be regarded as sheer magic,[2] has blinded men to the true nature of the rite.

When we attempt to assess the value of the Johannine baptism we ought to ask first of all why there was such a rite. Goguel has reminded us that the Gospel tradition preserves the recollection that Jesus Himself did not introduce baptism.[3] Why should baptism be taken for granted both in regard to the work of John and also in the story of the early Christian Church ? There is no

---

[1] *Vita.* 2.
[2] A recent illustration is Otto's *The Kingdom of God and the Son of Man*, pp. 76 ff.
[3] *Life of Jesus*, E.T., p. 199.

suggestion that a new rite is being introduced but only a demand that its true value should be recognized by a universal acceptance of it. The significance of this statement can be understood when we recall how carefully Paul explains the origin of the sacrament of the Eucharist to his readers (I Cor. xi. 23 ff.), and yet in his references to baptism appears to take it for granted that no instruction in the origin or meaning of this sacrament is required. Perhaps, however, some modification of this statement might seem to be required in view of Paul's reference to the Red Sea baptism (I Cor. x. 2) unless we recognize that the latter bears the marks of rabbinic exegesis and not sober history. Heathen initiatory rites might have made the Gentile converts familiar with some of the conceptions underlying baptism, but this fact does not explain why nothing was said of the origin of the Christian rite. Nor is any really satisfactory answer afforded by vague references to Jewish purificatory acts as antecedents of a Christian sacrament which differs from them in many vital respects.

Schweitzer suggests that John found the idea of baptism in the prophets.[1] But he makes the strange assertion that the question of its derivation is " comparatively unimportant, since in the originality of its significance it is not explicable by any other baptism ". After referring to the possible influence of Jewish proselyte baptism on John's act, which, on account of the scanty data [2] concerning the early history of the former, he leaves an open question, Schweitzer concludes : " in any case the significance of the Johannine baptism cannot possibly be derived from Jewish proselyte baptism ". It is interesting to put this

[1] *SMP*, p. 232. He refers to Isa. i. 15 f. ; iv. 3 f. ; Zech. xiii. 1 ; Jer. iv. 14 ; Ezek. xxxvi. 25 f. Schweitzer attaches special significance to the last " since sprinkling with water and the bestowal of the Spirit are mentioned together ".

[2] Schweitzer calls attention to the scantiness of the material shown in the summary of it given by J. Leipoldt, *Die urchristliche Taufe im Lichte der Religionsgeschichte*, 1928, pp. 1–25.

certainty regarding the significance of John's baptism against the admitted uncertainty as to its origin. Still more strange is the declaration of Schweitzer that one reason why the baptism of John has no parallels in Comparative Religion is that " it is the authoritative act of an individual who felt himself endowed with plenary powers. Its efficacy was not in itself but in him who bestowed it." As a proof of the power with which John invested the rite Schweitzer quotes the words uttered by the Baptist against the Pharisees and Sadducees who came to share it (Matth. iii. 7 ff. ; cf. Luke iii. 7 ff.). He understands these to imply that John considered his sacrament to be a guarantee of salvation at the Judgment. He finds too in the question concerning the authority of John's baptism [1] a proof that Jesus regarded the Johannine baptism as " a ceremonial act which works super-naturally ", and maintains that in the reply of the Master to the two ambitious disciples, in which He asked them whether they were able to be baptized with His baptism (Mark x. 38, 39), Jesus Himself implied that baptism was regarded as an effectual means of obtaining the glories of the Messianic Kingdom.

How strange all these references to magic and ritual appear when linked with the work of one who found his inspiration and guidance in the messages of the Old Testament prophets ! The witness of the New Testament account leaves us in no doubt of the influences of these writings on John. There were plenty of ascetics and charlatans in Palestine in the days of the Baptist. Did he belong to these ? Was he indeed in the prophetic succession as Jesus affirmed, or was he merely an ascetic who blended in his teaching a mixture of eschatology, ethics and magic ? If there is one impression which the reader of the Gospels gathers concerning John it is that of a man whose actions and words recall the ministries of the Old Testament prophets. Such is the effect left by the

---

[1] Mark xi. 28–33.

description of his dress, his fearless speech, his lofty spiritual teaching and not least the very quotations from the prophets themselves.

The one difficulty is the baptismal rite ! Is there any significance in the fact that the Synoptic writers while connecting the appearance of John and his proclamation of Jesus with Old Testament prophecy make no attempt to connect his introduction of baptism with any Old Testament prediction, although this is done in regard to the baptism of Pentecost ? Moreover, when we consider Hebrew history it is difficult to find a prototype for John the Baptizer. Apart from the incident of Naaman's " baptism " there would seem to be nothing in the acts and messages of the prophets that would be likely to influence John to put in the forefront a rite of baptism and to allow it such importance that his very name perpetuated the fact. This prominence given to a rite is not in keeping with the general attitude of the prophets towards mere ritual.[1] A. B. Davidson declared that ritual had no place in the prophetic teaching, only that which was moral had any meaning.[2] The prophets employed figures of speech derived from ritual when speaking of moral reformation, but for the rites themselves they appeared to show little regard. It is curious to note how from these symbolical references a direct link with John's baptism is discovered. But we need something more substantial in the way of proof before accepting a statement of the origin of baptism which builds itself mainly upon the supposition that out of this metaphorical and symbolical use a teacher, so akin to the prophets in spirit as John was, made a material rite and invested it with magical significance.[3]

---

[1] Isa. i. 11–17 ; Hosea vi. 6 ; Amos iv. 4 f. ; v. 21–5 ; Micah vi. 6–8 ; Jer. vii. 21–3.

[2] *HDR*, IV, p. 119.

[3] " For the greater prophets the rites have ceased to have vital importance, and the ritual vocabulary can now be used

In considering the prominence of baptism in the mission of John there is something very important which is apt to be overlooked. This is the Forerunner's own estimate of its value. The only recorded words of John himself regarding the rite are those which speak of it as a water rite, and suggest a certain depreciation of its value when compared with the more desirable Spirit baptism of the Messiah. If we leave aside for a moment the matter of the comparison we must recognise that the words, if authentic, whether used relatively or absolutely, demonstrate that John did not regard his rite as final or complete. Otto cast doubt upon the authenticity by suggesting that the words expressing the distinction between water and Spirit baptisms were probably not formulated until a later time.[1] But one cannot understand how they could have arisen without the support of a tradition which preserved some recollection of a stricture passed by John on his own rite. It is here that the words of Josephus may be a valuable witness, since they also offer confirmation of the belief that John taught men not to overvalue his baptism. Enthusiastic disciples might easily impute a far greater meaning to the act than that contained in the teaching of the Baptist. Both the Gospels and Josephus reveal that John sought to prevent any over-emphasis on the value of the rite.

The way in which the writers of the Gospels make reference to John's baptism permits the assumption that the novelty was less in the act than in the actor. There is no suggestion that anything strange was experienced, and one is left with the impression that however different

in prophetic exhortations, as supplying metaphors of moral cleansing (Isa. i. 16 ; Ps. li. 7). It may have been this metaphorical or symbolical language of the prophets that suggested to John the Baptist the adoption of an actual rite, with a moral significance attached to it " (A. B. Macdonald, *Christian Worship in the Primitive Church*, 1934, p. 175 f.).

[1] R. Otto, *op. cit.*, p. 81.

E

might be the significance of the rite the ritual itself was not unfamiliar. The popularity of the Johannine baptism supports too the idea that it met a need in a way which did not contravene but suited the conceptions of the time. We know that lustral washings were a familiar feature of Jewish life, as indeed among almost all nations of the ancient world. But while Levitical washings might offer some historical antecedents in purifications one is obliged to recognize that they are far from explaining the baptism of John. One striking contrast is suggested by the already noted fact that the latter was conferred but once, the Levitical rites needed constant repetition. Only one Jewish lustral washing known to us does not seem to have been repeated. That is the tebilah. Despite the lack of conclusive documentary evidence there are several important considerations which support the belief that the tebilah dates back beyond the beginning of the Christian era.[1] If this can be allowed it is practically certain that for some of their similarities the Johannine and Christian baptisms must be regarded as indebted to the more ancient rite.[2] There are differences [3] which must not be overlooked, but it is more than probable that the essential ideas arose in Judaism of the pre-Christian period, and when borrowed received a further development under the

[1] See chapter I.

[2] " le baptême des prosélytes . . . qui est universellement considéré comme étant sensiblement plus ancien et comme remontant sans doute plus haut que le baptême chrétien et même que le baptême de Jean-Baptiste. L'un et l'autre paraissent en être issus, en partie au moins." M. Goguel, *Jean-Baptiste*, p. 109.

[3] Much opposition to the connection has come because of the different meaning of the rites. Schürer, *GJV*, III, p. 185 note. Schweitzer, who leaves the connection an open question, remarks : " That a baptism intended to secure to Jews forgiveness of sins and the reception of the Spirit should have been suggested to John by the lustrations practised by Gentiles on their going over to Judaism is not easy to make intelligible." *SMP*, p. 232.

influence of more spiritual conceptions. While the New Testament makes no explicit reference to the tebilah it is possible that Paul's mention of those who were baptized unto Moses in the cloud and in the sea (I Cor. x. 2) preserves a memory of his pre-Christian training, and that the underlying idea was derived from some rabbinic teaching which found analogies with the tebilah in the manner in which Israel entered the Promised Land.[1]

In the previous chapter the view has been expressed that the tebilah was a natural development of the Jewish laws of purification, and that it assumed prominence as a rite at a time when the nation's racial and religious consciousness had been stimulated. A likely date is to be found somewhere in the period of the Maccabees when propaganda as well as fighting was a weapon of the Maccabæan princes.[2] The new interest in the foreigner revealed also a serious difference of opinion in the nation. There were two opposing parties. One wished to refuse all dealings with Gentiles, regarding them as sinners and idolaters doomed to destruction. The more liberal minded would not only allow these dealings but even sought them as opportunities for missionary effort, regarding the Jewish dispersion as part of the divine plan for the winning of the Gentiles to the Jewish faith.

A sample of the spirit of the uncompromising class is to be found in the Book of Jubilees which reveals the exclusiveness of the powerful Pharisaic party.[3] This

[1] B. Scott Easton, " St. Paul and the Sacraments ", *Constructive Quarterly*, VII, 1919, pp. 102 ff.

[2] Josephus, *Antiq.*, XIII, 9, 1 ; XIII, 11, 3 ; XIII, 15, 4. " The Maccabæan leaders, John Hyrcanus, Aristobulus and Alexander Jannæus, in waging their wars, paid as much attention to propaganda as to conquest. For them at least the two went together " (C. Guignebert, *The Jewish World in the Time of Jesus*, E.T., 1939, p. 228).

[3] *Jubilees* xxx. 7–17.

body had a keen sense of its own privileged position,[1] and associated its belief in a Messianic Kingdom [2] with the conviction that this latter would bring also judgment on the enemies of the righteous.[3] Men who belonged to this party of exclusionists not only had no thought of compromise but wished as far as possible to accentuate the distinction between Israel and the outside world. They had no desire to win converts among the Gentiles and regarded them as without hope, while they themselves looked forward to the coming Messianic era when all such sinners and idolaters would perish.

Side by side with this attitude of exclusiveness there was —as has been said—a missionary spirit which sought to magnify the nation by winning converts from paganism. There is plenty of evidence of widespread missionary work.[4] The path was made easier by the fact that Judaism, like other Oriental faiths, became a fashionable cult in the Roman empire. Josephus has described the inclination of the masses towards Judaism, and we have his boast that there was no city or nation where the Jewish laws regarding Sabbath observance, fasting, the use of lights and food prohibitions were not found.[5] This missionary activity was not always carefully directed, and a fanatical zeal resulted in the winning of adherents of doubtful quality. There were many cases of men whose conformity extended to external matters alone, and who proved to be undesirable converts of insincere motives, whose lives reflected little credit on the faith they had accepted. Josephus is a witness to the varying motives which made men seek the status of proselyte and

---

[1] *Jubilees* xv. 30.   [2] *Ibid.*, i. 29.

[3] *Ibid.*, xxiii. 30 ; cf. *I Enoch* xci.–xciv. *AP*, II, p. 49.

[4] Josephus, *Antiq.*, XIII, 9, 1 ; XIII, 11, 3 ; XVIII, 3, 5 ; E. Schürer, *GJV*, III, pp. 150–8. Jean Juster, *Les Juifs dans l'Empire Romain*, 1914, I, pp. 253 ff. For proselytism among the Romans, see Horace, *Sat.*, i. 4, 142 f. ; Tacitus, *Hist.*, v. 5 ; Juvenal, *Sat.* xiv. 96 ff.

[5] Josephus, *c. Apion*, ii. 40.

to the undesirable types which were included.[1] The
taunt of Tacitus [2] may be discounted as the utterance
of an embittered man and a recognized opponent of
Judaism ; but the bad name which proselytes bore among
the Jews themselves is full of meaning. A familiar
passage from Matthew's Gospel (xxiii. 15) gives words of
Jesus in which the proselytising zeal of the scribes and
Pharisees is stigmatised as making a man " a son of
Gehenna twice as bad as yourselves " (Moffatt's translation). While this reference of Jesus may be to a special
type of missionary activity it is very probable that the
language reflects the attitude of the more pious Jews
towards the abuse of missionary zeal.

This deprecation of a merely superficial proselytising,
which we can assume confidently would be the attitude of
every right-minded Jew, provides a partial clue to the
understanding of the mission of John the Baptist. Because of the age in which he lived and his environment
we are justified in assuming that he must have been
brought up against the question of proselytism. What
kind of attitude would be most likely in such a spirit ?
Devoted to the faith of his fathers John saw that religion
besmirched by the evil practices of many who professed
it, while the missionaries of Judaism were more eager to
secure outward conformity among their converts than to
remind men of the inwardness of the faith. John was
steeped in the teaching of the prophets, and the Old
Testament provides many illustrations of protests by the
nobler souls of Judaism against a blind trust in the efficacy
of a mere ritual. There are many reminders that these
acts were no real substitute for right living.[3] Circum-

---

[1] *Antiq.*, XII, 91 ; XIV, 10, 12 ff. ; XX, 7, 3.

[2] " Nam pessimus quisque, spretis religionibus patriis, tributa
et stipes illuc gerebant " (*Hist.*, V, 5). This taunt may be
a tribute to Judaism's message for the outcast. Cf. Celsus's
sneer against the Christians (Origen, *c. Celsum*, III, 59 ff.).

[3] Jer. vii. 1 f.

cision must be more than a cutting of the flesh.[1] Right living was of more value than material sacrifices.[2] Outward cleansing did not remove stains of moral pollution ; [3] and there must be seen the marks of true repentance.[4] These were some of the reactions of the prophets against the abuses of their age, and one cannot conceive John adopting a different attitude when confronting similar problems in his day. His special difficulty would be the abuse of proselytism which neglecting any higher demand exploited a ritual for its purpose, and by this very act encouraged a false emphasis in the value of race alone apart from righteousness.

Starting from this hypothesis we may consider afresh the message of John. He is represented in the Gospels as opposing a blind faith in the privileges of race and reminding men of higher spiritual needs (Luke iii. 8 ; Matth. iii. 8, 9). It is useful to consider his words from the point of view of his audience. Many Jews were looking forward eagerly to the day when the advent of God's Kingdom would bring them the long-desired relief from their present disabilities, and furnish the occasion of triumph over their enemies.[5] We can understand the

[1] Lev. xxvi. 41 ; Deut. x. 16 ; xxx. 6 ; Jer. iv. 4 ; ix. 25 ; xxxi, 31 ff. ; Ezek. xxxvi. 26 ; xliv. 7, 9.

[2] I Sam. xv. 22 ; Isa. i. 11 ff. ; Hosea vi. 6 ; Amos v. 21 ff.

[3] Jer. ii. 22 ; Isa. i. 16.

[4] Ezek. xviii. 31 ; Amos v. 24.

[5] Psalms xciii.–xcix. ; Isa. xxiv. 21 ff ; lii. ; Micah iv. 7. *The Wisdom of Solomon*, dating probably from the first century B.C. (*AP*, I, pp. 520–1) provides an excellent illustration of the Jews' confidence in their position as the chosen race. It contains the striking statement : " For even if we sin we are Thine, knowing Thy dominion." Then follows the confident affirmation : " But we shall not sin, knowing that we are accounted Thine " (*AP*, I, p. 559). It is interesting to recall that Paul, whose early training probably owed much to rabbinic scholarship, shows in his letters evidence of familiarity with this book. The claims of Jewish racialism form the background of many passages in Paul's writings, e.g. Rom. iv. ; ix., 6 ; xi. 13 ff. ; Gal. iv. 21 ff. Echoes of the idea are found in John viii. 33, 53 ;

readiness with which they welcomed the words of the prophet when he called men to prepare for the Messianic Kingdom, which to them meant the triumph of Jewish nationalism. But prominent in the message of John was the thought of judgment—not against Gentiles as naturally the sinners, but against Jew and Gentile, without consideration of race, against all who had sinned.

John's words reveal how much he owed to the inspiration of the Old Testament. Amos had told Israel that race privilege before God meant race responsibility not race immunity. " You only have I known of all the families of the earth ; therefore I will visit upon you all your iniquities." [1] Ezekiel stressed the individual responsibility before God. " The soul that sinneth, it shall die." [2] Throughout the writings of the prophets can be found many illustrations of the rejection of a narrow particularism,[3] most noteworthy being the messages of Deutero-Isaiah and the book of Jonah. Non-canonical writings also reveal the presence of this conception. The influential apocalypse of *Enoch* [4] describes the " Son of Man " as being not only " a staff to the righteous " but " the light of the Gentiles ",[5] and contains the promise that even " those who were born in darkness " will be transformed.[6]

In discussing the significance of John's baptism it can-

James ii. 21. In *The Psalms of Solomon* we have a racial interpretation of morality in which the alien is the sinner (i. 1 ; ii. 1 ; etc.). This attitude can be paralleled in the canonical Psalms (ii. ; ix. ; x., etc.).

[1] Amos iii. 2 ; cf. ii. 6 ff. ; v. 18–27.

[2] Ezek. xviii. 20.

[3] Zech. ii. 11 ; viii. 20–3. See *HDB*, extra vol., 1904, pp. 710 ff.

[4] " *I Enoch* has had more influence on the New Testament than has any other apocryphal or pseudepigraphic work " (R. H. Charles, *AP*, II, p. 180).

[5] *I Enoch* xlviii. 4 ; cf. Isa. xlii. 6 ; xlix. 6.

[6] *Ibid.*, cviii. 11 ; cf. verse 14, *Frag. of the Book of Noah*. *AP*, II, p. 281.

not be emphasized too much that neither he himself nor the writers of primary authority—Josephus and the Gospels—make any claim that there was a wonder-working efficacy in the rite. Everything that has been said in support of such a claim is a matter of inference based mainly on four known facts. These are : (i) John was of an ascetic disposition ; (ii) the rite of baptism was a prominent feature of his work ; (iii) he made stringent moral demands on those who came to share it ; (iv) in addressing the people who came to him he asked who had warned them to flee from the wrath to come. It is natural to presume from the last statement that those who received this baptism were supposed to have escaped the wrath to come. A distinction must be preserved however between the belief of the Pharisees and Sadducees (Matth. iii. 7) or of the multitudes (Luke iii. 7) who came in their unrepentant state to John and incurred his just censure, and the belief of the Baptist himself concerning his baptism.

The four facts must be read in the light of the whole teaching of John. The main feature of this was that it was character not lineage which matter before God. " Begin not to say within yourselves, We have Abraham to our father ; for I say unto you, that God is able of these stones to raise up children unto Abraham. And even now the axe also is laid unto the foot of the trees ; every tree therefore that bringeth not forth good fruit is hewn down and cast into the fire " (Luke iii. 8 ; cf. Matth. iii. 9). The absoluteness of the last phrase should be noted, since it takes no account of the value of the baptism which men sought. Throughout the recorded preaching of John the foremost place is given to the moral demand. The only words referring to baptism are those which term it a water rite, and on that very account contrast it unfavourably with a baptism in Holy Spirit which his Successor would employ (Mark i. 8).

The baptism of John is defined as " a baptism of

repentance for the remission of sins ". It is not said that these were words actually used by John. The form suggests rather that they are a summary of his message. The preaching of John centred in the demand for repentance. In recalling this we would remind ourselves that the contemporary proselyte baptism, with which John and his hearers were so familiar, was like other Jewish washings, essentially a ritual act. The emphasis was on the value of race and no high moral demand was associated with it. When men sought the baptism of John he left them in no doubt that it was the spiritual condition which was all-important. Little is said of the ritual. One is justified in assuming that the main purpose of baptism was to express by outward symbol an inward spiritual condition. This would be in harmony with that prophetic character which distinguished John from the mass of miracle-mongers and wandering teachers existent at the time. On this interpretation one can understand why John came to use the language he did in describing the Johannine baptism, and why the Jewish historian recognised that John attached no inherent virtue to the rite for the remission of sins but demanded righteousness which involved a complete change of life. He recognised too that John pointed out that his baptism was only a water baptism which touched the physical rather than the spiritual.

The words of the reference to the coming Spirit baptism may be placed side by side with the statement of Josephus. " I baptize you with water ; He shall baptize you with Holy Spirit." If we take the first sentence, leaving for the time the allusion to the Messianic baptism, we notice how the words of Josephus harmonise with this thought. The baptism with water was " not for expiating certain sins but as a purification of the body ". Yet, despite the superficial meaning it is clear that the Jewish historian did not intend to imply that the baptism was merely a water washing any more than the words of John contained in the Gospels. Both recognized a deeper significance. In the Gospel account this is seen in the care with which John guards his baptism from unworthy recipients, in Josephus the language used conveys a like hint. The phrase employed by the latter, βαπτισμῷ συνιέναι, "to come together through baptism ", is quite unlikely to have been applied to an ordinary act of assembling for bodily cleansing. It conveys the suggestion of an entrance into a community, and invests the purification with the character of an initiatory rite.[1] Judaism had only one such water rite of initiation which conferred once and for all a new status and enabled men to share the privileges of the chosen race. This was the tebilah offered to the Gentiles.[2]

[1] R. Eisler, *The Messiah Jesus*, p. 269. Goguel says : " Bien que l'intention évidente de Josèphe soit de faire de Jean un simple moraliste, on aperçoit nettement derrière ce qu'il dit, que Jean a été autre chose qu'un prédicateur de la vertu et de la justice. L'expression ' s'unir par un baptême ' qu'il emploie, est déjà caractéristique parce qu'elle implique l'idée d'une communauté ou d'un groupe, sans dire d'ailleurs sur quels principes, sur quelles idées, sur quelles conceptions ou sur quels buts ce groupe repose " (*Jean-Baptiste*, p. 19). He argues also (p. 16, note 3) against Brandt's translation of βαπτισμῷ συνιέναι " to meet together to receive baptism ", on the ground that it is most unlikely that John would have brought together all his disciples for baptism at one time. Moreover, if Josephus had meant to imply this he would have used the phrase εἰς or ἐπὶ τὸ βάπτισμα. Goguel combats the argument of Dibelius in support of Brandt's translation—in which he suggested that it was contrary to the custom of the historian to mention something which might give a hint of a conspiracy against Rome— by pointing out that by force of circumstances Josephus is compelled sometimes to make reference to these popular movements and revolts, and that the reference in this passage to the intervention of Herod offers some support for the idea that such a happening might be feared in the case of John's disciples.

[2] B. W. Bacon (*Story of Jesus*, p. 131) is among those who accept the identification. J. Weiss, however, suggests that the baptism of John had a meaning different from that of proselyte baptism (*The History of Primitive Christianity*, E.T., 1937, II, p. 631).

In studying the connection between John's rite and the tebilah we must recognize, as already stated, that proselyte baptism would be a familiar experience in the days when he grew to manhood. He would see—as Jesus saw —men seeking eagerly to win converts for their faith. It was impossible to avoid reflection on their work. He must have noticed—as Jesus did—how little was the moral improvement in converts begotten by the zeal of men whose own conduct left much to be desired. Wherein lay the fault ? Was it not that men accepted a mere rite without recognizing its true implications ? Did not the missionaries themselves need also a moral change ? Now would come into consideration the great call of John as the prophet of the new era, a call that cannot be explained, as no human reason can explain satisfactorily a divine call. But we can see why he could link with his work the challenge of a symbolic rite. It was an inspired interpretation of the tebilah, in which the emphasis was shifted from a narrow racial conception to the proclamation of a spiritual Israel prepared for the coming Kingdom wherein spiritual and moral, and not physical considerations, alone counted. John did not preach baptism because he desired to introduce some new rite of initiation without which men could not hope to enter the coming Kingdom. It is absurd to imagine that one of the greatest moral teachers should have put in the forefront of his teaching an appeal to men to accept an act of magic as the sure guarantee of a place in the Kingdom of righteousness, or as an assurance that their past misdeeds would no longer be charged against them before God.

Mention has been made already of the denunciation by Old Testament prophets of any reliance upon mere ritual in religion as a substitute for right living. Even paganism in its loftier moods revolted against such superficiality. We have the well-known jest of Diogenes concerning the notorious thief Pataikion who was entitled to a nobler destiny after death than Epaminondas because of his initiation. In familiar words the poet Ovid voiced the protest of the best minds of the age :

> Ah nimium faciles, qui tristia crimina caedis
> Fluminea tolli posse putatis aqua.
> *Fasti*, II, 45–6.[1]

Is it likely that here the spiritual discernment of paganism surpassed the prophetic insight of the Baptist, despite the high moral consciousness which is so apparent in his words ?

The theory that John did not create but adapted a Jewish ritual act and gave it his own significance may not solve all the difficulties, yet, we believe, it leaves less than any other supposition, and makes less demand on the imagination. It helps us to understand the unity between the message of John and the rite called by his name, and also the compatibility of both with the acts and teaching of Jesus. We can see too the value of such a ritual act against the background of John's eschatological teaching as a witness to membership in the spiritual Israel and the outward sign of a deep spiritual change which was attested by the fruits of repentance for which John called. In this the Johannine baptism was a symbol carrying with it a truly prophetic conception.[2]

In asserting that John's baptism belonged to the realm

---

[1] There is a good discussion with references in A. Oepke's article, " Religiöse Waschungen im Hellenismus " (*TWNT*, I, pp. 528–32).

[2] The prophets recognized a real value in symbol. Ahijah rent his mantle and gave ten pieces to Jeroboam (I Kings xi. 30). Jeremiah hid great stones " in mortar in the brickwork, which is at the entry of Pharaoh's house in Tahpanhes " (Jer. xliii. 9). These prophetic actions are not to be explained in modern terms as pictorial language. They are, in some way, an assurance of the accomplishment of what is predicted. The actions are not magical for they do not effect the desired end, which is accomplished by the Divine power, but they are regarded as an assurance that it is being carried out.

of symbol we do not dismiss it as a representation having no value in itself. The ancient connotation of symbol gave the term a closer connection than does the modern with the thing symbolized. But this is something very different from a piece of magic. The value of baptism depended not on a proper performance of the baptismal act but on the spiritual or moral condition of the recipient. Although John refused the conception of the tebilah which made it the means of entrance by ritual into an Israel based on a privilege of physical birth, and placed it in the category of a water rite when compared with the Spirit baptism of his Successor, he did not retain it as a mere representation.[1] If he had done this he could have viewed with indifference the question of its performance. There is not the slightest hint of this attitude. Instead we have a definite recognition of the value of baptism in the words addressed to Jesus : " I have need to be baptized of Thee " (Matth. iii. 14).

The language used in the New Testament of a much greater event may be applied to the message of John. It came in the fullness of time. The period covered by the life of the Baptist was one in which men were laying a greater stress on ceremonial purity, and were endeavouring to link it with a demand for a higher moral and spiritual standard. The movement was restricted to no one land. This impulse towards asceticism, as it has been termed,[2]

---

[1] Remembering the influence of apocalyptic teaching at the time one wonders if the Baptist found in his rite something after the type of the " mark of God " which the writer of *The Psalms of Solomon* affirmed " is upon the righteous that they may be saved " (xv. 8). It is interesting to notice that the fifteenth psalm deals with the positions of the righteous and sinners " in the day of the Lord's Judgment ". It is curious to see how these psalms express from their narrow standpoint much of the message of John. Thus in ix. 12 we have words which John himself might have used : " He cleanseth from sins a soul when it maketh confession."

[2] E. von Dobschütz, *The Apostolic Age*, E.T., 1909, pp. 70 ff.

was found not merely in Judaism but throughout the world. It revealed itself in many Greek and Oriental cults. In Judaism it gave rise to the Essenes, and was the cause of the appearance of characters like Banus. Montefiore has pointed out that this combination of moral and ceremonial severity was characteristic also, although in a less degree, of Pharisaic and Rabbinic Judaism.[1]

If John had limited his teaching to a demand for a baptism of purity linked with stringent moral conditions, such a message would have been understood and probably even welcomed. It would have been in harmony with the ideas of the age. We know that certain points of contact were recognized,[2] and we may assume that it was the belief that John's teaching followed these lines which caused the Pharisees to come to his baptism. Even the popularity of John and the possibility that, as in the case of Jesus, non-Jews were included also in the crowds, need not have aroused any antipathy among the Jewish leaders. It was, as we have seen, an age in which a certain type of universalism found considerable favour in many Jewish quarters, although it is perhaps a misnomer to use the word " universalism " of a particularism, applied to outsiders, whose sole purpose was to magnify the Jewish religion and the Jewish nationality.[3]

But the stumbling block for the Pharisees especially must have been John's insistence on the worthlessness of a trust in racial privilege, and the assignation to this people, proud of their heritage, of a position no better than that of the Gentiles whom they despised. One may suspect that previous to our Gospel account there had appeared evidence of the hostility of the scribes and

[1] *Peake's Commentary*, p. 624.
[2] Matth. ix. 14 ; Mark ii. 18 ; Luke v. 33.
[3] Even the obligations to the strangers laid down in the Pentateuch were limited to proselytes by rabbinic interpretations (G. Hoennicke, *Das Judenchristentum im ersten und zweiten Jahrhundert*, 1908, p. 75 ff).

Pharisees, and this may explain the sharp tone of John's message when some were discerned in his audience. The use of the phrase " generation of vipers " must have rankled. By it the boasted Abrahamic descent was scouted, they were placed in the category of outcasts, and likened to the wild creatures of the desert among whom an earlier prophet had found the type of his own crooked generation.[1]

Yet in view of the prevailing conditions when John began his ministry there is nothing surprising in the welcome that was given to it. The Gospels bear testimony to the early popularity of John. One can understand too how the novelty of the idea of a tebilah demanded from all without distinction of race or class would seize the popular imagination and even could cause men to forget or overlook the strictures which John himself passed on his rite. The spectators saw the many who came for baptism ; the inwardness of the prophet's message and the real place in his work assigned to the rite escaped their understanding. Thus we may suppose the popular title of Baptist arose ; although more discerning souls linked with the name of John that of Elijah, the expected messenger of the new era. This title bestowed—the one by which John will be known always—is an instance of one of the little ironies of history. The position that John claimed was that of a forerunner, not that of a baptizer. He was the " voice " preparing the way by his call to repentance.

In one way John's transformed tebilah must be regarded as a protest against the crude particularism signified by the earlier rite. This helps to explain the individual note in the Baptist's preaching and the stress laid on the need of preparation against the coming day of Judgment when racial privileges would count as nothing. There is an

[1] Isa. lix. 5 ; According to Matthew Jesus Himself used the same words regarding the Pharisees : Matth. xii. 34 ; xxiii. 33 ; cf. John viii. 44.

interesting probability that in his protest against a false trust in national privileges and the neglect of obedience to the divine commands John had in his mind the impressive illustration of Naaman. This Old Testament story describes a proud heathen who found that his salvation depended on absolute obedience to the words of the prophet. The vocabulary of the story is significant. The leper baptized himself (Greek ἐβαπτίσατο, Hebrew ויטבל) in the Jordan. The term recalls both John's baptism and the tebilah. We have also the word ἐπέστρεψε (Hebrew וישב) in the description of Naaman's " return " to the man of God to make his confession of belief (II Kings v. 15). It is very probable that this incident had influence on the preaching of John. There is no mention of it in our accounts which are too brief to allow such references, but there is significance in the use of the story by Jesus at the beginning of His ministry shortly after His separation from John (Luke iv. 27).

One point to be considered at this stage is that raised by the question of Jesus concerning the authority for John's baptism. This ought not to be taken as laying emphasis on the rite itself, and implying, according to Schweitzer, that the institution of baptism was based on heavenly authority.[1] The description is popular, and the interpretation of Swete is surely correct when he takes the phrase as referring to the Baptist's work and teaching as a whole, symbolised by its visible expression.[2] In support of this interpretation we have the explanatory words which follow in Mark xi. 32 : " all verily held John to be a prophet ". There is also a similar use of the phrase " the baptism of John " in the Acts.[3]

---

[1] *SMP*, p. 233.   [2] H. B. Swete, *St. Mark*, p. 263.
[3] Acts i. 22 ; xviii. 25. B. W. Bacon (*The Story of Jesus*, p. 131) has suggested that the question of Jesus probably bears witness to the fact that it was principally the ' unchurched ' element, the publicans and sinners, that responded to John's call and accepted baptism.

It needs little imagination to understand how the lofty message of John, with its statement that God was no respecter of persons, its demand for individual holiness and its reminder that men at the Judgment would stand or fall by their individual actions, would attract the young Jesus. In view of this early association of Jesus and John it is interesting to note how these same ideas repeat themselves in the Master's own words.[1] May there not be also some significance in the fact that the first recorded address of Jesus, given in the synagogue at Nazareth, was in one way a protest against a narrow provincialism or particularism and a reminder that God is no respecter of persons but extends His grace to all races ? The reference to Naaman might have been made familiar from the lips of John the Baptist himself.[2]

Terminology.

For a complete discussion of the nature of the Johannine baptism it is necessary to take into account the special terminology which is used to describe it.[3] Considerable importance centres in the use of the verb $\beta a\pi\tau i\zeta\omega$ and its cognates.

Usually Jewish ceremonial washings are described in the Old Testament by the Hebrew רָחַע, which is translated in the Septuagint by $\lambda o \acute{v} \varepsilon \sigma \theta a\iota$. This word is

---

[1] Matth. viii. 11, 12 ; Matth. xi. 20 ff. ; Luke x. 13 ff. ; Luke xiii. 23–30.

[2] Luke iv. 27. The broad world outlook attested by the appeal of John's baptism and the words of Jesus is obscured by a spirit of exclusionism found in certain passages of the Gospels, and which appears to find a certain justification even in the words of Jesus Himself (Matth. x. 5 f. ; cf. v. 18). J. Weiss thought that this exclusive tendency was an echo of a conservative movement in the early Church reacting against the broad-mindedness of the missionary work among the Gentiles (*The History of Primitive Christianity*, I, p. 171).

[3] An excellent summary of this is given in *TWNT*, I, pp. 527 f., 543.

found also occasionally in the New Testament, but there the special word applied to theocratic washings is $\beta\alpha\pi\tau\acute{\iota}\zeta\omega$. The form of $\beta\alpha\pi\tau\acute{\iota}\zeta\omega$ would suggest that it is the intensive and iterative form of $\beta\acute{\alpha}\pi\tau\omega$, and the few examples found in pre-Christian literature,[1] whether the use is literal or metaphorical, support this interpretation of the word. The few instances of the term in pre-New Testament times serve to call attention to its rare use. The word occurs in Josephus [2] in a metaphorical sense, and there are four examples in the Septuagint.[3] In some of the later Greek versions are other instances,[4] but the writers of these belong to the post-New Testament period. This rarity of the word in earlier times stands in striking contrast to its usage in the New Testament. Here are found seventy-seven examples, nearly one-half of which have reference to the ministry of the Baptist. When we consider the meaning we find that apart from metaphorical uses,[5] and one application to Jewish ritual washing,[6] the term refers solely to the rite of baptism, directly or indirectly. The context in almost every case would allow of a translation suiting the intensive form of the

[1] There are instances dating back to the time of Plato, who uses the word in a metaphorical sense. Most of the examples occur among the lesser-known writers (Liddell and Scott, *A Greek-English Lexicon*, New ed., Part II, 1926, s.v.). An instance in the Paris Papyri, dating back to the middle of the second century B.C., shows that it was already being used by the uneducated in a metaphorical sense (Moulton and Milligan, *The Vocabulary of the Greek Testament*, s.v.).

[2] Josephus, *BJ*, iv, 3, 3; *Antiq.* x. 9, 4.

[3] The word is used of Naaman washing in the Jordan (II Kings v. 14); of Judith bathing (*Judith* xii. 7); of cleansing after ritual pollutions (*Sirach* xxxiv. 25 (xxxi. 30); and metaphorically, of the effect of lawless conduct (Isa. xxi. 4).

[4] Job. ix. 31, *Aquila*; Psalm lviii. 3, *Aquila, Symmachus*; Jer. xxxviii. 22, *Symmachus*.

[5] Mark x. 38, 39; Luke xii. 50.

[6] Mark vii. 4, a disputed reading, but followed by the use of $\beta\alpha\pi\tau\iota\sigma\mu\acute{o}\varsigma$ (Luke xi. 38).

word "to immerse", although such a meaning could not stand in Luke xi. 38.

Two main explanations are given for the frequency with which the term appears in the New Testament. One reason put forward is that at this time the word was coming into use in Greek-speaking Jewish circles to denote ceremonial or religious washing.[1] On the other hand, Burkitt contended that the greater probability was that the word was brought into use through the practice of John himself.[2]

Turning to the cognates, we find that John's title βαπτιστής is unique. There is no instance of this word except as a description of John. Outside the New Testament it is found in the passage of Josephus which has been quoted already [3] and the impression left by a study of the use is that the term was a popular name for John and was peculiar to him. The meaning is doubtful. Βαπτιστής has generally been taken in the sense of "the baptizer", and this would appear to be confirmed by the substitution of the present participle of the verb in Mark i. 4 ; vi. 14, 24. It has been suggested that the title was bestowed on John because contrary to the Jewish custom of self-baptism he himself baptized others.[4] But the problem is not so easy of solution as this explanation would imply, and there are difficulties unanswered by such an interpretation. On the analogy of a similar form like σοφιστής it is possible to translate the word "the bather".

The two terms used for baptism, βαπτισμός, βάπτισμα,

[1] *JLBC*, I, p. 334.
[2] F. C. Burkitt, *Christian Beginnings*, p. 19.
[3] *AJ*, xviii, 5, 2. Abrahams (*Studies*, I, p. 33) thought that this use in Josephus might be an interpolation, since he argued that, apart from this epithet, the terminology of Josephus in this passage was quite independent of the New Testament. Reitzenstein thinks the reference is to a sect (*Die Vorgeschichte der christliche Taufe*, pp. 231-3).
[4] *TWNT*, I, p. 544.

are found in no writer before they occur in the New Testament.[1] Josephus has βαπτισμός in describing the work of John, but he introduces also another word, βάπτισις, which is not found in the New Testament. The fact that βαπτισμός and βάπτισμα are peculiar to the New Testament would lend support to the theory that their origin was due to the need that was felt of technical words to describe an entirely new phenomenon.

Why these terms which we have discussed were used rather than others is a question which cannot be answered with any degree of certainty. Perhaps the intensive form of the verb fitted the idea of immersion demanded in John's rite, and it is possible that the use of the term in the Septuagint version of the Naaman incident may have influenced its employment. Aramaic, however, would be probably the language which the Baptist employed in his preaching.

That John's baptism, following the tebilah,[2] was a complete immersion may be assumed from several facts. In the first place the rite took place at a river—the Jordan. Then in the description of Josephus the parallel demands an equally thorough treatment in both cases : " a purification of the body after the soul had been thoroughly purified already by righteousness " δικαιοσύνῃ προεκκεκαθαρμένης.

---

[1] Of these βάπτισμα is probably the whole act of baptism while βαπτισμός is the actual process of immersion. In the New Testament βαπτισμός is once used of Jewish ritual washing (Mark vii. 4 (8)). It is noteworthy that in the early Greek Fathers βαπτισμός is not used, in contrast to the fairly frequent employment of βάπτισμα ; Clement R., *Cor.* B. 6 ; Ignatius, *Polycarp.* 6 ; *Didache* 7 ; *Barnabas* xi. 1 ; Justin, *Trypho* xiv. 1 ; xix. 2 ; xxix. 1 ; xliii. 2 ; lxxxviii. 2; 7 ; Irenæus, *Haer.* I, 3, 3 ; 7, 2 ; 9, 4 ; 14, 6 ; 21, 1, 2 ; III, 12, 15 ; Clement A., *Pæd.*, I, 29, 5 ; 30, 2 ; etc. See J. B. Lightfoot, *Colossians*, ii. 12, note ; Moulton and Milligan, *Vocabulary of the Greek Testament*, s.v. ; Liddell and Scott, *Greek-English Lexicon*, New ed., s.v.

[2] That the Jewish tebilah was an immersion was shown by Abrahams in his discussion with C. F. Rogers, *JTS*, XII, pp. 437-45 ; 609-12 ; XIII (1912), pp. 411-14.

To maintain the parallel something akin to immersion would be expected. In the account of the baptism of Jesus it is said : ἐβαπτίσθη εἰς τὸν Ἰορδάνην ὑπὸ Ἰωάννου (Mark i. 9). Swete, who compared these words with the ἐν τῷ Ἰορδάνῃ of verse 5, thought that the former construction brought " the added thought of the immersion which gives vividness to the scene ".[1] It is very improbable, however, that any distinction was implied by the substitution of εἰς for ἐν. Moulton has pointed out that the New Testament provides clear examples of the tendency of εἰς to encroach on the domain of ἐν, which makes it unlikely that any importance attaches to the change. Some support of the idea of immersion might be found in the use of ἀναβαίνων in Mark i. 10 in contrast with the verb καταβαῖνον of the same verse describing the action of the Spirit.

A most difficult question is that concerning the agent who performed the rite. The Johannine baptism is regarded usually as one administered by John in person or by one of his disciples. This interpretation is supported by the employment of the Greek preposition ὑπο, and would appear to be confirmed by the conversation between Jesus and John, reported in the Gospel of Matthew. The problem unsolved by this explanation is that of giving a reason why John introduced this innovation. If the Johannine baptism was the Jewish tebilah adapted by John for his own purpose, one is at a loss to explain why baptism by an agent should have been substituted for the self-immersion of the Jewish rite. It is still more strange that such an action should have been accepted by the Jews and that there should be no hint of any controversy over the change, for we cannot think that there is any reference to the matter in the question of Jesus concerning the authority of John's baptism. The latter had to deal with John's credentials as a prophet,

[1] *St. Mark*, p. 8. For Moulton, see *A Grammar of New Testament Greek*, I, pp. 63, 234, 245.

and ought not to be limited to a query whether baptism by an agent, be he John or another, was permissible.

In heathen cults the act of the priest in the initiation of a candidate often was of vital importance, but this has no parallel in Judaism. Luke affirms that John was the son of a priest. The work of the Jewish priesthood was limited to the Temple,[1] and so far as purifications were concerned their part was that of giving instructions. In the tebilah the rabbis were merely witnesses. Nor in his character of prophet would John find any precedent in the Old Testament for assuming the rôle of baptizing others. Elisha did not even accompany Naaman to the Jordan. We know that in the period in which John lived Hellenistic mystery cults flourished, and these—as we have said—often laid great stress on the action of the priest in the performance of initiatory rites. But, whatever may be said for such mystery influence on later Christian teaching, there is no real evidence that John himself owed anything to it. Nor does his character, as revealed in the Gospels, lend support to the idea that he would arrogate to himself such an office.[2]

On the other hand, it is impossible to deny that the pictures given in the New Testament of the Johannine

[1] Even in the case of circumcision, which, as applied to children, naturally required an agent for its performance, it was recognized that any adult male Israelite was qualified for the task. There is even an instance of a woman performing the rite (Exod. iv. 25).

[2] One is puzzled to find the foundation for Schweitzer's description of John's baptism as " the authoritative act of an individual man who felt himself endowed with plenary powers ", whose belief in his own personal powers was such that it could be said of his rite : " its efficacy was not in itself but in him who bestowed it " (*SMP*, p. 232). It is not easy to derive this picture of John from the New Testament story of one who regarded himself as a prophetic " voice ", whose demands were essentially ethical, and whose character, even allowing for the exaggeration of the writer of the Gospels, surely revealed a deep and sincere humility.

rite, as well as those of early Christian baptism, indicate an act performed by someone other than the recipient. Yet it must be recognized that the first description we have of such a rite was written at least thirty years after the death of John, and there are not wanting signs that the writers who describe these earliest events are treating matters with which they are unfamiliar. We have an obvious example in the two passages of the Fourth Gospel which refer to baptism during Christ's earthly ministry (iii. 22–6 ; iv. 1, 2). There remain also traces of uncertainty in regard to the text. In Luke's reference to the multitudes who went to John's baptism (iii. 7), the Western text has a reading $\dot{\epsilon}\nu\dot{\omega}\pi\iota\upsilon\nu$ $\alpha\dot{\upsilon}\tau\upsilon\tilde{\upsilon}$ for $\dot{\upsilon}\pi'\alpha\dot{\upsilon}\tau\upsilon\tilde{\upsilon}$. If this text were correct the description is a true picture of a baptism performed after the manner of the tebilah. It is interesting also to find that in Mark i. 5, we have a verbal form which is both middle and passive, and the translation " they were baptized " is determined only by the words $\dot{\upsilon}\pi'$ $\alpha\dot{\upsilon}\tau\upsilon\tilde{\upsilon}$ the same phrase which in the Western text of Luke iii. 7 is substituted by $\dot{\epsilon}\nu\dot{\omega}\pi\iota\upsilon\nu$ $\alpha\dot{\upsilon}\tau\upsilon\tilde{\upsilon}$.

The historical problem of explaining the origin of John's rite as an act performed by an agent, and the textual and literary difficulties in the accepted text of the New Testament, affecting not only the descriptions of John's baptism but also its Christian counterpart, have given rise to the theory that both these rites which have much in common were administered originally, according to the Jewish custom, as self-baptisms. To explain the discrepancy between the accounts given in the New Testament and the method of the tebilah it has been suggested that the misinterpretation occurred in an age when men were familiar only with the developed form of Christian baptism administered by an outside agent. The tradition of the baptism remained, but its method had escaped them, and, unable to describe a form of which they were ignorant, they gave a picture of the later Christian baptism.

This theory is built on two main arguments: the use of the middle voice of the verb in places where it would not be expected, and the evidence in the language of liturgical differences from early Church baptismal practice which could be understood best if they were regarded as survivals from an earlier form which approximated to the Jewish tebilah. The latter argument is concerned with the form of the Christian rite, but we believe that there is no reason to suppose that this at first differed greatly from that of John. At any rate, if it can be shown that there has been a misunderstanding as to the earliest form of the Christian rite, the presumption is equally strong that a similar mistake has occurred regarding the baptism of John. It has been argued that the use of the middle voice may be explained by the possible interpretation that the form is used in the sense of " to get oneself baptized ". Such a translation is given for the middle form in Acts xxii. 16. Some, indeed, have found in every instance of this usage a special shade of meaning,[1] which is a convenient and not easily combated position. But the cumulative effect of the consideration of several instances tends to lead one in search of some more satisfying explanation.

An excellent statement of the case for self-baptism is put forward by B. S. Easton.[2] First he draws attention to the preservation in the New Testament of the instances of the use of the middle voice of verbs dealing with baptism. There are three such examples of $\beta a\pi\tau i\zeta\epsilon\iota\nu$.[3] There are also instances of the use of the middle voice of verbs which, from their employment in the Septuagint or elsewhere, may be regarded as technical baptismal terms : $\dot{a}\pi\dot{o}\lambda o\upsilon\sigma a\iota$ (Acts xxii. 16) ; $\dot{a}\pi\epsilon\lambda o\dot{\upsilon}\sigma a\sigma\theta\epsilon$ (I Cor. vi. 11) ; $\lambda\epsilon\lambda o\upsilon\sigma\mu\dot{\epsilon}\nu o\iota$ (Heb. x. 22) ; and $\nu\dot{\iota}\psi a\sigma\theta a\iota$

---

[1] J. C. Lambert, *The Sacraments in the New Testament*, 1903, pp. 136, 156–8 ; see also *TWNT*, p. 538.

[2] *American Journal of Theology*, XXIV, 1920, pp. 513–18.

[3] Mark vii. 4 ; Acts xxii. 16 ; I Cor. x. 2.

(John xiii. 10). B. S. Easton notes also that there are three cases where the middle appears as a variant. Although in regard to these the authority of the manuscripts concerned is but slight, the variant readings are not without significance in view of the present argument. There are also a number of cases where the forms can be read as either passive or middle.

Some of these instances carry little weight, but there are three which are vital to the discussion. First comes the passage in Acts xxii. 16, which professes to give Paul's own statement of the words used by Ananias when he visited him at Damascus. Here occur two instances of verbs in the middle form. There is every reason to suppose that the author of the Acts was a companion of Paul, and because of this a special value may be attached to this statement. It was an experience that Paul would never forget, and one can imagine that the vividness of the recollection would cause the speaker to give an almost verbatim report of the words that were uttered. Such a probability is confirmed by a close study of the passage since, as Easton points out, the language is " entirely Talmudic in its phrasing ".[1] This means that it approximates to the description of a tebilah experience in the very way we should expect early Christian baptism to do.

In regard to the other examples whose study is important, we have in I Corinthians vi. 11 : ἀλλὰ ἀπελού- σασθε, ἀλλὰ ἡγιάσθητε, words which remind us of the language of the *Sybilline Oracles*, iv. 165, ἐν ποταμοῖς λούσασθε ὅλον δέμας ἀενάοισιν, and of Isaiah i. 16, Λούσασθε, καθαροὶ γέγεσθε. There is no doubt too that the description of Israel's baptism at the time of the Exodus, given in I Corinthians x. 2, was written with

---

[1] He refers to Merx, *Die vier kanon. Evangelien*, II, 1902, i, p. 38, n. 1. It must be admitted that the expression one would have expected Ananias to have used for self-baptism would be βάπτισον σεαυτόν. Cf. *Corp. Hermet.*, iv, 4 : βάπτισον σεαυτὴν ἡ δυναμένη εἰς τοῦτον τὸν κρατῆρα.

obvious reference to the Christian rite. It is only by this assumption that we are able to explain the otherwise unintelligible εἰς τὸν Μωϋσῆν.[1]

Easton maintains that these passages offer evidence of a very archaic conception of baptism reaching back to the first divergence of Christian from Jewish ceremonial. He then proceeds to point out with what ease such grammatical forms could be changed in the Koine. In this latter the use of the middle to express reflexive acts was no longer absolutely essential. "Βαπτισθείς might be used to denote the fact of baptism without any reflection as to its agent." Easton illustrates his point from variant readings in Luke vii. 30 and iii. 7, and suggests that even where an agent is named this same explanation might be applied, since in reality the reference would be to the witness of the self-baptism. He maintains also that the phrase Ἰωάννης ἐβάπτισεν ἐν ὕδατι was not of Gentile origin, but was due to a special force given to the Hebrew hiphil form הטביל, which was translated by the Greek βαπτίζειν, and meant " to hold a baptism ". From this active use a passive might be formed in which the official witness would be spoken of as the agent.

In his hypothetical sketch of the evolution of baptism Easton goes on to suggest that the substitution of baptism by an agent in place of self-immersion would be furthered by confusion with the parallel rite of the Spirit which, of necessity, was not self-given. The actual words used to describe each action—both that of the Spirit, and of the

---

[1] Ἐβαπτίσαντο is the reading of B. Rec. and Tregelles, ἐβαπτίσθησαν is read by XACDEFG Tischendorf. The latter is common in the New Testament : Acts ii. 41 ; ix. 18 ; xvi. 15 ; xvi. 33 ; xix. 5 ; Rom. vi. 3 ; I Cor. i. 13, 15 ; xii. 13 ; Gal. iii. 27. It is impossible to imagine that the true reading was ἐβαπτίσθησαν with ἐβαπτίσαντο as the substitution. Lambert thinks that the use of the middle here implies that the act was a conscious and voluntary one (*op. cit.*, p. 159). The much-supported variant bears witness to the difficulty of interpretation felt by early scribes.

man himself—would be represented in Aramaic by the same causative form of the verb. A Gentile, who lacked the background of Jewish thought, would be confused and misinterpret it. This misunderstanding would be strengthened in the minds of those who were familiar with the initiation practices of mystery cults, where the priest, as agent, held a position of the utmost importance. The growth of the practice of exorcism would also assist the transformation of the rite of self-baptism. Finally, the merging of the witness into the agent would be completed in the time when the post-baptismal invocation of the convert—traces of which are still to be found in the New Testament writings, according to Easton [1]—was superseded by a pre-baptismal act, while the now recognized officiant laid his hand on the candidate at the moment of immersion.

These arguments offer a strong support to the contention that the original forms of both Johannine and early Christian baptisms were similar to, and derived from the Jewish tebilah. We do not think that any part of the evidence is decisive by itself, but the whole seems to present a cumulative force which compels a recognition of the true origin of the first Christian sacrament. One cannot regard, for example, as conclusive for self-baptism the argument which is based upon the instances of the middle voice of the verb. Although valuable, there is a danger of giving this form a significance which it does not possess in the New Testament where the proportion of really reflexive middles is very small.[2] But the real value of these instances is that they furnish a grammatical argument which can be linked with that based upon the

[1] Thus in Acts xxii. 16 it should be noted that it is the candidate for baptism who is commanded to utter the invocation, and not the officiant, supposing such had been present. The procedure also appears to find support in the language of I Peter iii. 21.

[2] J. H. Moulton, *A Grammar of New Testament Greek*, I, pp. 155 ff.

liturgical differences from later Church practice and the resemblances to the Jewish tebilah. We must also take into account the whole social and historical environment of early Christianity. These various considerations lead to one valid conclusion, and one only—that the three initiatory rites of the tebilah, the Johannine and the Christian baptisms, were not only originated by Jews, but have that even closer relationship which their common Jewish origin might suggest.[1]

ADDITIONAL NOTE A

Did John preach concerning the Kingdom of God?

It has been denied that John's message made any reference to the coming Kingdom. There is only one verse in the Gospels which states definitely that the preaching of the Baptist had to do with the Kingdom, and those who hold that the Johannine message was concerned only with the thought of the coming Judgment regard this passage (Matth. iii. 2) as an assimilation of the teaching of John to that of Jesus. R. Otto [2] dismissed the

---

[1] One writer who holds the view that there was probably " no direct connection between the baptism of John and Christian baptism, which came in naturally as soon as the Gentiles began to be converted ", has made the interesting suggestion that it was the seven deacons rather than the twelve apostles who were the first to practise baptism in the name of the Lord Jesus. This, he thinks, is implied by the narrative, and he argues further that such action " would correspond admirably with the probability that the seven represented Hellenistic Jews who had been influenced by the Diaspora ". He believes that in their mission to a heathen population like that of Samaria the seven followed the line of Jewish practice for the initiation of proselytes and baptized their converts, using probably the formula " ' in the name of the Lord Jesus ', to indicate that their converts were not merely proselytes to Judaism, but to that special sect which recognised the claims of Jesus " (*JLBC*, I, p. 341 f).

[2] *The Kingdom of God and the Son of Man*, E.T., 1938, pp. 69 ff. Doubt has been cast also on the proclamation by John of the

verse as an interpolation. He made no claim to manuscript support for his action ; and it should be recognized
at once that the evidence of the manuscripts is entirely
in favour of the genuineness of the words. The argument
for interpolation is based on the subject matter alone.

The question arises whether this is sufficient. Apart
from the fact that Matthew iii. 2 is the only verse which
declares this proclamation of the Kingdom there are some
further considerations. Most will accept the truth of
Goguel's statement that the thought of John seems to be
determined more by the idea of Judgment than by that
of the Kingdom of God.[1] There is also a strong probability that the description of the work and preaching
of John reveals a certain adaptation to Christian ideas.
But from these premises it does not follow that the
thought of the coming Kingdom had no place in the
Baptist's teaching.

One doubts indeed whether there was any Jewish
eschatology of this period which did not have to make
allowance for this idea. We know that it occupied
a special place in many apocalyptic writings, and John's
thought was cast in an apocalyptic mould. His knowledge
too of the Old Testament prophets from the days of the
great seers of the eighth century onwards must have made
the conception a familiar one. The proclamation of
severe judgments because of national guilt never caused
any of the prophets to overlook the possibility—and one
might almost say, the certainty—of a regenerate nation
realizing a reconciliation with Yahweh, and a kingdom
under His own personal direction or through the government of one whom He had called.[2] John's temperament

coming of the Messiah. This story has been attributed to later
Christian reflection. C. G. Montefiore, *The Synoptic Gospels*,
1927, I, p. 8.

[1] *Jean-Baptiste*, p. 43.

[2] A good discussion of the national hope is found in W.
Bousset, *Die Religion des Judentums im späthellenistischen*

and outlook made him stress the Judgment, but his message was uttered against a background of national belief in a Messianic Kingdom. Jesus proclaimed the Kingdom, yet He too preached Judgment and called men to repentance.[1] It must be remembered that our picture of John is but a partial one and is mainly concerned with his clash with the people who represented class privileges and unrighteousness. It is not surprising that he reiterated the ancient prophecies of Judgment and, in so doing, used the vivid figure of the consuming fire. But even the fire of Judgment could be regarded as an omen of the coming Kingdom. To this the Old Testament writings bear witness.[2]

Could John have afforded to ignore the conception of the Kingdom ? Speculations as to the date and duration of the Messianic reign held a prominent place in contemporary Jewish thought.[3] Although Luke makes no mention of the fact that the Johannine preaching was concerned with the Kingdom this Gospel shows how clearly the popular thought turned to Messianic expectations when a prophet like John appeared in the midst (iii. 15). The Baptist lived in an age of political and religious unrest, and although no definite Messianic movement may be pointed out, yet behind much of the unrest was a belief that a time was coming when either

Zeitalter, 3te Auf., 1926, pp. 213–42. See also C. Guignebert, *The Jewish World in the Time of Jesus*, E.T., 1939, pp. 122 ff. A brief but comprehensive list of books is included in the note, p. 122. There was a picture of the Judgment which included no hope of an earthly Messianic Kingdom. This arose from a pessimism which there is no reason to think was widespread, and which was due probably to special conditions. Such a scene is that depicted in some sections of the *Apocalypse of Baruch*, which was the outcome of a despair created by the tragedy of Jerusalem in A.D. 70. See *AP*, II, p. 479.

[1] H. Windisch. *Taufe und Sünde im ältesten Christentum bis auf Origenes*, 1908, pp. 79 ff.

[2] Ezek. xxxix. ; Joel iii. ; Daniel vii.

[3] C. Guignebert, *op. cit.*, p. 151.

directly or through His representative God would bring in His rule.

A study of the doctrine of the Kingdom furnishes a good introduction to a knowledge of the Jewish sects. It is interesting to observe that Josephus makes a description of the insurrection of Judas serve a similar purpose (*Antiq.* XVIII, i). The words of Josephus do not affirm that this movement was Messianic,[1] but doubtless it would make its appeal to the political Messianism of the time ; and we have no means of judging the full implications of the words of the Jewish historian in defining this Fourth Philosophy—as he terms it—which, he says, promoted violence under the name of liberty and proclaimed God as the only Ruler and Lord. No movement in Palestine at that period can be regarded as uninfluenced by these current beliefs. Even the mystical Essenes, who had no political hopes to cause a disturbance of existing conditions, have been described as men who endeavoured to prepare for the Kingdom of God by the organization of a community of saints.[2] The leaders and Rabbis frowned upon the turbulence of the people and despised their crude beliefs (John vii. 48, 49 ; Acts v. 35 ff. ; Josephus, *Antiq.*, XX, v, 1) but they were not untouched by the current eschatological hope.[3]

No student can approach the study of the thought of the period without being confronted with a strange mixture

---

[1] Foakes-Jackson points this out and appears to doubt the likelihood of there being any connection (*JLBC*, I, pp. 421–5).

[2] C. A. Briggs, *The Messiah of the Gospels*, 1894, p. 39. Philo regarded as worthy of comment the fact that the Essenes never came into conflict with the government (*Quod Omnis Probus Liber*, 13).

[3] " Auch die rabbinische Theologie bildet eine reiche Fundgrube für den eschatologischen Glauben jener Zeit, sowohl für die nationalen Hoffnungen wie für die erweiterte Eschatologie " (P. Volz, *Die Eschatologie der jüdische Gemeinde im neutestamentlichen Zeitalter*, 1934, p. 9).

of ideas.[1]   There are beliefs in a temporal and an eternal Kingdom, in a Messiah and in no Messiah, but out of the medley of ideas can be discerned the unshakable conviction that God will ensure the future of the race under His own power.   The apocalyptic writings offer a mine of information in this study, although it would be unwise to regard these as reflecting necessarily the popular mood, for the form of the literature scarcely suggests a popular appeal.   At the same time there is little justification for the attitude which dismisses this literature as a more or less negligible " excrescence ", having no connection with the main line of Jewish thought.[2]   The Book of Daniel was a part of the Jewish Canon and we have abundant evidence of the influence of apocalyptic teaching on the New Testament.   Much has been made of the Rabbinic attitude to these books, but it must not be overlooked that there were even Rabbis who indulged in apocalyptic speculations.   Moreover, one ought not to assume that Rabbinic Judaism was a more correct picture of the Judaism of the first century A.D. than that given in the New Testament which reflects the apocalyptic influence.[3] The New Testament may have been produced in a narrow circle, but it belonged to the period under review.

[1] See C. Guignebert, *op. cit.*, pp. 133 ff.

[2] C. G. Montefiore, *The Religion of the Ancient Hebrews*, 1892, p. 467.

[3] P. Volz, *op. cit.*, p. 10: " Will man ein Gesamtbild der damaligen Frömmigkeit und religiösen Anschauungswelt innerhalb des Judentums bekommen, so muss man die beiden führenden Kreise, Rabbinismus und Apokalyptik, zusammennehmen.   Ich halte es nicht für richtig, sie gegeneinander auszuspielen und den Wert der einen Erscheinung auf Kosten der anderen zuunterstreichen.   Beide sind gleich wichtig." To this may be added the words of G. F. Moore (*History of Religions*, 1920, II, p. 65): " There can be no doubt that in certain circles or strata of Jewish society, these (apocalyptic) writings had in their time a great vogue, and represented beliefs widely current among the people, notwithstanding the disapproval of scholars."

Montefiore pointed out that there was little Rabbinic literature which was as early as A.D. 50 and the period under consideration was " in a peculiar sense a time of transition ".[1]

Although it has been necessary to make reference to the critical attitude of the Rabbis towards apocalyptic teaching, we have no reason to suppose that the Rabbinic doctrine contradicted the main ideas of the apocalyptic writers. Fortunately for the purpose of our argument it is these main ideas with which we are concerned, and we are able to leave on one side the narrow partisan views peculiar to various authors, and the probable Rabbinic reactions to such fanatical teaching. Again, whatever the influence of the apocalyptic writings on the nation as a whole, there is no doubt of their influence on the people among whom Jesus grew to manhood. Otto has shown that *I Enoch* had much to do with guiding the conceptions of Jesus, and Burkitt has summed up the position in regard to the general influence : " The Jewish apocalypses themselves and the state of mind that produced them had a great and formative influence on the minds of the earliest Christians. I venture to think we can go so far as to say that without some knowledge of the Jewish apocalypses and a fairly clear realization of the state of mind in which they were composed, it is impossible to understand the earliest Christianity, impossible to enter at all into the hopes and fears of the ' multitudes ', of the crowd, that forms the background of the Gospels."[2] That this crowd which formed the background of the Gospels was the one to which not only Jesus appealed but also John is not a matter for conjecture alone, but is attested by the Gospel records themselves.[3]

[1] *Peake's Commentary*, p. 618.
[2] " The Apocalypses : their place in Jewish history ", *Judaism and the Beginnings of Christianity*, 1923, pp. 51, 52.
[3] Matth. xi. 7 ; xxi. 26 ; Mark xi. 32 ; Luke vii. 24 ; John iii. 26 ff. ; x. 40, 41.

It is through the apocalyptic writings we are able to understand how closely the ideas of Judgment and the Kingdom were associated in the minds of men of the period when John began his work. An excellent illustration is provided by the *Psalms of Solomon*. In the seventeenth and eighteenth we have a vivid picture of the triumph of the Messianic Kingdom and the Judgment on the nations, concluding with the prayer for the coming of the Lord's Anointed :

May God cleanse Israel against the day of mercy and
    blessing,
Against the day of choice when He bringeth back His
    anointed

    .   .   .   .   .   .

That He may establish them all before the Lord,
A good generation (living) in the fear of God in the days
    of mercy.[1]

Most of these psalms date probably from the middle of the first century B.C.[2] and reveal how out of the failure of hopes centred in the Hasmonæan princes there had developed in some circles a keener expectation of the coming Messiah.

It must be remembered that the prophetic writings [3] also provided part of the background for the work and

---

[1] The translation is that of G. B. Gray, *AP*, II, p. 651.

[2] Gray thought that Psalm ii., with its reference to the death of Pompey, was written about 48 B.C. He added : " None of the other Psalms refer to Pompey's death, and the majority may well be somewhat earlier than the second, and have been written soon after Pompey's invasion of Palestine (63 B.C.) " (*AP*., II, p. 630).

[3] " The idea of a judgment so severe as to render possible an entire breach with the guilty past, and of a subsequent complete realization of Yahweh's kingship in a regenerate nation, is common to all the prophets, but is expressed in a great variety of forms and images conditioned by the present situation and needs of Israel at the time when each prophet spoke " (W. R. Smith (and E. Kautsch) in *EBi*, " Messiah ", col. 3058).

teaching of both John and Jesus, and that these had much
in common with apocalyptic thought.[1] Here too the
conceptions of Judgment and the Kingdom were brought
into close connection.   Nevertheless, the belief that there
was this common background must not be understood to
imply that John invested the thought of the Kingdom with
exactly the same content as did Jesus. We can say
without qualification that the proclamation that the
Kingdom had come was a message which only Jesus could
give, and that its meaning was dependent upon Himself
alone.   But this does not prevent us from recognizing
that in the case of John it is scarcely credible that he should
have ignored so widely held a belief, and one which both
training and environment must have brought so often to
his notice.

   We turn now to a consideration of the New Testament
witness concerning John and his message. There are
two things which are significant for our present discussion.
The first is that John was welcomed by the people as
a prophet (Matth. xxi. 26 ; Luke xx. 6).   A message of
Judgment alone, directed against all classes without
exception, could scarcely be regarded as popular.   It is
true that according to Matthew (iii. 7) the Pharisees and
Sadducees are indicated as objects of the Baptist's
denunciation, and in Luke (iii. 12–14) unpopular classes
like the soldiers and publicans are mentioned, but Luke
also speaks of " the crowds " (iii. 7, 10). We may
assume that, like Jesus, the Forerunner felt, and even
expressed, a certain sympathy with the lot of the oppressed
masses, but we have no reason to assume that he showed
any discrimination in the application of the stern moral
content of his message. The second important fact is
that the words employed by Mark to describe the
entrance of John on the stage of history (i. 2, 3), include
a passage from the prophets which was associated in the

[1] The apocalyptic writers professed to proclaim a message
in harmony with that of the prophets ; see Daniel ix. 2.

popular mind with national deliverance and restoration.[1] If these words were also a part of the actual message of John, a conjecture which would appear most probable, their significance in this discussion is heightened.

Otto affirms that " if an account of the coming Kingdom had been present originally in the early records about John, it would have been impossible to suppress it later, for that account is just what would have shown him to be Christ's forerunner and pathmaker ". This argument is not very impressive, since it is not so much a question of suppression as of giving the idea a value and prominence which Otto thought it must have had. For the Church of the first decades of Christianity the significance of John as the forerunner of Jesus did not depend on whether he preached a similar message about the coming Kingdom, but whether he had proclaimed Jesus as the promised Messiah.[2] The records of the early Church show that the foremost interest of the men and women who composed it was not so much what Jesus said—much less a general statement of what his forerunner said—as what He was. If John proclaimed the coming Messiah they could take for granted the coming Kingdom that was inevitably bound up with His presence.

Supposing the early writers had felt that John had anticipated the message of Jesus, we cannot imagine that

[1] This Messianic expectation can be discerned in Josephus, *Antiq.*, IV, vi, 5 ; X, xi, 7. The ʿAlenu of the Jewish Prayer Book, which from its form is regarded as dating back to the pre-Christian era, is also a reminder of the importance of the Jewish conception of the Kingdom, and shows how the pious Jew looked forward to the day when the Lord would punish the wicked and reign as King over all the earth.

[2] The words of Dibelius may be applied equally to John's message of the Kingdom : " Mark is not concerned with the preaching of repentance by the Baptist, and it finds no place in his book. The Baptist is regarded only as a prophet of Jesus, i.e. as one of those who in consequence of divine illumination know of the status of Jesus " (*From Tradition to Gospel*, E.T., 1934, pp. 230–1).

they would have been eager—as the words of Otto imply—
to emphasize this fact.

They sought to point out the distinctiveness of everything concerning Jesus. Indeed, far from an attempt to
treat as similar the work of John and Jesus, there are not
wanting signs of an opposite tendency which might have
led to the suppression of this very phase of John's message
of which Otto speaks. Just as the Gospel writers make
a clear distinction between the baptism of water and that
of Spirit, so there is evidence of an attempt to make a clear
division between the preaching of John and that of Jesus.[1]
Swete recalls the comment of Jerome on this distinction :
" Joanne tradito, recte ipse incipit praedicare ; desinente
lege, consequenter oritur evangelium." This difference
from the point of view of outward form Jesus Himself
pointed out.[2] The evidence of the Evangelists leaves the
inference that the writers were so far from seeking to find
marks of similarity in the work of Jesus and John that they
emphasized the marks of distinction.

From the latter part of this discussion one may assume
that in view of the prominence of the thought of the
Kingdom in the teaching of Jesus this part of the message
of John would be allowed to fall into the background.
This suppression indeed had positive value. It not only
removed any danger of misunderstanding in regard to the
teaching of Jesus, but it was rightly realized that only
Jesus had given the message of the Kingdom its true place
and meaning. His unique position even more than His
words made it possible for Him to say, as none other
could : " The Kingdom of God is in the midst of you."

John had a different rôle, and the Gospel writers are
very definite about his position. He was the Forerunner.
Mark is content to affirm this with only a scanty reference
to the actual message which he delivered. Yet the Fore-

[1] Mark i. 14 ; Matth. iv. 12–17.
[2] Matth. xi. 16–19 ; Luke vii. 31–5. The quotation is from
Swete, *St. Mark*, p. 12.

runner who prepared the way of the Lord had not merely to announce His approach but to prepare men for that event. For this reason we have in the Gospels of Luke and Matthew a considerable amplification of the brief notice found in Mark, and the call to repentance is given a very prominent place. We have seen from a consideration of the prophetic and apocalyptic writings that repentance played its part in the preparation, and John would feel that the proclamation of it was a truly prophetic function.[1]

In support of his statement that John did not preach concerning the coming Kingdom Otto has called attention to a passage in Luke xvi. 16. He describes this as an early logion of Christ whose original form is found in Matthew xi. 13, and from his words suggests that it furnishes conclusive evidence for the position he has taken. The passage in Luke is : " The law and the prophets were until John ; from that time the gospel of the kingdom of God is preached, and every man entereth violently into it." In Matthew the words are : " For all the prophets and the law prophesied until John." The passage is one which has led to considerable discussion. Plummer [2] thought that Matthew xi. 12–15 was a comment of the Evangelist rather than a continuation of Christ's words, and referred to the phrase " from the days of John the Baptist until now " as offering support for this view. On the other hand, Goguel has argued that Luke's evident inability to appreciate the meaning of Matthew's quotation, for he substitutes " is preached " for " suffereth violence ", shows that we have a genuine utterance of Christ since no tradition could have created a saying which it did not understand.[3]

Even if we accept the utterance as that of our Lord it

[1] Jesus dwelt on this aspect of Jonah's work (Matth. xii. 41).
[2] *An Exegetical Commentary on the Gospel according to St. Matthew*, 1909, p. 162.
[3] *Jean-Baptiste*, p. 68.

does not follow that the interpretation is correct which makes it imply that John belonged entirely to the Law and the Prophets and had nothing to do with the preaching of the Kingdom. Certain doubtful points must be made clear. How shall we explain the words " until John " ? The " until " may include or exclude, the context alone giving the clue to the understanding. This is true both of the Greek and the English, and as far as the present text is concerned leaves matters just as they were. The same uncertainty surrounds the phrase " from the days of John the Baptist ". Was John entirely of the older " Law and Prophets " dispensation, or was he regarded as a go-between such as his title " forerunner " would suggest ? It is true that Jesus said : " He that is least in the Kingdom of Heaven is greater than he," but this points only to the fact that John had not experienced membership in the Kingdom. The failure to attain this experience is shown by John's lack of faith in Jesus, revealed by the question of the two disciples.[1] Yet Jesus paid high tribute to the Baptist. Do not His statement " there hath not risen a greater ", and the estimate that John was " more than a prophet ", refer to the latter's special part in heralding the Kingdom ? In Matthew xi. 14[2] Jesus Himself identifies John with Elijah, and this follows directly that passage which Otto affirmed to be the original logion of Jesus. Goguel, however, denies that this identification is the act of Jesus, and attributes it either to the writer of the Gospels or to early Christian tradition.

Not least of the arguments in favour of the belief that

[1] Matth. xi. 3, 6 ; Luke vii. 19, 23. R. Newton Flew says : " This final logion implies that some are not receiving the good news ; they do not understand the mysterion. These are not entering into the Rule of God " (*Jesus and His Church*, 1938, p. 91. Cf. p. 36).

[2] In Mark ix. 12 (cf. Matth. xvii. 11) Jesus declares that Elijah, i.e. John, restoreth all things. Acts i. 6 testifies to the Messianic ring in these words.

John preached the coming Kingdom is that which concerns the significance of his baptismal rite. Was it merely a method of safeguarding the future of the individual, or had it any reference to the formation of a community? Otto's theory that it was an act of magic for cleansing from sin has been mentioned, but it is an unsatisfactory explanation, for it leaves us with the problem why such cleansing was not repeated. John's baptism was bestowed once only; and this fact rules out the analogy of ascetic practices like those of Banus, who " bathed often, night and day, in cold water ". It is very difficult indeed to assign any meaning to John's baptismal act unless we can regard it after the manner of an initiatory rite connected with entrance into some community. This is certainly the impression given by the language of Josephus, as Goguel, who himself doubts whether the rite was an initiatory one, is obliged to admit.[1] In view of current belief, what community was more likely than that made up of men who looked for the Messianic Kingdom?

Perhaps greater significance than has been allowed attaches to the words of Jesus in Matthew xxi. 31, in which, after challenging the chief priests and elders on the question of the authority for John's baptism, He made the striking declaration that " the publicans and the harlots go into the Kingdom of God before you. For John came unto you in the way of righteousness, and ye believed him not; but the publicans and harlots believed him ", etc. The one obvious sign of belief would be the acceptance of baptism following the preliminary condition of repentance. From this it is difficult to see how one can dissociate John's baptism and the belief that his message included a proclamation of the coming Kingdom.

[1] *Jean-Baptiste*, p. 290.

ADDITIONAL NOTE B

The Rôle of John the Baptist

The question concerning the exact position which John held or claimed to hold is not easy to answer. The commonly accepted opinion regards him as the returned Elijah, but the acceptance of this view leaves serious difficulties. Chief of these is John's own denial of this identification, which is recorded in the Fourth Gospel : " And they asked him, What then ? Art thou Elijah ? And he saith, I am not. Art thou the prophet ? And he answered, No. They said therefore unto him, Who art thou ? that we may give an answer to them that sent us. What sayest thou of thyself ? He said, I am the voice of one crying in the wilderness, Make straight the way of the Lord, as said Isaiah the prophet."

Our task of discovering the position of John is rendered more difficult by the comparative scantiness of the information concerning him, which makes it impossible to determine with any degree of certainty his eschatological beliefs. Schweitzer,[1] who points out that in the time previous to the period of John there existed two distinct expectations of the future, described by him as the Messiah eschatology of the prophets and the Danielic Son-of-Man eschatology, admits that it is impossible to say which of the two was held by the Baptist. It is useful, however, to consider his estimate of John's position.

Schweitzer suggests that John combined the teaching of Joel in regard to the general outpouring of the Spirit with the teaching of Malachi that Elijah would come in the last days. Holding this amalgam of beliefs the Baptist expected that Elijah would baptize men with the Holy Spirit. He believed that it was his business to be the forerunner of this one ; and in the question to Jesus :

[1] *SMP*, p. 79.

" Art thou he that cometh, or look we for another ? " the " he that cometh " must be regarded as a description of Elijah and not the Messiah. To use the phrase of Schweitzer, John thought of himself as the forerunner's forerunner.[1] The belief that John was not Elijah finds support in the doubt inherent in the words of the disciples concerning the coming of Elijah, in Mark ix. 11 : " And they asked him, saying, The scribes say that Elijah must first come." It is true that Jesus follows this by a confident affirmation that Elijah is come ; but the question of the disciples implies that John himself had made no definite statement by which men could recognize the identification.

In the first chapter of his Gospel, Luke describes a visit of Gabriel to Zacharias, in which the angel foretells concerning the promised child that " he shall go before his face in the spirit and power of Elijah " (17). While no Messiah is mentioned, the phrase ' before his face ' must be interpreted in the light of the passages quoted in connection with John's mission (Isa. xl. 3 ; Mal. iii. 1).

Matthew records an identification of John with Elijah from the lips of Jesus : " If ye are willing to receive it, this is Elijah, which is to come " (xi. 14). But this passage which follows on John's question is not found in the corresponding section of Luke (vii. 18–35). Moreover, Goguel dismisses the incident of John's question as unhistorical. In the story of the transfiguration we have an account of a discussion by Jesus and His disciples on the coming of Elijah ; and it is to be noticed that Matthew again brings in the identification of the Baptist with the Old Testament prophet : " Then understood the disciples that he spake unto them of John the Baptist " (xvii. 13). Luke does not mention this discussion, and although Mark includes it his account has nothing of the identification of John with Elijah. In its place is the verse : " But I say unto you, that Elijah is come, and they have also

[1] *SMP*, p. 231.

done unto him whatsoever they listed, even as it is written of him " (ix. 13). These last words are difficult since nothing is said about a suffering Elijah in the Old Testament. The passages mentioned serve to show that it is the Gospel of Matthew which brings out most clearly the identification of John with the earlier prophet.

It will be observed that in the two references of Matthew one expresses the identification as a direct statement of Jesus Himself (xi. 14), the other makes it a surmise from the words of Jesus (xvii. 13). The former is naturally the more important. But while it gives the words as a direct affirmation by Jesus Himself and for that reason necessarily conclusive as far as the disciples were concerned there is an element of doubt introduced by the phrase " if ye are willing to receive it ". This implies that the author of the Gospel was aware that not all accepted the identification. Yet before these words can be considered in their relationship to other New Testament passages the doubt cast on their authenticity by Goguel must be discussed.[1]

Goguel appears to base his denial of the authenticity of the passage on the ground that nothing is said of the impression made on John by the answer received through his disciples, while the question itself could not have been asked by John since it refers to " un Messie historique " and not to " un Messie apocalyptique ". He adds : " L'idée que Jésus pourrait être ce Messie n'a pas pu se présenter à son esprit."[2]

Has this reasoning the force which Goguel suggests ? It is difficult to conceive that such a story of doubt, with its damaging reflection on the impression which Christ made upon His own contemporaries, and, above all, on His accepted forerunner John, had no historical basis. Could it have been invented by Christian writers ? With regard to the impression made upon John, the chief

[1] *Jean-Baptiste*, pp. 60 ff. ; *Life of Jesus*, E.T., pp. 278–9.
[2] *Jean-Baptiste*, p. 63.

concern of the incident was not the effect of the reply upon John but how Jesus reacted to the doubt of one with whom He had close relations. One might go further and surmise that if the story had been an invention it would most surely have contained an account of the impression the Master's answer made upon John. Invented stories usually are fairly detailed and complete. It is quite likely that the effect on John was unfavourable, as, strange to say, Goguel suggests. Such a result would not have caused the omission, if we are to judge by other sentiments recorded in the Gospels, and which the candour of the authors reveals to us. The question of John's disciples about fasting [1] bears witness to a dissatisfaction from the Johannine side with the methods of Jesus. The present incident might have created a similar feeling. But the fact, assuming it was so, that the impression was unfavourable would be a reason why the incident should have been suppressed entirely rather than a cause for the elimination of its ending.

An informing parallel is presented by the passage on ceremonial washing (Mark vii. 1–23 ; Matth. xv. 1–20). In Mark nothing is said about the effect on the Pharisees of Christ's answer to their question ; but in Matthew this latter is added. A comparison of the two accounts suggests the reason for the difference. Mark would appear to have no interest in this effect. In Matthew it is stated, not so much because it is important in itself, but because it furnishes an opportunity for giving a further utterance of Jesus, which Luke records in quite a different connection.

In regard to the discrepancy between John's apocalyptic Messiah and the historic Messiah of Jesus we may claim that this discrepancy is by no means proved, since the proof depends in great part on a knowledge of John's eschatological position, which mainly is a matter for conjecture. Yet even if this argument were allowed it

[1] Mark ii. 18–22 ; Matth. ix. 14–17 ; Luke v. 33–9.

does not deny the historicity of the incident. An inaccurate rendering of a story due to defective knowledge on the part of the reporter is no reason for denying absolutely its truth. Because of the very nature of the story, as already stated, we may affirm our belief in its authenticity.

The position of Schweitzer is of interest. He allows for the authenticity of the words of Jesus in Matthew xi. 14, but thinks that " Jesus does violence to reality by this identification ".[1] This brings us back to the implied doubt in the words attributed to Jesus, " if ye are willing to receive it ". It is most probable that not all in the early Church accepted the identification with Elijah. A possible reason for this doubt is not hard to find. The Gospels contain hints of certain difficulties which were experienced with disciples of John in the effort of the Church to establish itself. These have been discussed [2] already and it is sufficient here to remind ourselves that the Fourth Gospel represents the most obvious attempt to depress the position of John as contrasted with that of Christ. It is of great significance in this connection that the Fourth Gospel states John's own denial of his identification with Elijah (i. 20, 21) and protests against any attempt to magnify his position by the declaration that he is but a " voice ". May we not assume that the tendency shown in the Fourth Gospel reveals that there were some in the early Church who felt, in view perhaps of certain extravagant claims made by a few of the Baptist's disciples, that it was unwise to allow that John held the exalted position which prophecy had assigned to Elijah. Their denial did not affect the belief of many, otherwise one cannot explain the words in Matthew, but they caused certain doubts to be circulated of which the Gospels bear traces. When we recall the statement in the Fourth Gospel in which the Baptist denied that he was the Christ we should realize also that there is a certain inconsistency

[1] *SMP*, p. 163.   [2] Pp. 18 ff.

in the fact that the same writer relates an incident in which John states explicitly that he was sent before the Christ— the natural rôle of Elijah : " Ye yourselves bear me witness that I said, I am not the Christ, but, that I am sent before him " (iii. 28). A. Plummer has attempted to explain away the contradiction of each other involved in the two statements from Matthew xi. 14 and John i. 20 by proposing that we should accept the former as figurative and the latter as literal.[1] This avoids a difficulty, but we do not think it can be regarded as satisfactory.

Other names have been suggested for the character that John claimed to represent. Eisler says that John thought of himself as the reincarnation of Enosh—the Messianic figure mentioned in Daniel's vision (Dan. vii. 13).[2] Burkitt felt that there was a likeness to Elisha.[3] He made many attractive comparisons. John brought men to the same place to which Elisha sent Naaman and told them to do the same thing which Elisha commanded Naaman. Interesting points in the vocabulary have been discussed previously.[4] But when all the difficulties have been considered the identification of John as the second Elijah still would seem to be the most probable solution of the question.

[1] *St. John*, Cambridge Greek Testament, 1891, p. 78.
[2] R. Eisler, *The Messiah Jesus*, p. 232.
[3] F. C. Burkitt, *Christian Beginnings*, pp. 19 ff.
[4] P. 70.

CHAPTER III

THE BAPTISM OF JESUS

THE baptism of Jesus is one of the best attested facts of His life. Apart from any question of documents, it bears in itself the surest evidence of its genuineness.[1] No early Christian writer was likely to have invented such an incident which quite soon raised problems difficult to meet. The Gospels themselves show signs that the writers are aware of these problems, and the existence of critical or even hostile groups of Johannine disciples would serve to make the difficulty more acute. The author of the Fourth Gospel omits the story altogether. Perhaps more strange is the casual manner in which Luke alludes to it, as though it were merely incidental to the baptism of the multitude. Matthew's account, which is detailed, has an obviously apologetic purport. The description in Mark is of special importance since it gives what was in all probability the original or early form of the story [2] : " Jesus came from Nazareth of Galilee and was baptized of John in the Jordan. And straightway coming up out of the water, he saw the heavens rent asunder, and the Spirit as a dove descending upon him ; and a voice came out of the heavens, Thou art my beloved Son, in Thee I am well pleased."

[1] There have been a few who have doubted the historicity. See Goguel's criticism of Eduard Meyer, *Jean-Baptiste*, p. 139.

[2] Burkitt thought it unlikely that Q contained any reference to the baptism and held that " we owe it to Mark, and to Mark alone, that this remarkable historical fact has been preserved in the Christian tradition " (*Expository Times*, XXXVIII (1926–7), pp. 198–202).

The many ingenious explanations given by the early Fathers [1] indicate a measure of their difficulty in explaining the incident. In the New Testament we have not only the dialogue preceding the baptism in the account of Matthew, but the emphasis on the subordination of John to Jesus given in the Fourth Gospel. Perhaps equal importance attaches to the silence in other New Testament writings.[2] Moreover, it is interesting to note that early apostolic preaching based its argument for Christian baptism on John's prophecy concerning the Spirit baptism and not on the fact that Jesus Himself was baptized.

The undergoing of the Johannine baptism must be regarded as the recognition by Jesus of the prophetic character of John's mission—this is implied also in His question to the chief priests, scribes and elders in Mark xi. 30—but still more must His acceptance of it be taken as showing the desire of Jesus to range Himself with those who were willing to obey the prophet's message and seek membership in the new Israel. It was the preparatory condition of repentance demanded from all aspirants to baptism, which involved a recognition of a sinful past, that has created the difficulty in the case of Jesus.[3] This is probably the reason why Matthew makes

[1] See *Die Taufe Christi durch Johannes in der dogmatischen Beurteilung der christlichen Theologen der vier ersten Jahrhunderten*, J. Bornemann, 1896.

[2] Some have found a reference to Christ's baptism in I John v. 6, 8.

[3] This is shown by the apocryphal writings. In the *Gospel according to the Hebrews*, quoted by Jerome in his *Dialogue against Pelagius*, iii. 2, Jesus replies to His mother and brethren who suggest that He should be baptized by John : " Wherein have I sinned, that I should go and be baptized of him ? Unless peradventure this very thing that I have said is a sin of ignorance." In the pseudo-Cyprian " *De Rebaptismate* " (3rd cent.), there is reference to an heretical work, " *Pauli Prædicatio* ", in these terms : " in which book, contrary to every Scripture, you will find Christ, who alone never sinned at all, both con-

much of John's reluctance to baptize Jesus and records the statement of Jesus in accepting baptism : " Suffer it now : for thus it becometh us to fulfil all righteousness."

Although Goguel's theory that Jesus was at first a disciple of John is a fascinating one, we cannot allow that such a relationship is implied necessarily by the baptism, unless we give the term disciple an unusually wide connotation. Apart from the reference in John iv. 1, the use of the term disciple of John seems to be limited to a select band of intimate followers, whereas there must have been many who had experienced the baptism and afterwards returned to their usual occupations (John x. 40–2 ; Luke iii. 7, 12, 14).

What was the significance of baptism for Jesus ? Did it imply an endowment of Jesus with His Messianic gifts through the coming of the Spirit ? In support of this it has been remarked that the earliest of our Gospels commences with the story of the baptism, although the other two Synoptic writers begin with the story of the birth of Jesus.[1] The casual way in which Luke approaches the incident of baptism shows that he did not regard it as the supreme experience in the life of Jesus which the theory of endowment would suggest.

B. W. Bacon [2] has put forward the idea that primitive Christianity interpreted the baptism of Jesus in the manner of the early Christian rite. " Primitive Christians rightly conceived of Jesus' baptism as involving all that was involved in their own baptism and more. They were endowed at baptism with various ' gifts of the Spirit ',

fessing His own sin and being compelled almost against His will by His mother Mary to receive the baptism of John " Trans. M. R. James, *The Apocryphal New Testament*, 1926).

[1] E. F. Scott, *The Spirit in the New Testament*, 1923, p. 65. M. Dibelius says : " This idea of adoption, of course, could not remain in the two Gospels which had already described the child Jesus with full divine glory (as in Matthew and Luke) " (*From Tradition to Gospel*, pp. 272–3).

[2] B. W. Bacon, *The Story of Jesus*, 1926, p. 139 f.

the ' word of knowledge and the word of power '. Jesus too experienced this endowment with the Spirit of adoption ; only—as an ancient gospel expressed it—the ' whole fountain ' of the Holy Spirit, and not mere derived rivulets ' descended and dwelt in Him '." For support of this theory Bacon recalls the reference in Isaiah xlii. 1–4, which is found in Matthew xii. 18–20 and echoed in such passages as Matthew iii. 17 and xvii. 5.

Much has been made of the alternative reading by certain important manuscripts in Luke iii. 22.[1] They include D, the Old Latin, Justin, Clement. J. Moffatt, who accepts this text as the true one, translates : " Thou art my Son, the Beloved, to-day have I become thy Father " ($\dot{\epsilon}\gamma\dot{\omega}$ $\sigma\dot{\eta}\mu\epsilon\varrho o\nu$ $\gamma\epsilon\gamma\dot\epsilon\nu\nu\eta\kappa\acute{\alpha}$ $\sigma\epsilon$). He argues that the alteration in the other manuscripts was made " for harmonistic reasons ". But while assimilation to the text of Matthew and Mark is possible, it is more probable that the reading of the main Western texts is due to assimilation to Psalm ii. 7, influenced by a certain adoptianist Christology which was prevalent in the second century.[2]

The outstanding moment of the baptism was that in which the coming of the Spirit is depicted. But there is no special emphasis on this fact as indicating an endowment of Jesus such as is stated in the teaching of adoptianism.[3] No further reference to this experience is made throughout the New Testament. One finds it

[1] Dibelius says of this reading : " Contrary to my earlier view (*Die urchristliche Überlieferung v. J. dem Taufer*, p. 63), I now regard this form as old, but as precanonical and unjustifiably introduced into D from the unregulated tradition " (*op. cit.*, p. 231 note). At the same time he argues that the accepted text expresses the same idea of adoption in the case of Jesus, and that " Thou art my beloved Son " means in Oriental legal language : Thou shalt be so, " I have chosen thee "—and therefore the institution follows (p. 272).

[2] The evidence is found in A. Resch, *Agrapha*, 1906, pp. 223, 344, 346 f. See also " The Baptism of Jesus ", by D. Plooij, in *Amicitiae Corolla*, ed. by H. G. Wood, 1933, pp. 245 ff.

[3] See article " Adoptianism ", *ERE*, I, pp. 103–5.

difficult to gather any real support for the argument that because the narrative of Mark opens with the story of the Baptism the implication is that up to that time Jesus belonged to the rank of ordinary men, and His Messianic endowment was due to the baptism experience of the Spirit.[1]

It is significant that in the Gospel of Luke, where the work of the Spirit receives a prominence greater than in either of the remaining Synoptic Gospels, there is shown evidence of its activity long before the incident of Baptism. If it was said of John the Baptist that he should be filled with the Holy Spirit even from his mother's womb (i. 15), such an experience must have been true of Jesus also, and should be regarded as implied in the message of the angel to Mary : " The Holy Spirit shall come upon thee, and the power of the Most High shall overshadow thee ; wherefore also that which is to be born shall be called holy, the Son of God " (i. 35).

Goguel points out that there is little real difference between the Synoptic writers and the author of the Fourth Gospel regarding the teaching of the coming of the Spirit. It is a post-resurrection experience—an experience for the future rather than the present. This is expressed very definitely in the words of Jesus Himself (Luke xxiv. 49 ; cf. Acts i. 4, 5, 8), and may be regarded as implied in passages like Mark xiii. 11 ; Matthew x. 20 ; Luke xii. 12. Since the Christology of the Gospels is not a Christology of the Spirit, Goguel maintains that it is not permissible to explain the person and work of Christ by the fact of the outpouring of the Spirit upon Him at His baptism.[2]

---

[1] " It is apparently assumed that hitherto he had been an ordinary man, chosen no doubt by God for a supreme task, but as yet lacking the necessary qualification. In his baptism he received that plenitude of divine gifts which would rest, according to prophecy, on the Messiah " (E. F. Scott, *The Spirit in the New Testament*, p. 65.

[2] *Jean-Baptiste*, p. 200.

Ought not this manifestation of the Spirit at the baptism of Jesus to be regarded as a recognition rather than an endowment ? This would be in harmony with other divine manifestations in the earthly life of Jesus.[1] It was the completion of the period of preparation. The whole position has been well expressed by A. E. J. Rawlinson, who points out that from early days, as the incident in the Temple, when he was twelve years of age, bears witness (Luke ii. 49), Jesus was conscious of standing in a peculiar relation to God. To quote his words : " As He (Jesus) waited for some sign from the Heavenly Father, the rumour of the Baptist's preaching ran through the countryside—' The time is at hand.' Is it not likely that the Lord recognized His appointed Hour ? . . . as He came up out of those waters there burst upon Him, with renewed certainty, the conviction that He was indeed the Son of God (i.e. the Davidic King, Ps. ii. 7 ; II Sam. vii. 14), together with the consciousness of supreme endowment with the plenitude of spiritual authority and power." [2] Thus we may say that the visible expression of the Spirit was the outward sign of what Jesus had long realized as an inner experience, and this, together with the voice, marked the inauguration of the Messianic ministry.

Allowance must be made for the probability that the description of Christ's baptism has been assimilated in certain details to the rite of Christian baptism which was practised in the early Church. To take one recognized detail : in Christian baptism the convert after receiving his immersion offered a prayer of thanksgiving and dedication of himself to God. In Luke's brief account of the baptism of Jesus it is said that the latter received the Spirit after baptism while He was praying. As E. F. Scott says : " It can hardly be doubted that the evangelist had here before his mind the customary practice of the

[1] John xii. 28 ff. ; and the story of the transfiguration.
[2] A. E. J. Rawlinson, *St. Mark*, 1925. Additional note 2, " The Significance of our Lord's Baptism ", pp. 251–6.

Church."[1] But while making allowance for such assimilation it must be recognized also that there was no attempt to make the baptism of Jesus a model for other baptisms. For proof of this we may remark on the strange lack of interest in this event which the earliest Christian literature reveals. There is no reference to it before the time of Ireneus.[2]

On the other hand, it is possible that tradition has preserved some primitive details, and that some of the features found in the story of Christ's baptism are not a reflection of the later Christian type but are authentic, and a reminder of the older Jewish rite from which John's baptism originated. Thus the " praying " of Jesus, described by Luke in the passage to which we have just referred, has been likened to the proselyte's ascription on undergoing the tebilah : " Blessed art Thou who hast sanctified us by Thy commandment and commanded us concerning tebilah."[3] In the description of the vision Bacon believes we have to allow for the poetic imagery of Jewish midrash, with the vision and the voice as the expression of the message from the unseen.[4] Jewish influence is seen too in the association of the Dove and the heavenly voice, which shows definite traces of Rabbinic tradition.[5]

It is very interesting to note the differences in details in the narrative as set forth in the Gospel accounts. In Matthew, Jesus saw the vision, but the voice appears to have addressed someone else—John or the spectators. In Mark, the voice and vision are both parts of the experience of Jesus. According to Luke the words are addressed to Jesus, but the vision might be regarded as visible to

[1] E. F. Scott, *The Spirit in the New Testament*, p. 153.
[2] A. Schweitzer comments on this lack of interest. *SMP*, p. 240.
[3] T. B. Pesahim, 6, quoted from Abrahams, *Studies*, I, p. 42.
[4] B. W. Bacon, *The Story of Jesus*, p. 139.
[5] Abrahams, *op. cit.*, p. 47.

those around. The Fourth Gospel has no mention of the baptism ; but the words in i. 33 obviously refer to the vision that accompanied it, and here it is John who sees the Spirit descending on Jesus. Not much importance need be attached to these differences of detail. The different accounts in the Acts of the Apostles concerning Paul's vision on the Damascus road offer a similar variety in their reports.[1]

When we consider the story of the baptism of Jesus as a whole we are compelled to admit that there is nothing in the field of Old Testament incidents which can be adduced as a parallel to it, nor is there anything by which it can be explained. The various calls of the prophets, differing as they do from each other, contrast still more with this in form and meaning. The reason of the difference is to be found in the different character of the One to Whom the experience came. It was essentially, and of necessity, unique. This oft-abused word fits the situation most aptly. As Goguel says : " Le baptême n'est ni un appel, ni une vocation, c'est l'intronisation de Jésus comme Messie." [2]

[1] Acts ix. 7 ; xxii. 9 ; xxvi. 13, 14.
[2] *Jean-Baptiste*, p. 226.

CHAPTER IV

BAPTISM DURING THE EARTHLY LIFE OF JESUS

AMONG the books of the New Testament the Gospel of John alone makes any reference to baptizing as an act of Jesus, or of His disciples during His lifetime. Several references to this are to be found towards the beginning of the book. In iii. 22, we read : " After these things came Jesus and His disciples into the land of Judæa ; and there He tarried with them, and baptized." In verse 26 this fact is reported to John the Baptist by the latter's disciples in a statement declaring the success which was attending the new Teacher. " Rabbi, He that was with thee beyond Jordan, to whom thou hast borne witness, behold, the same baptizeth, and all men come to Him." In iv. 1, 2, we have a sequel to these references : " When therefore the Lord knew how the Pharisees had heard that Jesus was making and baptizing more disciples than John—although Jesus Himself baptized not, but His disciples—He left Judæa and departed again into Galilee."

These statements might appear decisive, although the correction in the last seems to suggest a certain hesitancy, yet in view of some serious difficulties there has been much argument as to whether baptism was practised during the earthly life of Jesus. It is necessary to take into account all the facts upon which these arguments are based. We will consider first those that tell against the belief that either Jesus or His disciples practised a baptismal rite during His earthly life.[1]

[1] See *TWNT*, I, p. 536.

1. The most important fact is the silence of the Synoptists. We have plenty of evidence that at the time our Gospels were written the Christian rite of baptism was very common, indeed one might say that then it was universal in the Christian Church, yet there is no mention of such a rite in the Gospels, apart from the last chapters of Matthew and Mark. What is the reason for this absence of any reference ? Is it due to a sense of historical perspective by which it was realized that at the time of which the Synoptists wrote the rite was non-existent ? The figure of baptism was actually used by Jesus (Mark x. 38, 39 ; Luke xii. 50), but this has been explained as a casual metaphorical use, a usage which later became much more frequent.[1]

2. In the commission to the disciples, set forth in detail in the Synoptic Gospels, there is no reference to baptism (Matth. x. 5–42 ; Mark vi. 7–11 ; Luke ix. 1–5 ; cf. Luke x. 1–16).

3. The forgiveness of sins, which is linked so closely with baptism, both that of John and that of the early Church, is bestowed on individuals by Jesus without any mention of baptism (Luke vii. 47–9 ; Mark ii. 3–12).

4. The enemies of Jesus challenged His claim to forgive sins (Mark ii. 7 ; Matth. ix. 3 ; Luke v. 21). We know too from His words that they were critical of the claim of John implied by his preaching and baptizing (Mark xi. 30 ; Matth. xxi. 25 ; Luke xx. 4), but we never read of any criticism of a baptism performed by Jesus or His disciples.

5. When men and women revealed that saving faith which later was associated with readiness for baptism,

[1] H. B. Swete, *St. Mark*, p. 237 ; A. Plummer, *St. Luke*, I.C.C. (1901), p. 334 ; Moulton and Milligan, *op. cit.*, p. 102, s.v. Goguel (*Jean-Baptiste*, p. 43, note) remarks on Matthew's omission of the reference to baptism while reporting the request of the sons of Zebedee (xx. 20–7). He suggests that the definitely ritual sense, which the word had acquired at the time of the writing of the Gospel, probably prevented it from being used metaphorically.

they were not called to undergo the rite but received a special commendation from Jesus. This has more significance when it is recognized that the outstanding examples of this possession of faith were found among Gentiles (Luke vii. 9 ; Matth. xv. 28).

6. " An attitude of detachment from the cultus on the part of Jesus is visible in the Gospel records." [1] There is evidence also in the Synoptic Gospels that the disciples themselves, apparently with the tacit approval of their Master, were rather indifferent to the claims of ritual (Mark vii. 2 ; Matth. xv. 2). This indifference led to a discussion with the Pharisees on the subject of purification in which the word βαπτισμοὺς, " washings ", occurs (Mark vii. 4), but yet there is no reference to baptism. The omission may be contrasted with the reference in the Fourth Gospel (iii. 25) to a discussion of John's disciples " with a Jew " concerning purifying, which led up to a talk on the popularity of the baptism which Jesus was offering.[2]

7. Prominent in the message of John was a statement that the mark of his Successor's work would be a baptism " with Holy Spirit " in contrast with his own water rite. If the words of the Fourth Gospel are correct we have a definite declaration that the Master, or, at least the disciples with His approval, baptized at the same time as John. Yet, according to this same Gospel, the Spirit was not yet given (vii. 39). Would not such an action on the part of Christ and His disciples tend to perplex the people and to discredit the Forerunner ?

8. The references to the baptism performed by Jesus

[1] V. Taylor, *Jesus and His Sacrifice*, 1937, p. 67. He adds : " It is remarkable that there is no evidence to show that He ever participated in the Temple sacrifices."

[2] Goguel, *Jean-Baptiste*, pp. 89, 250–1 ; *Life of Jesus*, E.T., p. 274. The text in all probability is corrupt and certain emendations have been suggested which, if accepted, would bring the incident into closer connection with Jesus and His disciples. *EBi*, 2504.

or His disciples occur in the early chapters of the Fourth Gospel. There is no mention of the subject in the greater part of the book.[1] Most significant is the fact that the later chapters contain the promise of the Spirit, which was to come only after the earthly life of Jesus had closed : " If I go not away, the Comforter will not come unto you " (xvi. 7).

9. Although the Fourth Gospel refers to a baptism by Jesus and His disciples it nowhere contains any statement that Jesus gave command that men should be baptized. We have, however, the problem created by the familiar passage in the Nicodemus incident in which Jesus declared : " Except a man be born of water and the Spirit, he cannot enter into the Kingdom of God " (iii. 5). It has been suggested that Jesus is speaking here in the light of His own baptismal experience. His words recalled to Nicodemus the teaching of the Baptist, and made him " wonder whether, if he was really in earnest in his desire for regeneration, it might not be his duty to become a candidate for the baptism of repentance in preparation for the coming of the Kingdom.[2]

The use of the phrase ἐξ ὕδατος καὶ πνεύματος instead of ἐξ ὕδατος καὶ ἐκ πνεύματος points to a single experience rather than two, and may be taken as an apt

[1] We do not overlook the fact that from the days of Irenæus, who found a reference to baptism in the story of the man at the Pool of Siloam (ix. 7 ; see *Adv. Haer.*, v, 15, 3), there have been many claims that the sacrament of baptism is referred to in the Gospel of John. Heitmüller, Loisy, Scott, and others mention such incidents as the washing of the disciples' feet, and the piercing of the side of Jesus at the Crucifixion. Schweitzer also detects references to the baptismal water (*SMP*, pp. 355–8). The matter, however, is too subjective to offer much scope for fruitful discussion. There is no doubt that the Fourth Evangelist held a strong sacramental belief and found its source in the life and teaching of Jesus. But here we are concerned with definite statements concerning baptism.

[2] J. O. F. Murray, *Jesus According to St. John*, 1936, pp. 78–81.

description of the way in which the Apostolic Church interpreted Christian baptism. An attempt has been made to rule out ἐξ ὕδατος as a Catholicising addition of a redactor.[1] In this way it is sought to avoid the difficulty raised by such an early reference to the Christian rite, since with the words as they stand it is almost impossible to controvert the argument that some reference to baptism is intended. For this reason it must be recognized that it is impossible to connect the passage with the author's references to the work of Jesus or His

---

[1] H. Wendt (*Gospel of John*, E.T., 1902, p. 120), J. Wellhausen (*Das Evangelium Johannis*, 1908). Among others denying the reference to Christian baptism we must include Th. Zahn (*Das Evangelium des Johannes*, 1908, pp. 186 f., B. Weiss (*Das Johannesevangelium*, 2te Aufl., 1902, pp. 110 f.), and Kirsopp Lake (*The Influence of Textual Criticism on the Exegesis of the New Testament*, 1904, pp. 13 ff.). Lake sets forth very clearly the arguments in favour of the idea of interpolation. He points to early citations of the passage in the *Clementine Homilies* (xi, 26) and *Apostolic Constitutions* (vi, 15, 3) as evidence that the text has been corrupted. In a quotation in Justin (*Apol.*, I, 61) the contested words are omitted. Again, neither verses 3 nor 8 of John, chapter iii, give support to the contention that water baptism was in the mind of Jesus. It is significant that in some authorities the suspected words have been inserted in verse 8. As a matter of interest it may be noted also that in a Christian interpolation in *The Books of Adam and Eve*, xlii, 4, the words " born again of water and the Holy Spirit " are found (*AP*, II, p. 144).

There is little reason to doubt that until Calvin's day the phrase was interpreted universally as indicating baptism ; and it must be remembered that the new life, suggested by ἄνωθεν, is connected with baptism in other parts of the New Testament. Wellhausen contended that the interpretation of the words, which associate the new birth and baptism by water, conflicted with verse 8, where there is a statement implying that the Spirit was not under man's direction. However, W. H. Rigg has met this contention by showing that in reality the statements do not conflict, since " baptism is coupled with faith, and faith in John is pre-eminently mysterious " (*Church Quarterly Review*, vol. 108, 1929, pp. 86–119). Lake's position in regard to interpolation has been criticized by Chase (*JTS*, July, 1905,

disciples in baptizing, even although they occur in the same chapter, since it would imply that they included Spirit baptism, an idea contradicted by the words of vii. 39. A not very convincing argument is that which would regard the statement of Jesus regarding the Spirit as anticipatory (xvi. 13).

10. While there is mention in the Acts of men who lacked the Spirit because they had experienced the baptism of John only, there is no mention in the Acts of those who had received the pre-Pentecostal baptism of the disciples. Yet if the statement of John iii. 26 is to be accepted there must have been many such persons. This argu-

---

p. 504), who thought that Lake's belief, that the omission of the contested words would yield a more consistent sense, had left out of account the baptism of John and the Jewish custom of proselyte baptism. Chase argued that there was reason for believing that Justin had verse 5 in a form similar to that which we know, since if he had not known of any mention of water in verse 5 he could not have connected the term " regenerated " in verse 3 with baptism in water.

Perhaps the balance of argument is with those who would retain as genuine the words ἐξ ὕδατος; but, at the same time, it must be confessed that the phrase makes the interpretation extremely difficult. W. F. Howard sums up the main possible interpretations as three : (i) The words ὕδατος καὶ are a restate-ment by John of the original saying of verse 3, and must be regarded as " a Johannine gloss to bring the saying of Jesus into harmony with the belief and practice of a later generation ".—J. H. Bernard, St. John, I.C.C., vol. I, 1928, p. 105. (ii) The Evangelist assumes the outward rite, but stresses the spiritual side which gives it value.—J. Moffatt, Theology of the Gospels, 1912, p. 197. (iii) The conception implied by ἐξ ὕδατος must not be interpreted by current baptismal teaching since this introduction of baptism destroys the continuity of the argument, which is concerned not with contrasting the baptisms of Jesus and John, but with two types of birth. It is a mystical con-ception and has to do with the spiritual process in which " water and spirit " form a contrast to semen and flesh.—H. Odeberg, The Fourth Gospel, 1929, pp. 48 ff. See W. F. Howard, The Fourth Gospel in Recent Criticism and Interpretation, 1931, pp. 207, 208.

ment would lose all its force if we accept the idea that the " baptism of John " was a generic name for the pre-Pentecostal rite, whether administered by the disciples of John or of Jesus. In favour of this belief is the statement recorded in Acts xviii. 25 concerning Apollos : " This man had been instructed in the way of the Lord ; and being fervent in spirit, he spake and taught carefully the things concerning Jesus, knowing only the baptism of John."

11. Finally, a vital question, which, although not directly concerned with the matter of baptism during the life of Jesus, yet is intimately bound up with it, is whether Jesus during His lifetime gave any command to His disciples to baptize after His death. The last chapters of Matthew and Mark contain passages which affirm that Jesus commanded His disciples to baptize as part of their future work. The command to baptize is introduced in the speech of Christ in a way which suggests that it is an experience with which the disciples are familiar, and if the words are genuine they make the previous silence of the Gospels still more difficult to explain. On the other hand, if the words are redactorial additions they bear witness to the need, which was felt quite early, for some authoritative utterance to explain the introduction of a practice which we know had become widespread. It is significant that Luke makes no mention of baptism in narrating the final words of Jesus (xxiv. 47 ff.), although in regard to the apostolic commission he uses terms very similar to those of Matthew. Yet this omission by Luke must not be unduly stressed since, if we accept the general opinion that this Gospel and the Acts are the work of the same author, we have proof that Luke held that Jesus commanded His disciples to baptize (Acts i. 5). The Fourth Gospel makes no mention of the command.

In our consideration of the genuineness of these words of Jesus we are able to rule out the passage from the final section of Mark's Gospel (xvi. 16). On very strong evidence this section has been rejected as a second-century addition.[1] The crucial question concerns the genuineness of the command in Matthew (xxviii. 19). Many scholars believe that the recognition of the Trinity which it contains is a sure sign that it is a later insertion, since they hold that this doctrine was a later development. The manuscript evidence is overwhelmingly in favour of its acceptance as an integral part of the Gospel of Matthew.[2] This does not carry with it a proof that the words were actually spoken by Jesus. Many critics accept the genuineness of the text as a part of the Gospel but maintain that it does not belong to the original tradition. They think that it was deliberately inserted therein to secure an appearance of Dominical authority for later doctrine and practice.

The arguments against the belief that this was a command of Jesus may be summarised as follows : If this was the direct command of Jesus associating baptism with the threefold name of the Trinity, it is strange that the Acts of the Apostles contains no mention of the formula, but in its descriptions speaks of baptism " into the name of the Lord Jesus " or a similar phrase. Moreover, if from the beginning the disciples had been sent " into all the world " by the direct message of Jesus, we have a serious difficulty created by those narratives in the Acts which imply that the breaking down of the narrow conceptions of their task was achieved only with much effort in the face of strong opposition. Still more strange is it that this achievement was mainly the work of one who would not have been present when Jesus was supposed to have given His command. Even in the case of Peter, who accepted, after some hesitation, the idea of the wider missionary call, it was the experience with Cornelius that

[1] H. B. Swete, *St. Mark*, pp. ciii–cxiii, gives a detailed discussion of the problem.

[2] F. H. Chase, " The Lord's Command to Baptize," *JTS*, July, 1905, pp. 481–521.

became decisive (Acts x. 34), and it was to this that he appealed when defending his action before his critics in Jerusalem (xi. 17). No mention is made in his defence of the words of Jesus, which he must have heard had they been uttered, and which would have been decisive in the dispute could they have been quoted.

Again, the apostles do not give baptism that position with which a command from our Lord would have endowed it. Paul appears to belittle his own part in baptizing (I Cor. i. 14). Peter deputed others for the work of baptizing in the house of Cornelius (Acts x. 48). The fact that so important a command had been given to the eleven should have marked them out above all others in such a way that not even Paul could have claimed on the ground of his experience of Jesus an equal apostleship (II Cor. xi. 5 ; I Cor. ix. 1). Finally it has been remarked that this command belongs to a series of post-resurrection speeches, which some think are a later tradition reflecting the ideas of the developing Church. Harnack has pointed out that Paul reveals no knowledge of these speeches of a risen Christ. The Gospel of Matthew contains other passages which are regarded by some as attempts to canonize later doctrine and practice, and it is thought that this belongs to these interpolated conceptions.

From a consideration of some or all of these arguments there are many who hold that baptism was neither commanded by Christ nor was it practised by Himself or even His disciples during His lifetime.[1] One writer puts the matter : " Few points in the problem of the Gospels are so clear as the improbability of this teaching,"— that baptism was introduced by Jesus.[2]

[1] For a discussion of the various arguments : F. M. Rendtorff, *Die Taufe im Urchristentum im Lichte der neueren Forschungen*, 1905, pp. 37 ff. ; J. C. Lambert, *The Sacraments in the New Testament*, 1903, Lecture II. K. Lake summarizes the textual, literary and historical criticism in *ERE*, II, pp. 379–81.

[2] *JLBC*, I, p. 335.

But the argument is by no means one-sided. While some may deny entirely any connection of Christ with the work of Christian baptism there is the indisputable fact that the disciples practised this rite very soon after the termination of their Master's earthly life. Is it probable that the rite could have obtained a complete recognition so early in the history of the Christian Church unless some authority from Jesus Himself was felt to be behind the observance ?

The question whether there was baptism during the earthly life of Jesus seems to be answered by the experience of the rite which Jesus Himself underwent. This statement is not controverted by the argument of Schweitzer, who has called attention to the silence of the early Church Fathers on the matter, that " it is completely wrong to think of early Christian baptism as a repetition, with similar significance, of the baptism of Jesus." [1] Whatever value we give to this argument it does not render unlikely the belief that the example of Jesus would be a spur to others, and especially to His disciples, to follow His action—unless there was some definite prohibition or discouragement from the Master Himself. Nowhere is there any hint of this refusal of Jesus to allow His followers to accept a rite which He Himself had experienced.

It is a likely conjecture that the disciples had been baptized. Tertullian makes a definite assertion in regard to this,[2] although it must be admitted that his arguments bring no conclusive proof and serve only to show that no such conclusive proof for the statement was forthcoming. The utmost that can be said with any degree of assurance is that some disciples of Jesus must have been baptized if, according to the tradition preserved in the Fourth Gospel, they had been previously disciples of John (i. 35).

Yet it is difficult to see how the rite of baptism could have been avoided in the ministry of Jesus unless we

---

[1] *SMP*, p. 234.   [2] *De Baptismo*, xii.

postulate a definite antagonism on His part to such a practice. According to the Gospels His message at first followed lines similar to those of John, and the statements in the Fourth Gospel imply that for a time Jesus and John worked side by side. In such circumstances was not the connection with baptism inevitable ? [1] One might say that the absence of this rite from the work of Jesus during those days of close association with the Baptist would have raised a controversy. Later we have a report of a discussion with John's disciples over the question of fasting (Mark ii. 18) ; is it not even more likely that there would have been a controversy over the matter of baptism ? [2] Yet, despite the proposed emendation of John iii. 25, we have not the slightest shred of evidence that disagreement on a matter of ritual brought about the separation of Jesus from His forerunner.

As a measure of the difficulty experienced in deciding the attitude of Jesus towards baptism, it is interesting to put side by side the views of critics who maintain diverse opinions on this matter.

Both Otto and Goguel have suggested that it was His rejection of the rite of baptism which caused Jesus to separate from John. Both believed that Jesus was at first a follower of John, and, while a fellow-worker, practised baptism but afterwards rejected it. The reason for this abandonment was that Jesus offered a new way of

[1] It is not without significance that Goguel, who believes that Jesus separated from John because he rejected the rite of baptism, and suggests that Christian baptism was not introduced in the very early days of the life of the Church, nor immediately became a widespread practice in all the groups affected by Christianity, is willing to admit, nevertheless, that previous to the introduction of Christian baptism there may have been " an archaic form of Christianity " in which the baptism of John was practised. The existence of this, he thinks, is confirmed by the incident of the disciples at Ephesus (*Life of Jesus*, E.T., 1933, p. 199).

[2] Goguel holds that we have evidence of such a dispute (*Jean-Baptiste*, pp. 250–1).

I

salvation in which there was no room for such a rite, or indeed for the ascetic practices which, according to Otto, were associated with the work of John.[1] Much of Goguel's position is built upon the acceptance of Oskar Holtzmann's emendation of John iii. 25, by which μετὰ Ἰουδαίου is changed to μετὰ τῶν Ἰησοῦ. He has argued that this incident marked the turning-point in Christ's relationship with John and His definite rejection of the Johannine rite.[2] A deep significance is found in the incidents of the Fourth Gospel which refer to matters of purification, the marriage feast at Cana (ii. 6) and the washing of the disciples' feet (xiii. 1–17). Goguel regards the latter incident as a succedaneum in the place of the Eucharist, and he lays stress on the words of Jesus in xv. 3 : " Already ye are clean because of the word which I have spoken unto you." In this speech he finds a contrast between ritual and spiritual purification, although he points out that the two conceptions were not mutually exclusive in ancient thought.[3]

B. W. Bacon[4] maintains that the baptism of Jesus had a very important influence on His life, and, in great part, determined its character. He argues that Jesus regarded this act as the consecration of Himself to the cause of the Kingdom of God. His belief is that the two sacraments are the " centres of interest " of the Gospel of Mark, and he terms the self-dedication of Christ in His baptism " an invaluable key to His whole career ". He finds in this an explanation of why Jesus began His work when He did, and also of many of the details of that work. " We understand why He makes judgment to begin at the house of God. . . . If, in submitting to the baptism of John, Jesus really consecrated Himself to the completion of John's work, He could not turn aside from this path. . . . There could be no reconciliation of the people of God until they purified His house. Therefore Jesus

---

[1] R. Otto, *op. cit.*, pp. 77–81.   [2] *Jean-Baptiste*, p. 89.
[3] *Jean-Baptiste*, pp. 92–4.   [4] *The Story of Jesus*, p. 192.

speaks of this work, and its perhaps fatal outcome, as the fulfilment of His baptism, a baptism of blood He must be baptized with. When it is done, and the inwardly furious priests demand His authority, He cites the divine authority of John. And when they had had their way and nailed Him to the cross, the rite by which His followers, rallying to the cause their cowardice had betrayed, made a new dedication of themselves, even to sharing His death, is the Johannine rite of baptism."

These opposite points of view are of value in showing what different interpretations the Gospel accounts may yield to different interpreters. Both profess to take into account the whole attitude of Jesus, and it must be recognized that this has great importance in view of our lack of definite data. The argument from silence cannot be regarded as conclusive.

In any consideration of the attitude of Jesus as revealed in the Gospels we are compelled to admit that " moral principles and spiritual ideals and not positive institutions are the characteristics of His Gospel ".[1] This supports the position of those who maintain that it is very improbable that He introduced such a rite. But that is not the question at issue. The contention is whether Jesus accepted a rite already in existence, not whether He created one for His need. Any discussion must take into account not merely the attitude of Jesus to ritual but the attitude of the age in which Jesus lived to such ritual as " washings " and " baptism ". There is much force in the assertion of Heitmüller that even without any express command of the Master the rite of baptism in the early Christian community might be regarded as a natural development.[2]

It is impossible to argue that Jesus did not have to face the question of His attitude to baptism. His environ-

[1] H. D. A. Major, *The Modern Churchman*, Oct. 1926, p. 257.
[2] W. Heitmüller, *Taufe und Abendmahl im Urchristentum*, 1911, p. 10.

ment and His own experience must have made this a live issue. We have His reply in the matter of obedience to the demand for ritual washings. But the baptism of John was not a ritual washing after the manner of those he rejected. It stood by itself. The only fair comparison is with the rite of circumcision and not with the daily washings of purification. It is perhaps significant that circumcision is mentioned only once in the Gospels (John vii. 22, 23) without any judgment being passed as to its value, and one ought not to read the Master's strictures on ritual purifications as a sign of His rejection of baptism. His words show that He disapproved of ritual washings because they placed an unnecessary burden on men which by the very frequency of its demand and its emphasis on the outward act caused them to forget the real need in the fulfilling of a custom. As an illustration of a different conception of Jesus we may recall the incident of the lepers in which Jesus sent the men to the priest to offer the sacrifice " for thy cleansing according as Moses commanded, for a testimony unto them " (Luke v. 14 ; Matth. viii. 4 ; Mark i. 44).[1] Although we can say with confidence that Jesus never allowed outward rites to obscure the inwardness of His message, His attitude did not rule them out entirely. Jesus never needlessly defied or denounced Jewish laws and traditions. He came not to destroy but to fulfil.

If the baptism employed by the disciples during the life of Jesus was the same as that of John there would be little need to draw attention to it. The story of the ministry of Jesus was introduced in each Gospel by a reference to the work of John, and we have the statement in the Acts that the true Messianic baptism of the Spirit was to be a post-Ascension experience. It was after Pentecost that the distinctively Christian rite was recognized. Those who believe that Jesus rejected baptism

---

[1] Plummer points out that it is the sacrifice which is the witness. *St. Luke, I.C.C.*, p. 150.

are obliged to assume that His attitude changed some time after His own baptism. We have no warrant in Scripture for this supposition. It is far more likely that His attitude when He taught the multitudes was the same as that in which He approached John on the day of His own baptism. He ought not to be accused of prohibiting an experience which in His own case had brought a divine revelation.

In Mark x. 38, Luke xii. 50, we have words of Jesus describing His life under the figure of baptism.[1] The language is probably metaphorical. There is a possibility that it has no connection with baptism at all, but is based on a familiar Old Testament figure denoting trouble and affliction (Ps. xlii. 7 ; lxix. 2, 3, 14, 15 ; cxxiv. 4, 5 ; Isa. xliii. 2, etc. ; cf. Isa. xxi. 4, Septuagint, for the use of $\beta\alpha\pi\tau\iota\varsigma\omega$ in this connection). But it must be admitted that quite early these words were understood as a reference to the rite of baptism,[2] and allowance must be made for the probability that such an interpretation was in the mind of Jesus. Granting for the moment this interpretation, we may say that the very fact that Christ could use such a metaphor would imply the recognition of the value of the baptismal act and also a background of its experience. The language would have a special appeal if it could remind those to whom the words were spoken of something they themselves had known. If previously the disciples had shared with their Master the experience of the Johannine baptism, we can appreciate the readiness

---

[1] According to Otto we have in these words the simplest form of Christ's anticipation of His end (*op. cit.*, p. 360). Would not the phrase be natural for one who had accepted baptism recognising all its implications ? Taylor thinks that Jesus used the words on more than one occasion. He says of Luke xii. 50 and Mark x. 38 : " There can be no reasonable doubt that the two sayings are quite independent " (V. Taylor, *Jesus and His Sacrifice*, p. 165). See the discussion in Taylor's book, pp. 165–7, also *TWNT*, I, p. 536.

[2] Irenæus, *Haer.*, I, 21, 2 ; Tertullian, *De Bapt.*, xvi.

of their reply to his question : " We are able." Indeed, Schweitzer has claimed that the reference of Jesus is a proof of the value of John's baptism. " If the baptism of John had had no real sacramental significance it would be unintelligible that Jesus should use this metaphor." [1] Before leaving this passage it may be remarked that the words closely associated with the Lucan reference, " I came to cast fire upon the earth ", recall the Baptist's message that his Successor would baptize with " Holy Spirit and with fire ".

Viewed as a rite which was witnessed and not performed in its earliest stage, we can understand why primitive tradition preserved no record of Jesus Himself baptizing as His disciples did in later days (John iv. 1, 2). It is very probable that baptism would be regarded by Jesus as permissible rather than obligatory. Certainly one cannot imagine that He ever gave to it a position of extreme importance. We have suggested that the Baptist himself did not give the rite the foremost place in his work which some have imagined because his name has been associated with it. But there is no warrant in the Gospels for the suggestion that Jesus rejected baptism or that this was a matter at issue between John and Himself.[2] We can assume with confidence that if the attitude of Jesus had been hostile to the rite two facts would have been impossible. The first is the significance attached to Christ's own baptism. How could they have explained that experience of ritual which brought to Jesus a manifestation of the Spirit ? Would Jesus from the basis of such a profound experience have evolved a doctrine of the futility of baptism ? Is it likely, moreover, that the disciples, knowing their Master's antipathy to baptism, would have made it central in their own teaching so soon after His death, and indeed have referred the prominence they gave to it to His own command ?

[1] A. Schweitzer, *Quest of the Historical Jesus*, p. 376, note.
[2] M. Goguel, *Jean-Baptiste*, pp. 257 ff.

Perhaps one does not go far astray in estimating that the attitude of Jesus to baptism was similar to that of the apostle Paul towards the Jewish rite of circumcision. The external act must never supersede the spiritual demand. We know that there were would-be disciples to whom Jesus had to unfold the exacting and imperative character of discipleship (Luke ix. 57–62 ; Matth. viii. 19–22). One can understand why He allowed to fall into the background a rite which might cause men to think that such could take the place of the inner spiritual demand as a means of entering into the new Kingdom. Perhaps too the experience of John may have shown that it was possible for men to misunderstand the purpose of baptism and seek a ritual for itself while forgetting the more important spiritual conditions for its observance. John had to warn the " generation of vipers " who sought his baptism that they must bring forth fruits worthy of repentance. In His attitude to the Sabbath, to rites of purification, to prayer, Jesus distinguished between the essential and the unimportant. Was not this the most likely attitude for Him to adopt in regard to baptism ? There were more important things than to ask men to accept a ritual that might be misunderstood ; but one cannot imagine that Jesus would have hindered earnest seekers of the Kingdom from undergoing a rite which witnessed to their belief that God had planned the redemption of His people.

The silence of the New Testament does not imply that there was no baptism in the later ministry of Jesus. It implies merely that the writers did not record it—probably because the teaching and life of Jesus overshadowed the observance of ritual or custom in its significance for their Gospel. We must not forget that the Gospels owed much to oral tradition and that they were written for people to whom baptism was a familiar Christian custom. There was nothing striking in the fact of baptism except as it concerned Jesus Himself, and the significance it attained in John's ministry. These are recorded. Nor is the absence of any command relating to baptism in the commission given to the disciples during the earthly ministry of Jesus a fact of great importance. The disciples were not asked to perform the transformed tebilah or to demand that it should be observed. Baptism was a natural development from the preaching of the Kingdom. To include it as a command of Jesus would have led to misunderstanding. In the eyes of the multitude it was still the Johannine baptism (Acts xviii. 25), and the days of John were past. However lofty the message of the Forerunner, his rite was no guarantee that men would understand better the Gospel which Jesus had brought in His own person. Was it not John himself who sent his disciples with the question : " Art Thou He that cometh, or look we for another ? " ?

CHAPTER V

PAUL'S TEACHING ON BAPTISM

PAUL'S letters [1] are the earliest known Christian literature, and we must regard the passages which make
mention of baptism as our earliest source of information
on the Christian rite. The first impression received from
a study of these references is that the apostle recognised
he was writing of something with which his readers were
familiar and which had been accepted by them as part
of their Christian experience. No attempt is made to
explain the origin of baptism. This contrasts with Paul's
action in the case of the Eucharist. The importance of
this omission can be realized best when we recall that there
were situations—envisaged in the letters—when it was
necessary for Paul to emphasize the significance of the
sacramental experience (Gal. iii. 27 ; Rom. vi. 3). In
the case of the Eucharist the apostle brought home the
full meaning of the rite by reminding men of its institution
by our Lord (I Cor. xi. 23 ff.). In the same letter he
introduces a reference to the baptismal act as an assurance
of the incorporation of the Christian in the mystical body
of Christ (xii. 13), but offers no explanation why there
should have been such a rite. The value of the recognition of this contrasted treatment of the two sacraments is
appreciated when we remember how ready Paul was in all
his letters to explain to his converts the historical significance of the Christian doctrines.

Although we must assume the familiarity of Paul's

[1] Ephesians, Titus, Timothy I and II are not included in
the letters regarded as of proved Pauline authorship.

readers with baptism, it is unfortunate that his epistles contain so few references to the rite. The danger is that we may be led to measure the importance in the eyes of the apostle by the amount of space devoted to mention of the sacrament. Paul gives much attention to other doctrines in his letters, and the brevity of his remarks on baptism might lead us to infer that he regarded this sacrament as of little account.

Few studies in the thought of Paul have called forth such varied opinions as that of the significance of his teaching on baptism. While some scholars have held that Paul interpreted the rite symbolically,[1] others have maintained with equal assurance that he regarded it as the actual means by which experiences vital in the Christian life were obtained.[2] The extreme opinion holds that Paul accepted baptism as a piece of magic. " Baptism ", one writer has declared, " is for St. Paul and his readers universally and unquestioningly accepted as a ' mystery ' or sacrament, which works *ex opere operato* ; and from the unhesitating manner in which St. Paul uses this fact as a basis for argument, as if it were a point on which Christian opinion did not vary, it would seem as though this sacramental teaching is central in the primitive Christianity to which the Roman Empire began to be converted." [3]

In discussing the Pauline doctrine it is important to realise that the fewness of the apostolic references is no real indication of the value he placed upon baptism. This is shown by the fact that some of these notices occur

[1] J. C. Lambert, *The Sacraments in the New Testament*, 1903, p. 191, cf. pp. 80, 126 f. See H. J. Holtzmann, *Lehrbuch der neutestamentlichen Theologie*, 1911, II, pp. 195-9.

[2] O. Pfleiderer, *Primitive Christianity*, E.T., I, p. 387 ; *SMP*, pp. 18 ff. ; W. Heitmüller, *Im Namen Jesu*, 1903, pp. 319 ff. Discussion in Von Dobschütz, " Sakrament und Symbol in Urchristentum ", *Theologische Studien und Kritiken*, 1905, pp. 1-40.

[3] K. Lake, *The Earlier Epistles of St. Paul*, p. 385.

in passages which are vital for an understanding of the
Pauline teaching. The cause of their fewness or brevity
should be sought not in any lack of importance but rather
in the lack of occasion or—still more—of need for discussion of baptismal belief. Other doctrines of the
apostle were given a larger place in the apostolic writings
since presumably they were more unfamiliar and needed
further discussion, while some also were matters of acute
controversy.

Before considering the main points of Paul's teaching
in regard to baptism there is one passage which needs
a preliminary discussion, for it is quoted often as evidence that Paul placed a low estimate on the rite. In
I Corinthians i. 13–17 we have the words : " Is Christ
divided ? Was Paul crucified for you ? Or were ye
baptized into the name of Paul ? I thank God that
I baptized none of you, save Crispus and Gaius ; lest any
man should say that ye were baptized into my name.
And I baptized also the household of Stephanas ; besides,
I know not whether I baptized any other. For Christ
sent me not to baptize, but to preach the gospel ; not in
wisdom of words, lest the cross of Christ should be made
void." This quotation, together with the recognition
that Paul lays much emphasis on faith and has few references to baptism, has led some to accept the position that
baptism held only a minor place in the Pauline theology.

It has been claimed that the picture of Paul's activity
in the Acts lends support to this conception. The
emphasis is always on Paul's work in preaching the gospel.
As one writer puts it : " We read that ' they preached the
word ', ' they preached the gospel ', ' Paul testified both
to the Jews and the Greeks repentance toward God and
faith toward our Lord Jesus Christ ' ; but we never find
it said in any of the summarized descriptions of evangeliz-
ing activity which occur from time to time, that ' they
baptized '." [1]

[1] J. C. Lambert, *The Sacraments in the New Testament*, p. 138.

In any discussion it should be admitted from the beginning that the teaching of Paul ought not to be regarded as governed necessarily by the general attitude of the Church of his day. The genius and religious experience of the apostle make dangerous any generalization which would treat his beliefs as typical of his age. We need to keep in mind the fact that succeeding generations of Christians failed utterly to appreciate his message or to follow his teaching. At the same time the other New Testament writings do furnish us with a background of thought and life which helps us to understand much of the apostolic doctrine and conduct. We have therefore to ask ourselves whether Paul wished to minimize the value of a rite which according to some passages in the Acts occupied a very prominent place in Christian experience.

The key to the study of the words in the first chapter of I Corinthians is the Pauline doctrine of faith. There is no doubt that Paul held that the supreme task of his life was the preaching of the gospel by which men could believe.[1] His great ambition was to make it possible for all to know the gospel so that a way might be opened for saving faith. This is the reason why preaching took the foremost place in his work. Looked at from this point of view his language in the present passage is seen not as an attempt to decry baptism but as a reminder to his readers of his main task. It is true he was relieved to think that his own action in baptizing had given little occasion to would-be schismatics, who—perhaps under the influence of " a formalistic sacramentarianism " [2]—were bestowing undue importance on the person of the agent in baptism, to boast of a close connection with himself. But the very reference to the rite after this manner implies a Pauline

---

[1] I Cor. xv. 11 ; Rom. i. 16.

[2] The phrase is from H. Lietzmann, *The Beginnings of the Christian Church*, E.T., 1937, p. 186, who refers to R. Reitzenstein, *Die hellenistischen Mysterienreligionen* (3rd ed., p. 40), in support of the idea that this condition was due to pagan influence.

recognition of its importance, since he stresses the fact that they were baptized not into the name of Paul, but of Christ.

It should be noted that when the apostle gives a definite reason why he did not baptize (17) he does not add, after the manner of his statement on circumcision in Galatians vi. 15, " for neither is baptism anything or lack of baptism ". Only on the ground of the consequences which might have ensued, if his past actions had lent any appearance of support to the schismatics, does he thank God that he baptized but a few. This passage must not be isolated and interpreted as a belittling of the baptismal rite. Paul preached and others attended to the work of baptizing,[1] and there is never the slightest hint or suggestion that the latter was not required. Perhaps the incident of Cornelius throws light on the method of Paul as well as Peter. After his preaching Peter himself did not perform the act of baptizing those who had received the Holy Spirit. " He commanded them to be baptized in the name of Jesus Christ " (Acts x. 48).

It must not be forgotten that there is much positive evidence of the value Paul gave to baptism.[2] Most of this will be considered presently, but we would mention here the curious reference in I Corinthians x. 2 to the Israelites of the Exodus who are said to have been " baptized unto Moses ".[3] Even if we allow that this is a figurative

[1] Moffatt suggests that the reason why Paul was able to state that he had baptized but few was due in part to the fact that at that time " most Christians seem to have baptized themselves (vi. 11), as Paul himself had done. It was only in an exceptional case that a convert would insist on being baptized by some apostle to whom he owed a deep personal debt " (*I Corinthians*, 1938, pp. 11, 12). In the period of transition from self-baptism to baptism by an agent there would be a time when both types were practised.

[2] E.g. Rom. vi. 3, 4 ; Gal. iii. 27 ; Col. ii. 12.

[3] Easton explains the words as " an addition of St. Paul's to the Haggadah, in order to make the parallel between Jewish and Christian baptism more complete. As the latter was per-

expression, the very figure used shows that Paul regarded baptism as an important and efficacious experience. This thought is emphasised when we couple with it—as does Paul—the mention of the spiritual nourishment which seems to foreshadow the Eucharist. It has been argued that the whole point of Paul's discussion lies in the uselessness of sacraments apart from that ethical obedience to which believers have pledged themselves in these sacred ordinances.[1] This brings us back to the position that it is difficult to assess the full significance of the ritual act in Paul's teaching since he takes for granted the presence of faith in those undergoing it.

In view of conditions prevailing in the contemporary heathen world it is instructive to commence our study of Paul's teaching on baptism with a consideration of his treatment of it as a rite of initiation. The only reference to such a connection is found in I Corinthians xii. 13 : " For in one Spirit were we all baptized into one body, whether Jews or Greeks, whether bond or free." In the eyes of the outside world the most obvious idea to be associated with baptism was that of initiation. The narratives of the Acts and the writings of the early Fathers show that this was fully appreciated. One Lord, one faith, one baptism, expressed the theological position of the apostolic Church. But from the language of Paul it was the possession of the one Spirit rather than the one baptism which indicated the unity, although the quotation given shows that the latter thought was not strange to him. In this passage it should be noted that the reception of the Spirit and the act of baptism are so closely linked together in the Pauline thought that they may be regarded as simultaneous experiences.

It is probable that Paul's neglect to stress the initiatory

formed ' in Christ ' Paul adds ' into Moses ' without much reflection as to meaning " (B. S. Easton, " St. Paul and the Sacraments ", *Constructive Quarterly*, VII, 1919).

[1] J. C. Lambert, *op. cit.*, p. 159 f.

significance of baptism was due to his desire to avoid a misconception which might have arisen because of contemporary pagan teaching regarding initiation into the mystery cults. Perhaps this feeling was responsible for the omission, to which Schweitzer refers, of the term " regeneration " [1] in the Pauline writings, and also of any direct reference to the teaching of rebirth. Everything implied in regeneration is found in the teaching of Paul,[2] but the significance is in the absence of the term.

There may have been also in Paul's attitude to the thought of baptism as initiation a reaction from his pre-Christian training. Judaism stressed both circumcision and the tebilah for proselytes. Christianity never adopted circumcision as a rite essential for entering the faith, even if at one time it seemed perilously near to following such a course. Paul knew from this experience the danger, and it is unlikely that he would seek to emphasize a side of baptism which brought it into line with circumcision and other outward acts of initiation. It is interesting to note that in one passage the Christian experience is likened to circumcision : " In whom ye were also circumcised with a circumcision not made with hands, in the putting off of the body of the flesh, in the circumcision of Christ ; having been buried with Him in baptism, wherein ye were also raised with Him through faith in the working of God, who raised Him from the dead " (Col. ii. 11, 12). Lightfoot, however, pointed out that the experience excels circumcision in character, " not made with hands ", in extent, not a mere mutilation but a complete " putting off of the body of the flesh ", and in authority, it is " of Christ " and not merely of Abraham or of Moses.[3] The exact part played by

---

[1] A. Schweitzer, *Paul and his Interpreters*, p. 191.
[2] " For the apostle every other aspect of baptism is practically swallowed up in this, that it is a rite of regeneration " (W. Morgan, *The Religion and Theology of Paul*, p. 210).
[3] J. B. Lightfoot, *Colossians*, 1880, p. 183.

baptism in this experience is difficult to define. The use of the phrase " not made with hands " prevents any restriction to a mere ritual act, but the aorist " ye were circumcised ", together with the other aorists in the passage, makes it most probable that the moment contemplated was the time of baptism.

In Paul's doctrine of baptism there are three main conceptions. These are concerned with cleansing from sin, the gift of the Spirit and union with Christ.

1. *Cleansing from Sin*

The apostle has little to say about the purifying power of baptism. Actually there is only one sentence which may be called a definite reference to the cleansing power of the sacrament. This treatment of a conception so often associated with baptism has brought forth an explanation [1] that since in Paul's theology the doctrine of justification by faith is prominent, and justification brought immediate forgiveness of sins, baptism was really superfluous from such a standpoint. Any emphasis on this side of the work of the baptismal act would have led to a confusion of the work of faith and the work of the sacrament.

But one cannot think that it was the attempt to create a harmonious system of theology which was the guiding principle with Paul, and caused him to make so little mention of the cleansing work of baptism. Although there is but one [2] reference it is most impressive. " And such were some of you : but ye were washed, but ye were sanctified, but ye were justified in the name of the Lord Jesus Christ, and in the Spirit of our God " (I Cor. vi. 11, R.V.). The tremendous change suggested

[1] B. S. Easton, *Constructive Quarterly*, VII, pp. 98–127.

[2] W. Morgan (*op. cit.*, p. 209) thinks that in Col. ii. 14 " blotted out " is a play on lustral washing. The word is used also in Acts iii. 19 in regard to the blotting out of sin. The other New Testament references follow the usual meaning. Moulton and Milligan *op. cit.*, s.v.) call attention to the use of the term in a Christian petition in the papyri : " blot out my sins " (*P. Oxy.*, iii, 407 [3]).

PAUL'S TEACHING ON BAPTISM

by the experience is seen not only in the contrast with the condition of many pagans, but in the linking with baptism of vital experiences like sanctification and justification. This passage is a strong argument against the symbolic interpretation of Paul's references to baptism. It is difficult to imagine that Paul would have ended the vivid contrast between the past and present conditions of his readers with a tame allusion to a symbolic rite. Nor would the thought have harmonized with his references to sanctification and justification.

But while it is impossible to restrict the apostolic conception to the realm of symbol, it ought not to be invested with the thought of a later sacramentarianism. It is true that Paul connects baptism with real and very vital experiences, but it is true also that according to other passages in his writings these same experiences are described as realized in a way that appears to have little connection with the rite of baptism.[1] An appreciation of the relationship to the Pauline doctrine of faith is necessary for a full understanding of the Pauline doctrine of the sacraments.

The appropriateness of an act of baptism as a sign of spiritual cleansing needs no comment, but it is not easy to see what foundation there is for the statement that for Paul baptism worked " according to the well-known idea that results could be reached in the unseen spiritual world by the performance of analogous acts in the visible material world." [2] This not only minimizes the Pauline emphasis on the ethical basis of life, but it ignores his demand for faith as the great essential in any act of salvation. Faith is never regarded as conditioned by baptism but as conditioning it. An excellent illustration of this statement is afforded by the passage from Colossians ii., a part of which has been discussed already in its reference

[1] See Von Dobschütz, " Sakrament und Symbol im Urchristentum ", *Theologische Studien und Kritiken*, 1905, p. 7.
[2] K. Lake, *ERE*, II, p. 382.

to circumcision. Reading from the twelfth verse, we have the words : " Having been buried with Him in baptism, wherein ye were also raised with Him through faith in the working of God, who raised Him from the dead. And you, being dead through your trespasses and the uncircumcision of your flesh, you, I say, did He quicken together with Him, having forgiven us all our trespasses ; having blotted out the bond written in ordinances that was against us, which was contrary to us ; and He hath taken it out of the way, nailing it to the cross," etc.

The passage reveals a close connection between the ideas of baptism, faith and forgiveness. Much discussion has arisen over the interpretation of " wherein " in the sentence of verse 12.[1] It seems most natural to take this with " in baptism " as its antecedent. The aorist participle " having forgiven " should be explained as implying coincident action with " did He quicken ". It would then be interpreted as referring to the act of baptism.[2] The relation of baptism and forgiveness must be considered in the light of the words in verse 12 " through faith in the working of God ". It is no mere generalization from one sentence to say that Paul could not contemplate the absence of faith in the forgiveness of sins through baptism. His whole system of doctrine demanded that faith should be present in every human experience of the divine grace.

2. *The Gift of the Spirit*

The belief in the close connection of baptism with the reception of the Spirit was widely held in the early

[1] See Abbott, *Colossians*, *I.C.C.*, s.v. ; J. B. Lightfoot, *Colossians*, s.v.

[2] J. H. Moulton, *Grammar of N.T. Greek*, I, pp. 130–1. A. Oepke says : " Die Aoriste Χαρισάμενος, ἐξαλείψας, προσηλώσας bezeichnen nach griechischem Sprachgebrauch weder einen begleitenden Nebenumstand noch einen vorangehenden Akt, sondern das Mittel, wodurch das im übergeordneten Verbum Ausgedrückte verwirklicht wurde " (*TWNT*, I, p. 540 n.).

Church,[1] and it is not surprising to find that it had a prominent place in the teaching of Paul. There are certain passages which bear witness to this : " For in one Spirit were we all baptized into one body, whether Jews or Greeks, whether bond or free ; and were all made to drink of one Spirit " (I Cor. xii. 13). " Who also sealed us and gave us the earnest of the Spirit in our hearts " (II Cor. i. 22). " But ye were washed . . . sanctified . . . justified in the name of the Lord Jesus Christ, and in the Spirit of our God " (I Cor. vi. 11).

It is very likely that Paul's own baptismal experience helped him in associating the gift of the Spirit with this rite.[2] Yet there is no reason to think that this experience led him to regard the ritual act as the important factor in the communication of the Spirit. As Deissmann has pointed out, the deciding factor in Paul's own case in bringing about communion with Christ was the Christophany at Damascus and not the rite of baptism, and he regarded the preaching of the gospel, not baptism, as the purpose of his apostleship.[3] We may say that in his teaching of the connection of the Spirit with baptism Paul was following the current doctrine of the Church. Allowance must be made, however, for the certainty that this belief, as every other which the apostle received, underwent a change in the light of Paul's personal experience. Paul never states or implies that the gift of the Spirit is conditioned by baptism. He has passages in his

[1] Titus iii. 5. The Acts of the Apostles bears witness to the extent of the belief, as also the tradition contained in the Gospels concerning the Spirit baptism of John's Successor.

[2] The passage in Acts which describes the meeting of Ananias and Paul has been interpreted in a sense which makes Paul's baptism the medium of his reception of the Spirit (R. J. Knowling, *The Expositor's Greek Testament*, l.c.). It is noteworthy that the author of the Acts ascribes to Paul the questions asked of the Ephesian disciples : " Did ye receive the Holy Ghost when ye believed ? . . . Into what then were ye baptized ? " (xix. 2, 3).

[3] A. Deissmann, *Paul*, E.T., 1926, p. 145.

writings in which its coming is ascribed to the gift of God without any mention of the medium of baptism.[1]

But while one may affirm with confidence that the apostle would never have agreed to any belief that made the gift of the Spirit dependent on a rite alone, there is another viewpoint from which to regard his attitude. This latter helps us to understand how Paul could regard baptism as a very suitable means for the conveyance of the Spirit, and the more so because it took the form of an outward action. The apostle would be familiar with that Hebrew conception of the Spirit which thought of it after the manner of a supernatural essence. The conception is strange to modern thought, but to the Jewish mind which accepted it the idea suggested naturally the need of some material form for its communication. It is along this line that we can find the explanation of Paul's use of the term $\dot{\epsilon}\pi\sigma\tau\dot{\iota}\sigma\theta\eta\mu\epsilon\nu$, " were made to drink " (Moffatt : " we have been imbued ").[2] This expression ought not to be dismissed lightly as a mere metaphor. Such a belief in the material vehicle for transmitting the Spirit would be encouraged by the Johannine tradition, with which Paul must have been familiar, which associated the Messianic baptism with the coming of the Spirit.

[1] I Cor. ii. 12 ; II Cor. v. 5 ; Gal. iii. 5 ; iv. 6 ; Philip. i. 19.
[2] I Cor. xii. 13 (cf. Matth. x. 42 ; xxv. 42, etc.). Moffatt adds the explanatory term " saturated " (*I Corinthians*, p. 186). It is useful to recall the frequent employment of the term in irrigation. Instances of this are to be seen in the Septuagint and the Papyri. Moulton and Milligan, *Vocabulary of the Greek Testament*, s.v. H. Lietzmann reminds us that we must not ignore the possibility that " were made to drink " might refer to something other than the rite of baptism—the Eucharist (*I Korinther*, II, 1925, p. 64). In I Cor. x. 4 Paul follows up his enigmatic reference to the baptism of the Israelites " unto Moses " by the statement that these Israelites " did all eat the same spiritual meat ; and did all drink the same spiritual drink ". This latter figure is interpreted usually as prefiguring the Eucharist. See Moffatt, *I Corinthians*, 1938, pp. 129–30.

3. *Union with Christ*

The teaching of Paul on baptism has one phase which may be regarded as pre-eminently the apostle's own. This is his conception of union with Christ, in which he found the deepest significance of baptism, and in the light of which the rite appears to take on the nature of a mystery. We have the familiar passages : " Or are ye ignorant that all we who were baptized into Christ Jesus were baptized into His death ? We were buried therefore with Him through baptism into death ; that like as Christ was raised from the dead through the glory of the Father, so we also might walk in newness of life " (Rom. vi. 3, 4). " For as many of you as were baptized into Christ did put on Christ " (Gal. iii. 27). " Having been buried with Him in baptism wherein ye were also raised with Him through faith in the working of God, who raised Him from the dead " (Col. ii. 12).

The attempt to derive the Pauline Christusmystik, as it has been termed, from the pagan mysteries is a failure, and has been discredited as having no basis in fact. Paul's knowledge of the mystery cults is very doubtful,[1] even if at times his language seems to introduce words and phrases used to express the great mystery conceptions. The assumption that we have here the infiltration of mystery ideas into Christianity, which were accepted by Paul and used by him, is incredible, if only for the fact that it would imply that the opponents of Paul, who fought strongly against his liberalising tendencies in regard to the admission of the Gentiles and the observance of the Law, raised no objection, since silence here would be full of meaning, against the even more dangerous acceptance of heathen mystery conceptions. The belief in mystery influence is not needed to explain the Pauline

[1] A. D. Nock suggests that Paul's neglect to use the idea of rebirth, though thinking of baptism as a death, is a striking illustration of his unfamiliarity with the mysteries (*Essays on the Trinity and the Incarnation*, p. 116).

thought or terminology. H. A. A. Kennedy affirms :
" The Old Testament evidence makes it superfluous to
seek for the explanation of Paul's use of any of these terms
in the Hellenistic mystery religion. What we do learn
from the parallels is the ability of many of his readers to
catch the meaning of a more or less technical terminology,
due not merely to a course of instruction in the Old
Testament, but to their acquaintance with a religious
vocabulary already current among the mystery associations ".[1] This similarity of background made it possible for the convert from paganism to understand in
part, with but little teaching, the rites of his new faith,
and yet rendered it easy for him to misunderstand their
full ethical and spiritual meaning.[2]

From its outward form the Pauline doctrine of union
with Christ would seem more closely allied to pagan
mysticism than to Judaism.[3] The conception of identification with deity through initiatory rites is foreign to
Judaism. Moreover, in the Unio Mystica of the Platonic
philosophers and the lower ritual union with the mystery
god we have much that reminds us of the doctrine of Paul.
But the parallel is illusory, and, apart from the probability
of Paul's unfamiliarity with the mysteries, there is no real
resemblance to the Pauline conception in the familiar
figure of the pagan initiate dying and being reborn. No

---

[1] H. A. A. Kennedy, *St. Paul and the Mystery Religions*, 1913,
p. 198.

[2] I Cor. x. 14 ff. ; xi. 27. When we consider the previous
pagan condition of many of Paul's converts we feel that some
slight modification is needed in Deissmann's statement that " the
ancient Christians were able easily to understand the mystical
meaning of the several stages of baptism (Col. ii. 12 ; Rom. vi.
3 ff.) to the death, burial and resurrection with Christ, because
having been baptized as adults, they had an indelibly vivid
recollection of the ceremony performed upon them by immersion. . . . The usages and sentiments attached to other cults of
their environment may have rendered the mystical interpretation
of their sacrament easier " (Paul, E.T., 1926, pp. 182–3).

[3] R. Reitzenstein, *Poimandres*, 1904, p. 220.

known pagan mystery taught of an initiate dying and rising with his deity after the manner suggested by Paul's words. Also it is an error to imagine that Paul connected his doctrine with the rite of baptism because he saw in the latter a symbolical submerging of the old and sinful self and a rising into a new life. His linking of baptism with the experience of union with Christ resulted from something which had happened to himself, and which others also had shared.

In arriving at this doctrine of union with Christ it is most likely that Paul was influenced by the early Church teaching of the gift of the Spirit in baptism. We have called attention to the apostle's acceptation of the Hebrew conception of Spirit as a supernatural essence, but this does not express his only, or indeed his main interpretation. Despite the apparent inconsistency we find him frequently alluding to the Spirit as someone personal. In this he was in harmony with the teaching of his fellow-apostles. Although it was recognised that the Baptist had proclaimed the coming of a Spirit baptism, the early Church which recalled the words of Jesus about the gift of the Spirit always associated the work of the latter with a post-Ascension experience of the presence of Christ. The Johannine Gospel bears witness to this (John xv. 26) as also does the Acts (viii. 39). At times Paul identifies the Spirit with Christ (Rom. viii. 9, 10). When he speaks of the " indwelling Spirit " (Rom. viii. 11 ; I Cor. iii. 16) it is not an essence but a person of whom he thinks, and that person is none other than the One who revealed Himself on the road to Damascus.[1] Thus we come to the profound spiritual experience which is described as " in

[1] " To treat this presence (indwelling Spirit) as the ' influence of a vague and semi-physical something is altogether to miss the truth ; for Paul, life is so identified with Christ that to live is Christ, and the fellowship of the Spirit is intensely personal, with nothing between the believer and his Lord " (H. Wheeler Robinson, *The Christian Experience of the Holy Spirit*, 1928, p. 19).

Christ ", or similar words.[1] It was the divine Spirit which accomplished this vital sharing in the Christ life (I Cor. xii. 12, 13).

This conception of the mystical life in Christ is Paul's contribution to the baptismal teaching of the early Church. We may regard it as the outcome of the doctrine of the gift of the Spirit in baptism which was accepted throughout the early Christian communities, and which, in the case of Paul, had been transmuted in the crucible of his own personal experience. There was nothing spectacular about the results of this union. Its fruits were to be seen in the graces of the Christian life rather than in the abnormal glossolalia.

Before leaving this doctrine of union with Christ in baptism we may ask whether the idea is due entirely to Paul alone. Does the figure of the Vine and the Branches (John xv.) preserve an echo of the Master's own teaching, or is it a reflection of later Christian belief ? In words of Jesus on the subject of His death there is used the figure of baptism (Luke xii. 50 ; Mark x. 38 f.). Some regard these words as the earliest form of His approach to the subject. If we accept the suggestion that the figure was employed by Jesus on more than one occasion, might not its message have lived with His followers ? The full implication could easily escape dull minds, but to the spiritually sensitive Paul it might come as a revelation.

Throughout the consideration of the Pauline teaching on baptism it has been necessary to remind ourselves continually that at the background of all his thought is the great doctrine of faith. This cannot be separated from any part of his belief which concerns the plan of salvation, and nowhere does the truth need greater emphasis than in his sacramental thought. There is a theory that Paulinism embraces two systems or principles of salva-

[1] For a discussion of these words and their meaning, see A. Deissmann, *Die neutestamentliche Formel " in Christo Jesu "*, 1892.

tion, the one entirely sacramental, the other dependent
on faith. But the sixth chapter of Romans does not
as alleged introduce a sacramental principle which contrasts with the doctrine of justification by faith. Faith
and the baptismal conception are joined in an indis-
soluble union. However different the two ideas may seem
to be, Paul links them together " in a perfectly real if
undefinable way ", to quote a phrase of Wrede, which
aptly expresses the connection.[1] We have found, when
discussing the work of baptism in ensuring forgiveness,
the gift of the Spirit and union with Christ, that all these
conceptions were built on a basis of faith as well as
baptismal efficacy. How far faith and the ritual act affect
each other in producing the experiences associated with
baptism we cannot tell since the apostle gives no
indication.

The Pauline doctrine of faith is a sufficient guarantee
that the apostle accepted no ritual act as the sole means of
cleansing from sin or of obtaining any other of the
benefits associated with salvation. There are other
reasons too for maintaining that he laid no undue stress
on the efficacy of the sacraments. Galatians ii. 19, 20,
embodies the Pauline teaching on redemption, yet it contains no mention of baptism. More significant is the fact
that in the apostle's great doctrinal treatise—the epistle
to the Romans—baptism is mentioned only once and the
Lord's Supper not at all. It would have been impossible
for an advanced sacramentalist to have written in this
manner.[2]

In summing up Paul's doctrine of baptism we may have
confidence in affirming our belief that he allowed it no

[1] W. Wrede, *Paul*, E.T., 1907, p. 122.

[2] Schweitzer gets over the difficulty by postulating a " remarkable duality in Paulinism " which reveals the sacramental idea
" intensified to an extreme and unintelligible degree " and yet
recognizes that " the necessity of the sacred ceremonies does
not logically result from the system as a whole " (*Paul and His
Interpreters*, p. 214).

mere mechanical or magical efficacy. This is not disproved even if we recognize that he gave a certain significance to the formula used in baptism.[1] Indeed, there is something to be said for the position of J. Weiss, who drew attention to Paul's use of the sacred name on important occasions, including baptism, and argued that it revealed his belief in its potency. Weiss maintained that in the utterance of the name in baptism Paul must have felt that a Power had assumed control over the baptized which snatched them from the domination of Satan and the demons into His own possession. On the other hand, he thought it was impossible to maintain that Paul regarded the act of baptism as entirely magical, since in his play with the idea that Christians might be baptized into the name of Paul (I Cor. i. 13), he showed that this relation of ownership was dependent upon the will of the baptized, and therefore non-miraculous and non-magical in the full sense of the term. His summing up of the Pauline position was that there was " a certain hesitation between the sacramental and the symbolical modes of thought ".

The value of the statement of Weiss is the reminder it gives us that, although possessed by lofty spiritual ideas, Paul was in some ways a man of his age and influenced by many of the conceptions of that age. It must be recognized that our picture of Paul is not that of a theologian with all his ideas logically set down, but of a preacher speaking out of the fullness of his own experience and yet working within an organization which although opposed to the spirit of the world without had many ideas and practices which were common to the age. There is, however, nothing in the language or reported actions of Paul which can lead us to assume that he relied on the repetition of any form of words, or the performance of any ritual act to secure special results, except in as far as these same words and acts were associated with and revealed the saving faith which was indispensable.

[1] W. Heitmüller, *Im Namen Jesu*, pp. 65 ff.

It is important to note that this saving faith is revealed not by mere affirmation but by actions. Paul never regarded faith as a cold assent to theological ideas. It was much more than intellectual agreement and included a strong emotional experience in which the convert gave himself in self-surrender to Christ. No moment expressed this so completely as that which witnessed the baptism of the convert ; and no one sought more earnestly than Paul to enable the baptized convert to realize the full implications of this experience. Thus in Colossians iii., when writing to men who had undergone baptism, Paul uses terms which speak not only of union with Christ but of the need for revealing the reality of this union : " For ye died, and your life is hid with Christ in God. . . . Mortify therefore your members which are upon the earth ; fornication, uncleanness, passion, evil desire and covetousness, the which is idolatry . . . But now put ye also away all these ; anger, wrath, malice, railing, shameful speaking out of your mouth ; lie not one to another ; seeing that ye have put off the old man with his doings, and have put on the new man, which is being renewed unto knowledge after the image of Him that created him." There is no inconsistency in this language ; the one experience is the basis of the appeal for the other.

A similar conception is found in Romans vi. 3, where the apostle states very definitely : " We who were baptized into Christ Jesus were baptized into His death." Then without any pause or explanation he adds : " We were buried therefore with Him through baptism into death ; that like as Christ was raised from the dead through the glory of the Father, so we also might walk in newness of life." This call to be baptized to walk in newness of life, and later the reminder that they must reckon themselves as dead unto sin (verse 11), are eloquent testimony to the recognition that for full experience of the baptismal blessings there must be a life willed for good, a faith revealing itself in action.

The reference in I Corinthians xv. 29 to the strange practice of baptism for the dead has been the subject of much controversy and has brought forth innumerable explanations. Most of these are far from helpful and some are fantastic. It cannot be said that any real evidence has been adduced which enables us to form a definite opinion as to the origin and meaning of the custom. The most likely suggestion is that of Meyer,[1] that the purpose of the rite was to enable the dead to secure admittance into the Kingdom of God and bliss in Paradise ; although it is very doubtful if this arose out of an early Christian idea of baptism, derived from the significance of the Johannine rite. One suspects that it owed much to pagan conceptions which still exercised their influence in the minds of Christian converts. Patristic thought appears to be as perplexed about the matter as we are, and keeps an impressive silence. The earliest known reference to such a practice as Paul mentions is found in Tertullian,[2] who ascribes it to the Marcionites. But it is quite likely that the custom observed among the heretics may have been founded upon this passage ; and therefore it offers little help.

The Corinthian reference is so isolated in its context that the whole subject is one of uncertainty. To mention one matter alone : who are the dead on whose behalf baptism was undergone ? Weinel thought that they were those who had died before conversion.[3] On the other hand, McGiffert and Moffatt assume that they were converts who happened to die before receiving baptism.[4] There is also the question whether the words should be taken to mean that the believer underwent one additional baptism or many, according to the number of the dead.

[1] *Ursprung und Anfänge des Christentums*, 1923, III, p. 246.
[2] *De Resurrectione Carnis*, 48 ; *Adv. Marcion.*, v, 10.
[3] H. Weinel, *St. Paul : the Man and his Work*, 1906, p. 120.
[4] A. C. McGiffert, *History of Christianity in the Apostolic Age*, 1897, p. 272 ; J. Moffatt, *I Corinthians*, 1938, l.c.

Also, are we sure that Paul had in mind a practice of the Christian Church ? Is it not possible that he is referring to a purely heathen practice for an illustration of his argument ? In that case the suggestion would be that Paul, who, it should be noted, makes no comment on the validity of the custom, is employing an *argumentum ad hominem*.[1] However, there is no evidence in contemporary paganism of any custom of baptism for the dead [2] ; and one may assume from the silence of later Greek Fathers on that point and their interpretation of the passage that they knew of no such custom. Schweitzer is critical of those who without a shred of proof assign this practice to pagan sources. He points out that pagan baptism of the dead was not a baptism for the dead.[3]

We come back to the probability that it was a Christian custom which the apostle had in mind. Schweitzer [4] has argued that it was Paul's own teaching concerning baptism which caused the custom to arise. Holding what he terms " the quasi-physical " conception of the being-in-Christ, relatives of the unbaptized dead were baptized on their behalf so as to make them capable of taking part in the resurrection at the return of Jesus. It

[1] W. Morgan, *The Religion and Theology of Paul*, p. 211. H. A. A. Kennedy (*St. Paul and the Mystery Religions*, pp. 253 ff.) thought there was value in Von Dobschütz's suggestion that the superstition belonged to the circle of the " sceptical " at Corinth since lack of faith and superstition come of the same lineage.

[2] R. Reitzenstein has quoted as an ancient Mandæan parallel the pouring of water upon a dying man (*Das mandaische Buch des Herrn der Grösse und die Evangelierüberlieferung*, 1919, p. 88). H. Lietzmann refers to " evidence from a later period in regard to a similar custom. The corpse was baptized and another person gave the answers to the liturgical questions instead of the dead " (*The Beginnings of the Christian Church*, E.T., 1937, p. 185). A study of the evidence, however, leaves one with the feeling that none of the so-called parallels is satisfactory for offering guidance in the interpretation of the custom. See list in H. Lietzmann, *I Korinther*, II, 1923, p. 83.

[3] A. Schweitzer, *St. Paul and his Interpreters*, E.T., pp. 210-12.

[4] *SMP*, pp. 283 ff.

is not clear that Paul approved of the custom ; and Schweitzer's reason for its discontinuance—that being wholly bound up with the eschatologic-Pauline view of baptism it became obsolete with it—is not too convincing, since customs persist long after the reason for them is past and forgotten.

In view of the obscurity which surrounds both the meaning of the passage and the origin of the custom to which it refers, one feels that the soundest critical position is that adopted by A. J. Maclean, who felt that the problem was insoluble with our present knowledge.[1] Yet if we could be sure that this was a Christian and not a pagan practice, it would show that some Christians had a kind of magical conception of baptism in which they believed that the act of the living could influence the condition of the dead, but the vital link is missing to show whether this doctrine had anything to do with Paul's own teaching, as Schweitzer alleges, or was a superstition of which he made use in his argument.

[1] *DAC*, I, p. 129.

CHAPTER VI

LATER NEW TESTAMENT DOCTRINE

A STUDY of the epistles regarded as later than those Pauline letters which have been considered makes us aware that we are dealing with a developing doctrine and that the sacramental position represented by them presents certain differences from the ideas found in Paul's teaching. The change may be expressed in general terms as a tendency to greater precision of statements and a certain hardening of ideas. The implications of some underlying conceptions have been accepted as matters of faith. A good illustration of the kind of change involved is shown by the passage from Ephesians iv. 5, which makes mention of " one Lord, one faith, one baptism ". Here baptism becomes a sign of the unity of the Church. The conception follows closely the Pauline thought in I Corinthians xii. 13, but it is more definite. It is also in harmony with a similar argument used by Paul of the Lord's Supper (I Cor. x. 17).

An important statement of the work of baptism in the Church is contained in Ephesians v. 25–7 ; for there seems little doubt that the sacrament of baptism was in the mind of the writer.[1] " Christ also loved the church, and gave

---

[1] This is not negatived by the statement of T. K. Abbott (*Ephesians, I.C.C.*, p. 168) that in τῷ λουτρῷ τοῦ ὕδατος there is probably an allusion to the usual bath of the bride before marriage. Such a play on words is not unknown in Paul's writings. S. Cave believes that the washing mentioned is not baptism but the bride's bath, and that the reference to baptism can only be of a metaphorical kind (*The Gospel of St. Paul*,

Himself up for it; that He might sanctify it, having cleansed it by the washing of water with the word, that He might present the church to Himself a glorious church," etc. Here there is attributed to baptism a cleansing and—if we allow an interpretation of ἐν ῥήματι accepted by Augustine and some Greek commentators—a sanctifying power.[1] In the phrase " washing of regeneration," λουτρόν παλιγγενεσίας (Titus iii. 5), we have language that brings us into touch with that realm of Hellenistic thought which later exercised considerable influence over Christian teaching.[2] The theology of the developing Church makes more clear the tendency to stress the importance of baptism, and in so doing reveals

1928, p. 218). The allusion to the bridal bath is denied by J. Armitage Robinson (*Ephesians*, 1904, p. 207).

[1] For a discussion of the meaning of ῥῆμα, see T. K. Abbott, *Ephesians*, pp. 168, 169, and J. A. Robinson, *Ephesians*, pp. 206, 207.

[2] The idea of regeneration through baptism probably lies behind the words in John iii. 5. See A. D. Nock, *Essays on the Trinity and the Incarnation*, pp. 116–18, for Hellenistic references. " All the contemporary religions centred in a sacred rite, which was supposed to effect a marvellous change ; and Gentile converts inevitably thought of baptism in the light of those ideas with which they were familiar. It was acknowledged that in Christianity a man was renewed ; he was set free from all past sins and became spiritual instead of carnal. How could this mysterious change have come about except through a regenerating rite ? The act of baptism was singled out as that which affected the transformation. In later baptismal doctrine the influence of the Hellenistic mode of thought was decisive, but from this we cannot argue, with some modern writers, that baptism first acquired its mystical significance as a result of the Gentile mission. The alien ideas served only to develop, in a peculiar direction, beliefs that can be traced back to John the Baptist, and through him to Old Testament prophecy. The Messiah was to baptize with the Spirit—with the heavenly power which God would pour out on his people in the last days. This Hebrew conception now adapted itself to Gentile modes of thinking, but was the underlying motive in all baptismal theory " (E. F. Scott, *The Spirit in the New Testament*, pp. 153–4).

how ideas current in pagan initiatory rites have been absorbed in it. The introduction into the sacramental vocabulary of the term "enlightenment", which afterwards became very prominent in Clement of Alexandria as a synonym for baptism, may be traced back to the New Testament; although this does not imply that the word when employed there has all the implications of its technical meaning in paganism or later Christian thought. The writer of Hebrews speaks of "those who were once enlightened (τοὺς ἅπαξ φωτισθέντας) and tasted of the heavenly gift, and were made partakers of the Holy Spirit" (vi. 4), and bids his readers to remember the former days "in which after ye were enlightened (φωτισθέντες) ye endured a great conflict of sufferings" (x. 32). In the Hermetic literature enlightenment is the result of gnosis, but there is little proof of any New Testament connection with the usage found in the mysteries. Nock inclines to the belief that the use was commonplace and derived from mysticism.[1] In the later Greek Fathers the employment of the word reveals definite evidence of pagan influences, but then it was part of the vocabulary of a Church which, being no longer predominantly Jewish but Gentile, had received many ideas from the Gentile world. A study of the Septuagint helps to an understanding of the figure of enlightenment and shows that the thought was familiar in Judaism,[2] while numerous references in the Gospels [3] and elsewhere in the New Testament [4] prove that the conception made a strong appeal to the early Christians. It is very probable that this appeal was reinforced by a remembrance of Christ's own teaching.[5] Of the passages in Hebrews we

---

[1] *Essays on the Trinity and the Incarnation*, p. 120 note.
[2] Psalm xxvi. (xxvii.) 1 ; Psalm xxxiii. (xxxiv.) 5 ; Isa. lx. 1, etc.
[3] Matthew iv. 16 ; v. 14 ; Luke ii. 32 ; John i. 4, etc.
[4] II Cor. iv. 4, 6 ; Ephes. i. 18 ; v. 8 ; I John i. 5, 7 ; ii. 9 ; I Pet. ii. 9.
[5] Matth. v. 14–16 ; John viii. 12 ; ix. 5 ; xii. 36, 46.

may say that although the word had not yet become a technical term for baptism its employment affords some indication how this technical usage was acquired.[1]

In any reference to the growth of a sacramental vocabulary there is one term which must not be overlooked. The verb " seal ", $\sigma\varphi\varrho\alpha\gamma\acute{\iota}\zeta\omega$, occurs in several passages which are thought to refer to the rite of baptism. In II Corinthians i. 22, Ephesians i. 13 and iv. 30 this sealing is connected with an experience of the Spirit. Yet although the application of the term to baptism may be accepted in these passages, it would be a mistake to suppose that in this period the word itself suggested baptism. This limitation was a later development due to the continual association of word and rite.[2] Before leaving this term it is instructive to consider it as an illustration of the way in which words change their meaning by the influence of the conceptions of an age which has made use of them. In the New Testament " seal " recalls a definite eschatological interest, and there is no trace of the mystery conceptions which later are so closely bound up with it. Its early Church use as a synonym for baptism enshrined the eschatological hope of the Christian convert in the Messianic Kingdom. This shows plainly that the place of its origin was Judaism ; but afterwards mystery ideas gave a new direction to its meaning. Lake remarks on this eschatological content and suggests that it " helped to unite the two, logically somewhat inconsistent, ideas of sacramental and eschatological salvation ".[3]

---

[1] A. D. Nock thinks the use of the word in Hebrews should be understood in a more general sense (*op. cit.*, p. 120 note).

[2] See H. B. Swete, *The Apocalypse of St. John*, 2nd ed., 1907, pp. 96–7 ; *DAC*, II, pp. 465–6 ; G. Anrich, *Das antike Mysterienwesen*, 1894, pp. 120 ff. ; J. B. Lightfoot, *Apostolic Fathers*, I, ii, p. 226.

[3] *ERE*, II, p. 385b.

CHAPTER VII

BAPTISM IN THE ACTS OF THE APOSTLES

THE Acts of the Apostles professes to carry forward the story of Christianity from the time of the Ascension. If we adopt the usually accepted view that the author of this book is the same as that of the third Gospel we might take the words in Luke xxiv. 47–9 as a kind of introduction to the Acts. Probably also we ought to regard this passage as a counterpart of the more familiar commission to the disciples found in Matthew xxviii. 19, 20. Here we are confronted with a difficulty. While Matthew contains the much-discussed injunction to baptize, Luke makes no mention of baptism. Yet the subject of preaching is given in the third Gospel as repentance and remission of sins—a phrase whose intimate connection with baptism Luke had recognized in the case of John the Baptist (iii. 3), and which he recalls also in the Acts on several occasions (ii. 38 ; xiii. 24 ; xix. 4). Moreover, against the complete silence of the Gospel regarding any command to baptize we find that in the Acts the work of baptism holds a prominent place, and the references to it are more numerous than in any other book of the New Testament. We must recognize, of course, that it is most natural that a book which sets forth the history of early missionary enterprise by the Church should make frequent mention of the rite by which converts entered into the new community.

In view of the belief of some that baptism was not practised in the Church from its inception,[1] it is important

---

[1] Although he admitted the difficulty of fixing the time of its introduction, J. Weiss thought that baptism was not in use

to note that the author assumes the existence of this custom at the very beginning of the apostles' missionary labours. He interprets its existence as the fulfilment of the Spirit baptism foretold of his Successor by John, and he associates it with the happenings of the day of Pentecost, which must be regarded as the beginning of the apostolic mission. Some have suggested that by his treatment of the subject of baptism the author shows a good sense of historical perspective, since although the book was fairly late in composition, certainly much later than the letters of Paul, they think that it presents a sacramental position less developed than that found in the Pauline epistles.[1] From the other side Kirsopp Lake has argued that in the manner in which the writer distinguishes between baptism and the gift of the Spirit we have the reflection of a later age.[2]

The book begins by setting forth the previously predicted difference between the Johannine and Spirit baptisms (i. 5) ; and the words of Jesus in which this is given anticipate that the Holy Spirit will be bestowed upon His disciples very soon. The second chapter presents a vivid narrative of the Pentecostal gift of the Spirit. But it is curious that the description of the actual experience contains no mention of the gift as a baptism, nor does Peter in his speech immediately following make any reference to the figure. Further, the apostle finds the anticipation of Pentecost not, as one might expect, in the words of the Baptist concerning the Messianic baptism, but in the prophecy of Joel on the outpouring of the Spirit. Following the first speech of Peter comes a second in which the connection between baptism and the gift of the Spirit is established, but still there is no mention of the Johannine promise.

The gift of the Spirit is offered to all (ii. 38) who accept

in the Church at the beginning (*The History of Primitive Christianity*, I, 49).

[1] *FJBC*, I, p. 344.   [2] *ERE*, II, p. 383.

the new baptism, and one may regard it as the outstanding feature of the rite as depicted in the Acts. Moreover, despite the omission in the narrative of Pentecost of any mention of John's baptism and the prophecy relating thereto, the book contains several references in which the contrast between John's rite and Christian baptism is taken for granted. It is assumed also that the promise of the Spirit baptism has been fulfilled in the new experience.[1] One incident appears to be introduced deliberately to bring out clearly the distinction between the Johannine and Christian rites (xix. 4). This story has been used by some to give support to a theory that at first there was considerable difficulty in making converts understand the difference between the two initiatory experiences.

Such passages as xviii. 25-8, xix. 1-7 reveal a difficulty in differentiating between the two rites. But some critics believe also that they uncover a deep antagonism which it is alleged existed between the followers of John and the disciples of Jesus. One cannot feel that this theory of a bitter conflict finds support in the passages under discussion, which leave the impression that the men concerned willingly accepted instruction in the Christian way. Much significance is attached to the statement in xix. 5, that " the disciples ", as they are designated, were rebaptized into the name of the Lord Jesus, although nothing is said of rebaptism in the case of Apollos. Goguel has used these incidents as an argument for the existence of a Johannine sect,[2] yet he

[1] Acts xi. 16 ; xviii. 25 ; xix. 4.

[2] " Même si Apollos et les douze hommes baptisés par Paul n'étaient pas des disciples de Jean-Baptiste, il reste que le rédacteur des Actes a cru qu'ils en étaient et ceci déja est important parce que, par la, est établie la persistance d'un groupe de disciples du Baptiste jusqu'a la fin du premier siècle " (Jean-Baptiste, p. 104). One fails to follow the reasoning of Goguel that the editor of the Acts mistook these men for disciples of John, since he uses the word " disciple " only of the followers

admits the possibility of the men being disciples of Jesus but ignorant of the new baptism.

An important fact to note is that these Ephesians are called disciples (xix. 1). The words " disciple " and " disciples " occur thirty times in the Acts, apart from the present instance ; only once is there any addition to the title,[1] and every time it means Christian disciples. Moreover, it is said of Apollos that " he spake and taught carefully the things concerning Jesus ". Despite the statement about rebaptism there is every reason to accept the plea of Lietzmann that these Ephesians were already disciples of Jesus and not of John.[2] The baptism of John would then be understood as the generic name for the rite which was originated by John and practised during the lifetime of his Successor (John iii. 22 ; iv. 1, 2). The implication is therefore that these disciples had received the earlier form of the Christian rite—simple baptism in the Johannine mode for " repentance and forgiveness of sins "—and were ignorant of that supplementary experience of Spirit baptism which was the fulfilment of the promise of Jesus. The difficulty concerning rebaptism remains, but there are signs through-

---

of Christ (see above). What the paragraph proves is not that there were groups of Johannine disciples in existence at the end of the first century, but that the author was at a loss in describing early Christian baptism. We have confirmation of this latter fact from other sections.

[1] " Disciples of the Lord " (ix. 1). There is probably a special purpose in this designation since in the story the voice says to Saul, " Why persecutest thou *me* ? " In the dialogue the Lord identifies Himself with His disciples.

[2] H. Lietzmann puts forward the theory that " John's baptism was taken into primitive Christianity in its original significance of a washing away of the uncleannesses of the old æon, a cleansing necessary for the entry into the new Messianic world ". He thinks that later this was not regarded as sufficient, and a more exact liturgical formula was added with the name of Jesus named over the candidate (*The Beginnings of the Christian Church*, pp. 80, 81).

out the Acts that the author was at a loss in describing the early form of the gift of the Spirit, and the Ephesian incident must be regarded as an illustration of his failure to appreciate the full significance of the story which tradition had handed down to him.

This brings us to the question concerning the nature of the earliest Christian baptism. There appears to be no uniform type. Although endowment with the Holy Spirit is said to be the special sign of the new rite, there are instances given by the author in which baptism is performed and yet no gift of the Spirit follows immediately. A short study of the relationship of the two is necessary.

In the story of Pentecost no mention is made of baptism in the case of those who were gathered in the " one place " and received the gift of the Holy Spirit. It is of course possible to assume that, since they were disciples, they had undergone already the earlier type of baptism. In any case the occasion must be regarded as unique. But it is interesting to notice that Peter calls on the multitude to be baptized " unto the remission of your sins ; and ye shall receive the gift of the Holy Ghost ".[1] Whatever might be in the mind of the writer in penning this description, there is an obvious practical difficulty in the way of the assumption of a water baptism of three thousand people in Jerusalem in one day, especially when consideration is given to the presence of the huge crowds assembled for the celebration of the feast.

There are important instances in which baptism with the Holy Spirit and the water rite are shown as two separate experiences, although perhaps regarded as complementary. Apart from the incident of the Ephesian

---

[1] This reference to baptism is declared to be redactorial since it is alleged that the words of Jesus in Acts i. 4 imply a baptism in Spirit as a substitute for baptism in water, not as a consequence of it (*JLBC*, I, p. 340).

disciples already discussed, we have the stories of the converts at Samaria (viii. 16, 17), and the friends of Cornelius (x. 44–8). In the former of these, as in the case of the men at Ephesus, there is mention of a separate and definite act of the apostles, who laid hands on the baptized converts and thereby conferred the gift of the Spirit. The story of Simon introduces a man who had been baptized, but from whom the act supposed to confer the gift of the Spirit was withheld, perhaps because his past demanded greater evidence of his sincerity. The fact that the imposition of hands was withheld suggests a certain discrimination on the part of the apostles. On the other hand, in the story of Cornelius the Spirit was given without any human agency save the spoken word of Peter. There was no outward act, but the preliminary conditions of baptism—faith with repentance—may be assumed from the phrase " heard the word ".

The explanation why the author of Acts, who undoubtedly seemed to believe in a close connection of baptism and the gift of the Spirit, should have emphasized these exceptions is a matter for conjecture. Possibly some part of the answer is to be found in the sharp controversy between the narrow Jewish party in the Church and those of the more liberal spirit. The author is a Christian with a world outlook. His object may have been to show that even before the Council of Jerusalem (xv.) the contention of those seeking to limit salvation to men who observed certain ritual had been refuted by actual experience which showed that men who were neither circumcised (xi. 3) nor baptized (x. 47) had received the greatest of all the divine gifts—the gift of the Holy Spirit. Perhaps it ought not to be overlooked that Luke, the supposed author of the Acts, was a companion of Paul, whose teaching concerning the Spirit gave it a wide and almost unrestricted field of operation. In view of later developments, which caused the Church to reject circumcision but demand baptism, it is interesting to observe that the incident of Peter and Cornelius concludes with the performance of the baptismal rite.[1]

The assertion that these incidents were employed to show that the Spirit was essentially a divine gift and not dependent on or directed by human will alone finds a kind of confirmation in the story of Simon Magus. Just as the story of Cornelius revealed the error of those who contended that the Spirit was limited by ritual and human action, so the story of Simon may have been told as a protest against a conception, fostered by pagan initiatory rites, that spiritual power could be obtained by other than spiritual means.

The difficulty of reconciling the various accounts in the Acts has led to the theory that the book contains three different descriptions of Christian baptism, due to the fact that the editor has combined his own view with those of the sources he has used.[2] These views are supposed to be three in number and may be stated briefly :

1. Christian baptism was entirely a baptism in Holy Spirit, thus being distinguished from the water baptism of John, with which it is contrasted both in the Gospels and the Acts. That this coming of the Spirit was regarded as a baptism is shown by the language of Acts i. 5. The promise in this verse was made to the disciples themselves and cannot be taken as referring to the experience of the three thousand who heard Peter at Pentecost. It is obvious that water baptism was not included in that sudden revelation which came upon the disciples as they were gathered together in one place ; and by his description of the " tongues parting asunder like as of fire " the author seeks to give the idea of a baptism of Spirit and fire

[1] Foakes Jackson contends that the reference to baptism in the narrative of Cornelius was introduced by the editor in view of later Church teaching. He points out that the parallel report of Peter suggests something quite different, and that his reference to the words of Jesus are strange as an argument for water baptism (xi. 16) (*op. cit.*, I, p. 341).

[2] *JLBC*, I, pp. 337-42.

similar to that predicted in the Gospels and contrasted with the baptism of John. It is argued that in both Peter's Pentecostal speech and the incident of Cornelius redactional interpolation is responsible for the references to baptism. It is also pointed out that the impression derived from Mark is that Christian baptism does not go back to the time of Jesus or His immediate disciples.

2. There was a baptism with water which conferred the Holy Spirit, but only on condition that the rite was administered in the name of Jesus the Christ or the Lord Jesus. Support for this view is claimed from the incident at Ephesus and the story of Paul's conversion. In this latter the laying on of hands comes first, but it is not stated whether the gift of the Spirit is conferred by baptism or precedes it. The laying on of hands may be presumed to have a connection with the giving back of Paul's sight which preceded his baptism.

3. A third belief has been noted in which baptism was given in the name of the Lord Jesus, but the actual gift of the Spirit depended on the laying on of the apostolic hands. The incident of viii. 9–19 implies this.

While no one denies the confusion of statements, the evidence for the different types of baptism based on a theory of different sources is too subjective and therefore not very satisfactory. Both Schweitzer [1] and Lake [2] criticize this attempt to find a solution by postulating different strata of narrative. Lake thinks the solution lies in recognizing that the doctrine of the writer of the Acts separates baptism and the gift of the Spirit, and that while baptism was the regular and general initiation into Church membership the gift of the Spirit was due to the laying on of hands. He believes that the acceptance of these facts does away with the necessity of postulating a variety of sources in the Acts with different views on baptism.

Another explanation of the different descriptions of

[1] *SMP*, p. 235.　　　[2] *ERE*, II, p. 383.

baptism in the Acts is furnished by J. Weiss,[1] who treated the matter more from the point of view of known doctrinal development. His starting-point was the situation in I Corinthians xii. 13, in which membership in the community depends upon the conferring of the Spirit in baptism. He linked this idea with the calling and election in I Corinthians i. 26 ff. and argued that baptism was regarded less as an act of the individual than as an experience in which he was entirely receptive and almost passive.[2] This conception, he believed, carries us back to " the enthusiastic period of the beginnings of the Church ". He affirmed that the differences found in the Acts of the Apostles reflect most instructively the development of the relationship between baptism and the gift of the Spirit. There were three stages.

The first and oldest is seen in Acts x. 44, 47, where God sends down His Spirit on men to show that He has chosen them. " Baptism must follow this heavenly indication, and carry out in an earthly manner that which God has already determined ". Weiss held that this stage was represented in the Pauline teaching where the gift of the Spirit is the seal of God's adoption, and the sign of membership in Christ, without reference to baptism.[3]

The second stage is seen in Acts ii. 38, of which Weiss said that it was firmly hoped that he who had been baptized would receive the Holy Spirit, although he added : " But it is very striking that in a following verse (ii. 41), although it is recorded that three thousand souls were baptized and that they ' were added ', no further mention is made of the reception of the Spirit." For a commentary on this incident he referred to the story of Acts xix. 5 f., where the coming of the Spirit followed

---

[1] J. Weiss, *The History of Primitive Christianity*, E.T., 1937, II, pp. 622 ff.

[2] Weiss found significance in the fact that the verb " to baptize " is usually in the passive form.

[3] Rom. v. 5 ; viii. 9 ; II Cor. i. 21 ff. ; Gal. iv. 6.

baptism, but only after the imposition of Paul's hands on the baptized. He regarded this story as illustrating the transition stage to the third position found in Acts viii. 12–17, in which, after baptism had been given, the reception of the Spirit depended on prayer and the laying on of the apostolic hands.

Although this third stage finds its justification in the later historical condition of baptism, the other processes are by no means so sure. The charismatic stage found in Paul may have belonged to the earliest form of the experience of the Spirit, but what then is the relationship with the work of John and the story of Christ's own baptism ? Do we accept these latter as the interpretation of a later belief ? The distinction drawn between Acts ii. verses 38 and 41 is not justified by the language. What is the full meaning of the author's words " were added " ? Can we paraphrase the definite language which is employed in ii. 38 : " ye shall receive the gift of the Holy Ghost " by " it is firmly hoped that he who has been baptized will also receive the Spirit " ? If the writer of the two verses is the same one can have no hesitation in affirming that, despite the omission of any mention of the Spirit in verse 41, it must be assumed to have been experienced in view of the emphatic language of 38. If the words in verse 41 come from a different source the editor must have thought that they implied the same condition as promised in verse 38. One feels that this silence in 41 lacks significance, and the more so as we notice the author's interest in numbers when recounting the progress of the infant Church.[1] It is the thought of the increasing numbers which here is the main interest, and little stress need be laid on the mention of baptism only and not the gift of the Spirit.

The various views that have been considered serve to remind us of the difficulty of finding a completely satisfactory solution of the problem of the earliest form of

[1] Acts i. 15 ; ii. 41 ; iv. 4 ; cf. ii. 47.

Christian baptism from the details supplied in the Acts. The book, however, gives us one very valuable piece of information in its assumption of a direct connection between the baptisms of John and of the early Church. Goguel has drawn a sharp distinction between the two and has regarded the former as a baptism of Judgment,[1] but in the Acts it is the gift of the Spirit which makes the only distinction. It is perhaps to meet this difficulty that Goguel makes the suggestion that at the beginning of the apostolic age there may have been " an archaic form of Christianity " the outcome of preaching which was directly connected with the ministry of Jesus, and supported by personal recollections of His life, which knew no other form of baptism than that of John.

It is very probable that the mission to the Gentiles helped to make more clear in the mind of the disciples the meaning of baptism. They were winning converts in a heathen world and the Messianic Kingdom seemed more clearly defined against a background of heathenism, yet the conceptions underlying the baptism still revealed their Jewish origin. To this not only the ritual but the references to the baptism of John testify. One authority who has maintained that baptism came in naturally as soon as the Gentiles began to be converted adds the qualifying words, " but it is also probable that many of the disciples of John were themselves converted to Christianity and that they brought with them their own baptismal custom ".[2] This recognition that the two rites have a close relationship is affirmed by Schweitzer, who declares that Christian baptism is identical with that of John except that " the bestowal of the Spirit is now contemporaneous with the baptism by water, and that baptism takes place with the name of Jesus as the expected Messiah ".[3] There would seem to be little doubt that the purpose of the author of the Acts is to present Christian

---

[1] *Jean-Baptiste*, pp. 39 ff. ; *Life of Jesus*, E.T., p. 199.
[2] *JLBC*, I, p. 343. [3] *SMP*, p. 236.

baptism as a continuation of the work of John and to view it as a supplementing of the Johannine rite by a gift of the Spirit rather than as an entirely new phenomenon.

Having regard to the fact that there are many who contest the truth of the divine command to baptize, the question arises whether there is any other reason which could have caused the disciples to carry forward this rite into the new conditions which obtained after the death of Jesus. In studying the message of the early Church to the world without we cannot but be struck by the confidence with which the apostles spoke of the work achieved by Jesus. He was to them a triumphant and victorious Christ, and the Kingdom which He had preached was seen by them in the light of His own life. Dodd has shown how identical in purport the apostolic preaching in the Acts is with the description given in Mark of the preaching of the Kingdom by Jesus. The Holy Spirit in the Church is the sign that the new age of fulfilment has begun. In the exaltation of Christ God had vindicated the cause for which He came. The Kingdom of God was no longer to be regarded as an event in the future but as a present experience which had entered the world through Jesus.[1]

It is not surprising, therefore, that the apostles turned to the rite which had been regarded as preparatory for the coming Kingdom. It became to them an assurance of its possession, and this feeling was strengthened by the experience of the Spirit so closely associated with baptism. Several times in the Acts is there mention of the prediction of John concerning the Spirit baptism, whose fulfil-

[1] " We must remember that the early Church handed down as a saying of the Lord, ' The Kingdom of God has come upon you ' (Matth. xii. 28 ; Luke xi. 20). This means that the great event, the eschaton, has already entered history. In agreement with this, the preaching both of Paul and of the Jerusalem Church affirms that the decisive thing has already happened " (C. H. Dodd, *The Apostolic Preaching and its Developments*, 1936, pp. 66–7).

ment was now realized.   Jesus Himself must have spoken
of baptism in regard to His work (Mark x. 38 f. ;
Luke xii. 50), and while the significance of this must
not be over-estimated, it has a special value when put
with the recorded baptism at the Jordan.   Men bereaved
of the visible presence of Jesus found a comfort in
symbolic acts whose value was increased by the knowledge that their Master Himself had once shared them.
Moreover, these acts not only encouraged their eschatological hopes, but it was felt that they had the express
sanction of Jesus for their performance.   Such was the
feeling in regard to the Eucharist ; such it was also concerning the rite of baptism.

In whatever way the rite of baptism came into prominence, there was no better medium for bringing home to
men the thought of the immediacy of the Kingdom.   The
influence of John's work still remained among his country-
men.   The conception of initiation was familiar throughout the Gentile world, and in an age of mystery cults the
sacrament brought a special appeal.   The message of the
early missionaries and the significance attached to their
rite were one.   When the men of Samaria were baptized
after being convicted by the preaching of Philip, the
author mentions that the subject of his message was
" good tidings concerning the Kingdom of God and the
name of Jesus Christ ".   Perhaps too there must be
reckoned as not least among the factors encouraging the
revival of the Johannine rite the fact that it was so closely
associated with the preaching of repentance and the
remission of sins.

These statements do not take into account the possibility of any direct command of Jesus on the subject.
We have the words of Matthew which have been discussed, but the question now concerns the language used
in Acts i. 5.   Had Jesus in mind the rite of baptism when
He referred to the coming of the Spirit under that figure ?
Lake has suggested that the use in this passage is meta-

phorical and has no reference to Christian baptism.[1] It is argued that the disciples misunderstood Christ's message, and that in the passage quoted the idea of Jesus was to supersede water baptism by an endowment of the Spirit, whereas the disciples linked this Spirit baptism with the rite of John.[2] The difficulties in details supplied by the Acts have been discussed already and do not appear to be lessened by this theory. But there is little to support the belief that Christian baptism was due to a misunderstanding. The message of John bears witness to the conception of and preparation for an experience greater than that which his own rite offered. With his knowledge of the message of John it seems scarcely credible that Jesus should use the figure of baptism concerning His own gift of the Spirit if he meant to reject the symbol entirely. It was called a " baptism " and under that term it is most natural to include the material symbol as well as the spiritual experience. If Jesus had meant to reject John's water rite we should have expected more definite language. We cannot conceive that such was used by Him and suppressed by a ritualistic band of followers. Nor, if it is merely a case of misinterpretation, can we know whether modern criticism is better able to gauge the mind of Christ in this than the men who passed on His message. Jesus never rejected symbol even if He denounced reliance on empty ritual. He must have known that in speaking of baptism and the Spirit the thought of John's prediction and His own baptismal experience would be in the minds of His disciples. Because of this and the lack of any qualifying word in the promise we are justified in accepting the language as referring to an experience which supplemented and did not supersede the previous rite.

---

[1] K. Lake, *ERE*, II, pp. 382-3.
[2] E. Haupt, *Zum Verständniss des Apostolats im N.T.*, pp. 44 ff.

CHAPTER VIII

BAPTISM AS A RITE

WHATEVER may be the results of investigation in determining the origin of baptism there is no doubt that very early the rite had assumed such importance that everywhere it was accepted as the act of initiation which marked the entrance of the convert into the Church. The earliest New Testament documents confirm this belief. No one can read the first letter of Paul to the Corinthians without receiving that impression. It is not a question of the value attaching to the rite but of its universal validity. Much controversy has arisen over the meaning of Paul's statements on baptism in the first chapter of this epistle, but it must not be overlooked that in the twelfth chapter we have the sweeping affirmation : " For in one Spirit were we all baptized into one body, whether Jews or Greeks, whether bond or free ; and were all made to drink of one Spirit." Such a sentence taken with other references of Paul to the baptismal rite leaves the unmistakable impression that all the members of the Corinthian Church had been baptized.[1] If, too, we could be sure that the difficult passage on baptism for the dead (I Cor. xv. 29) referred to a custom among the Christians in Corinth, it would be a sign that the necessity of baptism was felt so strongly that a vicarious form of the rite had been introduced to cover the case of those who had died before they could receive the rite. Although not re-

[1] H. J. Holtzmann, *Lehrbuch der N.T. Theologie*, 1911, I, pp. 450-1.

ferred to elsewhere there is no proof that this custom was confined to Corinth.

Despite its prevalence in the Church it is difficult to answer with any degree of assurance the question as to the earliest form of baptism. We have referred already to the hypothesis of three different kinds of baptism in the Acts. We certainly need stronger evidence before accepting the statement that Christian baptism was at first a non-water rite ; nor do the words of John imply that baptism by water would be superseded by a baptism in Spirit in which the act of sprinkling or immersion had no place. If we regard the baptism with Spirit as supplementary to the rite of John we are justified in supposing that so far as their form was concerned the two baptisms had much in common. Apart from the reference to the laying on of hands the details found in the New Testament appear to confirm this belief.

The element of water was very prominent in the baptism of John and this also is true of the Christian rite.[1] No mention of any special kind of water is found in the New Testament. This fact should be noted in view of the statement in the *Didache* concerning " living " or running water, which—so far as documentary evidence goes—must be regarded as marking a later development, although the similarity to the Jewish tebilah must not be overlooked. Nothing is said about the place for Christian baptism. John's converts went to the Jordan, but, as already pointed out, there is no declaration that this was essential, and we have words which allow the inference that it was practised elsewhere. Much of the Christian missionary work was carried out in distant lands where baptism in the Jordan would have been

---

[1] Acts viii. 38 ; x. 47 ; Ephes. v. 26 ; Heb. x. 22. We have indirect suggestions conveyed by the references to washing and cleansing in Acts xxii. 16 and I Cor. vi. 11 and the mention of the " laver of regeneration " in Titus iii. 5. There is also the much-discussed passage of John iii. 5.

impossible. In the case of the baptisms in Samaria there is no reference to the river. The declaration of the Ethiopian eunuch, " Behold, here is water : what doth hinder me to be baptized ? " suggests that the rite was performed in any convenient place whenever there was a demand for it. There is, however, no known instance, either from the pages of the New Testament or from early Church literature, of a baptism in a church.[1]

Following the form adopted in the tebilah and the rite of John the Baptist we may regard immersion as customary in the primitive Christian sacrament. This is supported by the descriptive words in Acts viii. 38, 39, " went down . . . came up ". We have also the figurative language of Paul to describe the effects of the rite : " We were buried therefore with Him through baptism into death " (Rom. vi. 4), " having been buried with Him in baptism " (Col. ii. 12). This figure is only complete if we can picture baptism as an immersion. Yet in stating that immersion was probably the customary form of baptism we are compelled to recognize that certain situations portrayed in the Acts must have made such an action difficult if not impossible. It is not easy to imagine immersion in the cases of the 3,000 converts on the day of Pentecost, or the midnight baptism of the household of the Philippian gaoler. Perhaps we ought to assume that from the beginning some less difficult form of baptism than total immersion was accepted in certain circumstances. A pouring out of water could be taken as expressing the outpouring of the Spirit, and thus justify the act of sprinkling. In Acts ii. 17, 18, the Greek ἐκχεῶ is applied to the pouring out of the Holy Spirit as a translation of the Hebrew אֶשְׁפּוֹךְ (Joel ii. 28 (iii. i).

One cannot enumerate with any degree of certainty the details of the early Christian ritual. Yet we may

[1] F. J. Foakes-Jackson, *Studies in the Life of the Early Church*, 1924, p. 233.

say that the informality and spontaneity implied in the New Testament incidents leave little room for elaborate details. With the abandonment of self-baptism and the introduction of an agent a more elaborate ritual would tend to grow. It is possible that behind the references in the New Testament which describe the apostles as leaving the work of baptizing to others there is a hint of men specially employed in such work.[1] Their duties might consist in interviewing the candidates and administering the rite. Such a procedure would tend to make the act one of greater formality and lead to elaboration. The complete form of the second century is a development which has required a considerable period of time.

An important question concerns the relationship of baptism to the act of the laying on of hands. There is mention of such an act following baptism in Acts viii. 14–17 and xix. 1–6, and the words in viii. 16, 17 give the impression that it was quite distinct from the actual baptismal ceremony. But in this latter incident it is stated that the laying on of hands was followed by the gift of the Holy Spirit, and, since Christian baptism, as distinguished from John's rite, was essentially a Holy Spirit baptism, the laying on of hands must have been regarded as connected with the baptism. The incident of Cornelius in which the gift of the Spirit, presumably without any imposition of hands, preceded baptism should be regarded as exceptional, for we must recognize a special purpose in the narrating of such a story. Ananias laid his hands on Paul before baptism and told Paul he had been sent " that thou mayest receive thy sight and be filled with the Holy Spirit ". It is difficult to say what are the implications of this story, whether the laying on of hands was to cure the blindness or to confer the Spirit ; perhaps it was connected with both. In Hebrews vi. 2 baptism and the laying on of hands are mentioned together, although the context gives no

[1] Acts viii. 16 ; x. 48 ; I Cor. i. 17.

indication of what is meant by the latter. It may be the post-baptismal act or it may refer to something different —a kind of ordination (Acts vi. 6 ; II Tim. i. 6).

The figure of anointing is found in II Corinthians i. 21 ; I John ii. 27, and while it is unlikely that it refers to any existing custom it sheds perhaps some light on the origin of the latter practice, which may have given a literal interpretation to metaphorical language.[1] It has been suggested that the aorist form χρίσας in II Corinthians i. 21, has reference to a definite act in the baptismal rite.[2]

The mention of sealing in II Corinthians i. 22 ; Ephesians i. 13 ; iv. 30, ought to be interpreted metaphorically since there are many instances [3] of the figurative use in the New Testament, including one referring to the Jewish rite of circumcision (Rom. iv. 11). The three examples that are cited afford, however, a good illustration how the term came later to be employed in a technical sense of baptism. Once again the use of the aorists indicates a definite moment in the spiritual experience, and we should accept the reference to baptism although no special part of the ceremony may be designated.

One act that we hear of later as a part of the baptismal ceremony, and which may have been used in the New Testament ritual, is the kiss. The practice of kissing as a sign of affection and fellowship is well attested both in the Old and New Testaments,[4] and it can be under-

---

[1] See F. E. Warren, *The Liturgy and Ritual of the Ante-Nicene Church*, 1897, pp. 20 f. Darwell Stone, *Holy Baptism*, 1912, pp. 23 f.

[2] F. H. Chase, *Confirmation in the Apostolic Age*, 1909, pp. 53 ff.

[3] John iii. 33 ; vi. 27 ; Rom. xv. 28, etc. See A. J. Maclean in *DAC*, II, p. 129.

[4] Gen. xxix. 13 ; xlv. 15 ; I Sam. x. 1 ; xx. 41 ; cf. metaphorical use in Ps. lxxxv. 10. It is suggested that the early Christian habit of promiscuous kissing as a symbol of friendship was an application of pagan social practice (A. E. Crawley,

stood readily how such a custom came to be included in the baptismal ritual as an expression of the common brotherhood in Christ. The letters of Paul supply evidence of the use of the kiss at the ordinary church meetings.[1] One is justified therefore in assuming that early in the history of the Church it would be employed as a symbol of welcome into the fellowship for those new members who had undergone the ceremony of baptism. The description given in Justin's *Apology* lends support to such an assumption. But we should look for its origin in a spontaneous expression of welcome rather than in the adoption of a formal act.

The casual manner in which baptisms take place in the Acts supports the belief that at first no special garment was worn by the candidate. Nor is it likely that the metaphor which Paul employs in Galatians iii. 27, " For as many of you as were baptized into Christ did put on Christ "—where the latter part may be translated " clothed yourselves with Christ "—has reference to a use

ERE, VII, p. 740). But while Judaism offers no trace of a practice of kissing in the synagogue (Moffatt, *I Corinthians*, p. 280) and certainly the promiscuous kind would have offended Jewish sentiment (*EBi*, 1914, col. 4254), yet in view of the fact that this salutation was customary among the Israelites and Christianity professed to abolish the Jewish emphasis on sex distinction (Gal. iii. 28 ; cf. John iv. 27) it would not appear necessary to seek an origin in paganism for something which might be described as the abuse of a practice which based itself on a high conception of equality before God. The weakness of human nature led to this abuse as also to abuses in regard to other early Church practices. The Church Fathers, who realized fully the danger that had been incurred by a departure from the old Jewish form, were at pains to stress both the religious significance of the act and the spirit in which it should be performed (*Const. Apost.*, ii, 57 ; Tertullian, *De Orat.* xviii ; *Ad. Uxor.*, ii, 4 ; Athenagoras, *Legat.* xxxii ; Clement Alex., *Pæd.*, III, 81). Moffatt compares the baptismal kiss to the formal kiss bestowed upon the emancipated Roman slave.

[1] Rom. xvi. 16 ; I Cor. xvi. 20 ; II Cor. xiii. 12 ; I Thess. v. 26 ; cf. I Pet. v. 14.

of special baptismal robes. The metaphor is a favourite one with Paul,[1] and it is improbable that the custom of special garments at baptisms had become so established in his day as to call forth this figure.[2] At the same time this statement must be qualified by a recognition of the oriental habit of adapting dress to character and expressing by the outward garb an inward spiritual condition. If such a custom could be proved as existing in the days of the apostles it would invest with a new significance some passages in the Apocalypse.[3] But there is no definite evidence that any particular kind of dress was worn for baptisms during the period covered by the New Testament.

The two preliminary conditions of faith and repentance were demanded from each candidate for baptism, and much stress was laid on these in the apostolic preaching and teaching.[4] While we may assume that the authority for such a demand was based on the teaching of Christ Himself the call to repentance reminds us of the work of the Baptist. In words that John himself might have used Peter is described in Acts ii. 38 as calling the multitude to " repent and be baptized unto the remission of sins ". In some of the passages in the Acts there is no mention of repentance, only the demand for faith, but we can assume that both conditions are present. Thus Paul told the Philippian gaoler to believe on the Lord Jesus and thou shalt be saved, but the attitude of repentance is obvious both from his previous question

[1] Rom. xiii. 12, 14 ; I Cor. xv. 53, 54 ; II Cor. v. 3 ; Col. iii. 10, 12 ; I Thess. v. 8.

[2] J. B. Lightfoot showed that the figure is common in the Septuagint (*Galatians*, p. 148). Swete suggested that ἱμάτια (Rev. iii. 4) had reference to the baptismal profession which many in Sardis had allowed to be besmirched (*The Apocalypse of St. John*, 2nd ed., 1907, l.c.).

[3] Rev. iii. 4 ; vii. 14 ; xvi. 15 ; xxii. 14.

[4] Acts ii. 38 ; viii. 12, 37 (Western Text) ; x. 43–8 ; xvi. 31, 33 ; xviii. 8 ; xx. 21 ; xxvi. 18.

to Paul and the washing of the apostle's stripes. It is probable that each candidate was required to make some open confession of Jesus as Lord and an affirmation of belief in His resurrection (Rom. x. 9).

According to the words of Paul there were teachers in the churches (I Cor. xii. 28). One may surmise that part of their work at least was to establish in doctrine the candidates who had accepted baptism, sometimes also to prepare men for baptism or to check any incipient error. Priscilla and Aquila expounded unto Apollos the way of God more carefully. It is possible that in the incident of Apollos we ought to regard the work of Priscilla and Aquila as that of evangelists or even apostles. Work such as Philip did in " guiding " the Ethiopian eunuch before baptism would be regarded as belonging to the sphere of missionary activity of the apostles. " Philip preached unto him Jesus " (Acts viii. 35).

The question of the agent in baptism has been discussed at length. If we accept the theory of self-baptism as the earliest form of the rite we must also consider the question of what happened after this practice had been discontinued. It has been suggested that there may have been a special class of baptizers. Peter commanded Cornelius and his fellow-converts to be baptized (Acts x. 48). Paul states that he himself baptized only a few in Corinth (I Cor. i. 17). Might we surmise that this duty of baptizing belonged to the " helps " (I Cor. xii. 28) ? But there is no sure evidence that men were especially set apart for the work of baptizing, and from the New Testament references we are justified in assuming that any disciple of standing might perform the rite. There is certainly no sign that the command in the Gospels led men to insist on apostolic baptism.

The New Testament contains no mention of the baptism of children. This is true also of the earlier rite associated with the name of John. The omission in regard to the latter is of little significance since there

is no suggestion that a complete and detailed account of
the work of the Baptist has been attempted. However,
the life of Jesus gives definite evidence of the interest
in children and we might expect to find this reflected in
the work of the apostolic Church. Much has been made
of the dubious argument from silence. That we have
no recorded baptism of a child is regarded by many as
a sure proof that there was no child baptism. Some
have found confirmation of this belief in Paul's statement regarding the spiritual status of children of " mixed
marriages " (I Cor. vii. 14). Paul declares that the
children of " mixed marriages " are to be accounted
" holy " on account of one parent's faith. This is
thought to indicate that in early times the baptism of
children was not regarded as necessary, since their
spiritual status was determined by that of their parents.
It is obvious that if the children of " mixed marriages "
were accounted " holy ", those who had both parents
Christians would be equally so. Moreover, the words
of Jesus in His declaration concerning the children who
were brought to Him that " of such is the kingdom of
God " (Mark x. 14, 15) might appear to lend support
to the belief that in the case of children no baptism was
necessary. It has been argued also that this absence of
child baptism was natural in the conditions obtaining at
the beginning of the missionary work of the apostles.[1]

[1] " That is precisely what might have been anticipated. . . .
The Church was a Mission Church, coming slowly into existence
through the preaching of the Gospel ; it was being built up
as a result of the faith of individuals. Only by degrees did it
change into a Christian community with the faith of individuals
built up out of it. Even to-day the baptism of infants is in
place only where the children grow up in the midst of a living
Church. The reason is that baptism exhibits its meaning and
unfolds its spiritual consequences not all at one moment but
gradually as the child lives and grows in vital interaction with a
Christian environment " (H. R. Mackintosh, " Thoughts on
Infant Baptism." *Expositor*, vol. XIII, pp. 193–203).

Goguel suggests that the passage from I Corinthians proves that the rite of baptism was practised only for those who entered the Church from without and not for those born within it.[1]

Any discussion of the question must take into account first of all the environment in which Christianity began its work. The solidarity of the family was a far more real thing in antiquity than in modern life, and the idea found its strongest expression in the religious and political relationships. In Judaism circumcision was a rite applied not only to the proselyte but also to his children. The Talmud gives information concerning the tebilah, stating that infant baptism was to be employed in the case of the children of proselytes [2]; and on the analogy of the custom of circumcision one is justified in assuming that this rule would have been observed in the earliest period of the rite. In view of these conditions it seems most unlikely that Christianity adopted a practice which would have seemed a denial of the family solidarity.[3] Moreover, we have definite statements recording the baptisms of households—Lydia, the Philippian gaoler, Crispus, Stephanas—and it is impossible to imagine that no children were included in their numbers. Tertullian [4] did not like child baptism, which was very prevalent in his day, but in expressing his opposition he gives no hint that he believed the practice to be at variance with early custom. This argument would have been invaluable, and one feels he must have used it, had it been available. There were baptismal disputes in the early Church. Would it have been possible to have avoided one over the matter of child baptism if those who

---

[1] *Jean-Baptiste*, p. 102.   [2] A. J. Maclean, *DAC*, I, p. 136.
[3] J. V. Bartlet points out that there was a distinction drawn in proselyte baptism of children in the cases where the father, as the head of the household, brought his children, and where the mother alone brought them. See *ERE*, II, p. 379.
[4] *De Baptismo*, xviii.

disliked this custom had known that it was an innovation ?

The arguments that seem to deny child baptism are
seen to be less powerful than their advocates will admit.
A close examination of Paul's words in the seventh
chapter of his first letter to the Corinthians leads to the
reflection that they offer no support to either side in the
question of infant baptism. The apostle is discussing
holiness, not baptism, and there is no statement in the
New Testament that baptism makes the baptized holy.
Doubtless some indirect connection can be claimed
between holiness and baptism, since holiness was associated with the gift of the Spirit and the latter with baptism, yet the last two are not identical. Weiss suggested
that baptism did confer the status of holiness.[1] But

[1] " According to the analogy of Jewish baptism of proselytes
(Schürer, *GJV*, III, pp. 182 ff.), it (Christian baptism) served
as a bath of purification in which the sins of the past were
washed away, and at the same time as a bath of consecration
through which the converts became ' holy ', that is, God's
property (I Cor. vi. 11) " (J. Weiss, *The History of Primitive
Christianity*, E.T., I, p. 172). In reverting to this reference
in vol. II, p. 633, he states : " In I Cor. vi. 11, along with
' washing ' and ' justification ', ' sanctification ' is mentioned,
yet it is not inherently necessary to think of this as being directly
connected with baptism. For Christians become ' sanctified ',
i.e. are drawn into the sphere of the divine nature, and are made
the property of God, by the impartation of the Spirit, and, as
we have seen, this need not necessarily coincide with baptism."
Weiss however follows this statement by an argument for
regarding I Cor. vi. 11 as referring to " a single act of dedicatory
nature " in which baptism is also thought of in connection with
sanctification. He thought that the emphasis was on the unity
of the act because of the words which follow, which link together
two ideas : " in the name of the Lord Jesus Christ, and in the
Spirit of our God ". On the basis of this expression he argued
that through its connection with the " washing away " the word
" sanctified " took on a tone which was more cultic and ritualistic
than spiritual and religious. It is difficult to accept this interpretation which contravenes the usual teaching of Paul with
regard to the Spirit, unless it can be supported by other evidence,

until more definite proof is forthcoming his position cannot be accepted. In the seventh chapter of Corinthians Paul makes no mention of baptism but confines himself to the question of holiness. Since holiness is the subject of discussion the most likely explanation of the Pauline statement is to be found in the teaching of Judaism—or more particularly Pharisaism—in which the apostle had been trained. The Pharisees held that not only were Gentiles unclean, but a Jew became unclean by his marriage to a Gentile, and, as a natural consequence, the children of the marriage were unclean. The problem with which Paul had to deal at Corinth may have arisen because this Jewish attitude was being applied in Christianity, perhaps by members of the Peter party (I Cor. i. 12 ; cf. Gal. ii. 11 ff.). In a smaller way it was a difficulty resembling that which confronted the Jerusalem Council (Acts xv.). From their narrow Jewish standpoint some Christians may have contended that mixed marriages were disastrous on the ground that the spiritual experience of the Christian was brought to nothing through contact with the heathen partner. Ought a rule of separation to be enforced in the case of Christians similar to that mentioned in the Book of Ezra (x. 3) ? Paul combats this narrow attitude by an argument which brings out his high conception of the power of faith. Despite the unequal yoking, Christianity is the more powerful factor making for holiness. Moreover, the reference to the unbelieving wife or husband being sanctified in the Christian partner must be taken with the statement concerning the children. There is one principle for both. Since there is no suggestion that Paul inferred that the unbelieving husbands and wives, who were sanctified in their believing

which does not appear to be forthcoming. A more natural explanation would be that the Pauline expression is a trick of style in which compression is used for the sake of brevity. This is not unknown in Paul's letters.

partners, had no need of baptism if they should accept
the faith for themselves, we have no right on the analogy
to say that Paul held that children need not be baptized.
It is difficult to imagine that Paul's argument conceived
of any moral or spiritual quality which an individual
could receive without any effort on his part. The unbelieving husband is said to be " sanctified " in his wife ;
but it is certain that Paul did not believe in vicarious
goodness. Each shall give account of himself to God
(Rom. xiv. 12). The apostle does not suggest how this
holiness works, and perhaps it is best to regard it as an
influence or atmosphere which enabled the unbeliever
to share in some measure the Christian fellowship.
Much of our difficulty in following the full meaning of
the discussion is due to the fact that in Judaism the
conception of holiness had at bottom a ritual rather
than a moral connotation.

Yet while this passage in Corinthians may be dismissed
as irrelevant to the discussion of baptism it is probable
that attention ought to be given to the references to
" children " in the letters (Col. iii. 20 ; Ephes. vi. 1)
in passages where the context has a physical rather than
a spiritual meaning. Although the word " children "
may be applied to those of older years, τέκνον suggests
a time before years of discretion have been reached.
Additional support for this interpretation comes from
language like " obey in all things ". These children
must have been regarded as Church members for they
are included in a letter addressed to " the saints and
faithful brethren in Christ which are at Colossae ". If
members we must assume that they had been baptized.
There is no hint of any other way into the Church save
that of baptism.

Finally we must take into account the heathen environment of Christianity. Paganism found a place for
children in its cults. There were mystery societies in
which children were appointed priests. In view of its

rivalry with paganism could the Christian Church have afforded to ignore the children and let slip the opportunity of enrolling the child in its membership by its own recognized rite ? In answering this question we must keep in mind the Jewish rite of circumcision. The value of a symbol was too important to be overlooked. Moreover, it was not the case that baptism of a child would have denied the conditions demanded in every conferring of the rite. A young child might appear to lack the understanding faith demanded of the adult, but he lacked also the unbelief which shut men out of the Kingdom of God. The words of Jesus treasured by early tradition which affirmed that it was necessary to " receive the Kingdom of God as a little child " might be a powerful argument for maintaining that the absence of an active faith should be no real deterrent in the case of a little child. We have no means of estimating what weight the words of Jesus had in determining the attitude to child baptism in the earliest days, but certainly it would encourage rather than discourage such a practice.

The Form of Words used

Despite the manuscript attestation of the genuineness of Matthew xxviii. 19, it is most unlikely that the trine formula presents the earliest form of the baptismal dedication. One may go further and assert that there is no evidence for any definite form of words except what may be read into the expression " in the name of the Lord Jesus " or similar words. There are prepositional variations of this phrase. We have " in " (x. 48), " into " (viii. 16 ; xix. 5), and " on account of " (ii. 38). All these occur in the Acts of the Apostles, and some have inferred that the variations have significance. " In the name " has been referred to the use of the name in the baptismal invocation, and " into the name " to the act of dedication to, linked with reception of, the power invested in the name. Yet in view of numerous instances of the interchangeability of these prepositions in the Hellenistic period it is most probable that little or no distinction was intended by the varying terms.[1] This does not mean that the phrase as a whole lacked significance. To rebut such a suggestion it is sufficient to recall Paul's declaration to the schismatics of the Corinthian Church that the baptism of his converts was not carried out " in the name of Paul " (I Cor. i. 13, 15 ; cf. I Cor. vi. 11). This argument would have had little meaning for us had we no knowledge of the expression in the Acts " in the name of the Lord Jesus ".

The age in which Christianity arose revealed a widespread belief in magic, and some have maintained that the use of the expression just quoted provides an illustration of its presence in the Christian communities.[2] Heitmüller, in his well-known monograph, has called attention to the mysterious power of the name in the beliefs of antiquity, and has brought together many illustrations from Christian, Jewish and pagan sources to show that these beliefs were common to all.[3] He argued that the use of the name was held to invest the person concerned with the power of the deity named, a close relationship being established involving perhaps ownership by the deity. Is it possible to accept this solution in interpreting the baptismal phrase ? Abrahams denied that the primitive meaning in Christian baptism had any magical significance.[4] According to his argument the words of the Christian phrase approximated more nearly to a Roman legal term by which men were entered on the patron's roll of dependants. This practice was well known at the time when Christianity was

---

[1] J. H. Moulton was willing to accept the possibility of there being a certain difference of meaning in some instances (*Grammar of N.T. Greek*, I, 1908, pp. 62 f., 68).

[2] *JLBC*, V, p. 123.

[3] *Im Namen Jesu*, pp. 12, 51 f., 106 f., etc.

[4] *Studies*, I, pp. 45 f.

spreading throughout the ancient world ; and there are many other examples from the literature of the New Testament of familiarity with the legal and political procedure of the Roman empire. Abrahams also recalled the late Hebrew expression describing the baptism of the proselyte " in the name of Heaven " and the rebaptism of slaves on attaining their freedom " in the name of Freedom ".

The work of A. Deissmann has revealed a series of illuminating parallels from the papyri in which the idea of personal relationship is covered by this phrase.[1] Yet while due regard must be paid to the environment of the Church when considering any idea or custom found within it,[2] there is a danger lest the early association of Judaism and Christianity should be overlooked and no attempt made to consider a more obvious explanation in Jewish thought. In the present case we may recall an Old Testament conception by which the use of the name of the deity suggested possession or ownership of the person or thing in connection with which it was used.[3] Thus in the prophecy of Jeremiah God speaks of the house which is called by My name (vii. 10 ff.), the message of Moses to Pharaoh is given in God's name, and David tells Goliath " I come to thee in the name of the Lord of hosts " (in Septuagint ; ἐν ὀνόματι Κυρίου Θεοῦ κ.τ.λ. I Sam. xvii. 45). This usage was not contrary to that of the world around, but was a case where the Hellenistic and Semitic viewpoints were very similar. Although a certain idea of magic cannot be ruled out

---

[1] *Bible Studies*, E.T., 1909, pp. 146 ff., 197 ff.

[2] This influence of environment must not be underestimated in assessing the value of words and phrases. " There cannot be the slightest doubt that in Antioch and in churches like it, baptism ' in the name of Christ ' or ' with the name of Christ ' took on a much greater significance than it ever did in the Jerusalem church " (J. Weiss, *op. cit.*, I, p. 177).

[3] P. G. S. Hopwood, *The Religious Experience of the Primitive Church*, 1936, pp. 283–5.

entirely, for we must remember that the case of Simon shows (Acts viii. 13, 18, 19) that there were professing Christians who were not entirely freed from the superstitions of their former pagan life, yet it must be recognized that the value of the affirmation in the Christian formula was dependent in great part on the faith and life of the person who employed it. This is brought out by the strange story of the Jewish exorcists (Acts xix. 11 ff.).[1] It is possible that we owe the emphasis in Hebrews x. 22, 23 on faith, " a true heart in fullness of faith ", and the appeal to hold fast the baptismal confession—for such is the natural reference of the words " the confession of our hope "—to the need felt by the writer of combating a magical conception of the baptismal ceremony. The obscure and difficult passage in I Peter iii. 21 probably should be explained as a protest against a material and magical interpretation of the baptismal act and a reminder of the inwardness of the experience : " Baptism, the counterpart of that, saves you to-day (not the mere washing of dirt from the flesh but the prayer for a clean conscience before God) by the resurrection of Jesus Christ " (Moffatt).

It was natural that in the earliest form of Christian baptism words should be used which associated the ceremony with the name of Jesus. Yet we may be certain that the phrase " in the name of the Lord Jesus " would never have been introduced if the trinitarian formula had been recognized from the beginning. It is very likely that the words we are discussing were the original formula at baptism since the original expression would be marked by simplicity. In the time of self-baptism the candidate would make the invocation as a confession of faith, and in a spirit of self-dedication. One is much inclined to

---

[1] Cf. Mark ix. 38 ff. ; this linking of faith with the achievement is not negatived by the words of Matth. vii. 22, where the claim comes from men who are described by Christ as " ye that work iniquity " (23).

the conjecture that in the passage from Ephesians v. 26, " having cleansed it by the washing of water with the word ", " with the word " should be understood as implying the solemn mention of the Lord Jesus Christ in connection with the rite of baptism, either as the confession made by the candidate or as the formula employed by the ministrant.[1] This would harmonize with the thought in James ii. 7, where an allusion to the baptismal rite is the most likely explanation of the language : " Is it not they (the rich) who blaspheme the noble name which was called over you ? "[2]

There is a suggestion[3] that the formula " in the name of Jesus the Christ " or " in the name of the Lord Jesus " might have originated through the missionary work of Hellenistic Jews like the seven deacons, who in preaching in heathen cities would use words like these to indicate to their converts that they were not merely proselytes to Judaism but had joined that particular sect which recognized the claims of Jesus.[4] This theory maintains the historical connection of the Christian rite with Jewish baptism, but it does not explain the difficulty, to which

[1] J. Armitage Robinson, *Ephesians*, 1904, p. 207. The expected expression would be καὶ ῥήματος, but Abbott points out that ἐν is quite admissible. He adds : " The objections from the absence of the article, and from the fact that ῥῆμα has not elsewhere this meaning, fall to the ground when we consider that it is not alleged or supposed that ῥῆμα of itself means the formula of baptism ; it retains its indefinite meaning, and it is only the connection with the reference to baptism in the preceding words that defines what ῥῆμα is intended " (*Ephesians and Colossians*, I.C.C., T. K. Abbott, p. 169).

[2] There is a good discussion of the passage in J. B. Mayor, *The Epistle of St. James*, 1897, pp. 84–6.

[3] *JLBC*, I, p. 342.

[4] Jesus was central in the preaching of the early missionaries. We may dismiss viii. 37 as a later insertion, but there is ample evidence for the truth of this statement. Paul " proclaimed Jesus, that He is the Son of God " in the synagogue at Damascus (Acts ix. 20).

184

J. Weiss called attention, that former Jews like Paul were baptized.[1] We have no ground for assuming that the case of Paul was exceptional, and in view of the geographical as well as the social and religious conditions it is most probable that the greater part of the early converts came from the ranks of Judaism.

Whatever may have been the origin of this formula which mentioned only the name of Jesus, there is no reason for believing that long familiarity with its use caused it to be regarded as a technical expression for

ERRATUM

p. 185, line 8, for "no" read "now".

formula had come into use. In the section dealing with baptism we read : " Baptize in the name of the Father and of the Son and of the Holy Spirit in living water." The phrase is repeated in the same section, and yet, although this use would prove it to be the accepted formula, we have an injunction in the section on the Eucharist stating : " But let no man eat or drink of this eucharistic thanksgiving, but they that have been baptized into the name of the Lord." [3]   The solemn invocatory form of the trinitarian formula previously given makes it impossible to regard the phrase " into the name of the Lord " as an alternative.   Fortunately, the New Testament usage throws light on the subject and enables us to realize that a phrase which later had become a stereotyped form and a synonym for Christian baptism was in the earliest times a solemn formula invested with the deepest significance.

[1] J. Weiss, *op. cit.*, II, p. 631.
[2] This is how Rendtorff understood the words in the New Testament passages and not as a formula used in baptism (*Die Taufe im Urchristentum*, 1905, p. 43).
[3] *Didache*, vii, ix.   The translation is that of J. B. Lightfoot, *The Apostolic Fathers*.

CHAPTER IX

MAIN FEATURES OF THE NEW TESTAMENT DOCTRINE OF BAPTISM

THE summing up of the main features of the early doctrine of baptism raises problems which are due to the impossibility of finding in the books of the New Testament a completely coherent and logical system. However, there is nothing disconcerting in the absence of such logical coherence, for it is just what would be expected from the circumstances of the origin of the rite. Baptism was received as an experience before there was any attempt to explain all its implications. We regard it as a development from the tebilah through the Johannine rite, and a close examination will reveal that the Christian form in its early days bore traces of the journey it had taken. While due allowance must be made for an assimilation of the various rites to each other, we believe the Christian type was marked by certain definite features.

Of necessity some of the features were common to both the baptism of John and that of the early Church. We have indisputable evidence that the Christians of the apostolic age believed that their baptism was the successor of that of John the Baptist, and this very fact proves that although there were distinguishing marks there must have been also recognized points of contact. Moreover, rites are usually more persistent than beliefs, and although the Church proclaimed its initiatory act a baptism in Spirit—distinguishing it from the baptism with water offered by John—it does not appear from a consideration of the two that there was much difference as regards the outward form. Little weight need be given to the fact that there is evidence of a difficulty in bringing into a right connection the gift of the Spirit and the water baptism. This does not imply that a distinct Spirit baptism preceded the introduction of a water rite. Such a difficulty serves only as a reminder that the early missionaries were not men of education, but artisans, peasants and fishermen. They were preachers rather than theologians and witnesses rather than philosophers. They had no doubt about the experience, but they found it difficult to define the exact relationship of the gift of the Spirit with the act of baptism. For the first real advance to a doctrine of Christian baptism we must turn to the writings of Paul.

The details in the Acts serve to show how readily—in contrast with later practice—allowing for certain preliminary conditions, baptism was granted to all who sought it. There is no proof that it was regarded as obligatory, but the inference to be drawn from passages in the Acts and from the writings of Paul is that it was a rite bestowed on all who fulfilled the necessary conditions and sought to enter the new society. Was this the position at the first ? In view of the Master's attitude to ceremonial acts and the silence of the Gospels regarding any baptizing during the earthly ministry of Jesus, it has been suggested that baptism was permissible in the lifetime of Jesus although not demanded. Probably we ought to assume the existence of a similar state of affairs in the earliest Christian society. But the experience of the value of baptism and the recognized unwisdom of too great laxity in methods of organization, together with an increasing conviction that our Lord's promise of the Spirit in a baptism was given so that all Christians should enjoy the privilege of this rite, would lead in time to a demand that it should be shared by all. This would be the stage represented by the Dominical injunction of Matthew xxviii. 19.

It has been argued from such passages as Acts iii. 19

and x. 43 that there was a time in the history of the infant Church when baptism was not accounted essential for salvation, and that these sections belong to a source earlier than the rest.[1]   One is disposed to regard with suspicion source theories which are built upon an argument from silence regarding expected details ; but it certainly seems most unlikely that Christianity began with a demand for a ritual which Jesus Himself did not make obligatory in His lifetime.   Yet we must admit that there is no indication that baptism was ever regarded as an innovation in the early Church, and also that there is never any attempt to explain its significance save by recalling its association with the Johannine rite and the prediction of the Messianic Spirit baptism.

The clue to the understanding of our facts, however, comes when we recognize that what the primitive Church sought was not a rite but an experience—the fulfilment of the promise of the Spirit.   Whether Jesus used the term baptism concerning it, as Acts i. 5 avers, or whether the idea was derived from the Baptist's prediction may be a matter of argument, but there can be no doubt that the preliminary conditions demanded in baptism—repentance and faith—made the acceptance of this rite a very suitable preparation for the work of the Spirit.   From a recognition of its value as a preparation one could pass to a belief that it was essential for the experience, since the rite itself was so expressive of that outpouring associated with the coming of the Spirit.

Perhaps there is a deeper significance than we are able to prove in a phrase of Hebrews vi. 2—the teaching of baptisms.   The natural interpretation of these words is that which regards them as indicating the different types of baptism familiar at that period.   The Acts of the Apostles is a witness to the fact that the apostles distinguished between the baptism of John and the Christian rite, and we can understand how necessary it would be to

[1] J. Mackinnon, *The Gospel in the Early Church*, 1933, p. 16.

instruct a Jewish convert concerning the differences between Jewish purifications (including the tebilah) and Christian baptism.[1] This reference to the distinction between the Christian and other rites suits the conception of " first principles of Christ " spoken of in the previous verse in the chapter of Hebrews. Another possible explanation is to take the plural as denoting the dual baptism of water and Spirit (John iii. 5).[2]

The phrase in Hebrews serves to call attention to certain generally accepted beliefs which later were brought together in the formation of a doctrine of baptism.

The first is that which emphasizes the completeness of the break symbolized in the rite. Here both Judaism and Christianity stand together in contrast with pagan mystery cults. Peter called men to save themselves from this crooked generation (Acts ii. 40), and there is Paul's vivid reminder to his readers of their past moral condition (I Cor. vi. 11). Lightfoot has pointed out that Paul's expressive word $\mu\epsilon\tau\acute{\epsilon}\sigma\tau\eta\sigma\epsilon\nu$ in Colossians i. 13 gives a picture of the wholesale transportation of peoples from one country to another, of which the Oriental monarchies supplied so many examples, " who delivered us out of the power of darkness, and translated us into the kingdom of the Son of his love ".[3] There is also the strong metaphor of Colossians ii. 11, which speaks of the putting off of the body of the flesh in the circumcision of Christ.[4]

From the idea of separation we pass to the thought of baptism as the expression of a new moral status. The

[1] A. S. Peake, *Hebrews, Century Bible,* l.c.
[2] E. F. Scott, Hebrews, *Peake's Commentary,* l.c.
[3] J. B. Lightfoot, *Colossians and Philemon,* pp. 141–2.
[4] For $\mathring{\alpha}\pi\acute{\epsilon}\kappa\delta\upsilon\sigma\iota\varsigma$. see Lightfoot, *op. cit.,* pp. 189–91, who argues that the aorist forms of the verbs point to the time of baptism. The difficulty due to the use of $\mathring{\alpha}\chi\epsilon\iota\rho\sigma\pi\sigma\iota\acute{\eta}\tau\psi$, " not made with hands ", may be explained perhaps by understanding Paul's contrast to be between physical circumcision and the baptismal act regarded not as an outward ritual but as a spiritual experience.

precise relationship of the rite to forgiveness may be difficult to define, but the close association of the two is undoubted (Acts ii. 38; xxii. 16). This connection of forgiveness with baptism receives much greater prominence in the Acts than in Paul's writings, due probably to the fact already noted, that Paul approached the question of forgiveness by way of his great doctrine of justification by faith. There is no real difference of belief regarding the means by which forgiveness is obtained; it is merely a matter of viewing the question from another angle. No passage in the New Testament can be quoted in support of the contention that forgiveness was held to depend on a ritual act alone. From this standpoint it is important to observe how repentance and faith are linked with the act of baptism not only in the writings of Paul but also in the Acts (ii. 38; x. 43), and possibly the first epistle of John (i. 9). In asserting this necessity of faith we should bear in mind too the fact that baptism was administered in the name of Jesus (Acts x. 48; cf. iv. 12).

But it is not surprising to find that the close association of baptism with cleansing from sin gave rise to a tendency to treat the two conceptions as identical. Perhaps it was a looseness of phrasing which was partly responsible for this tendency. In the story of Paul's conversion reported in Acts xxii. 16 the words of Ananias are given as " Arise and be baptized and wash away thy sins, calling on His name ". A still more emphatic illustration is found in I Corinthians vi. 11, where the apostle marks the dividing-line between the pre-baptismal and post-baptismal state of his readers by the use of the significant word ἀπελούσασθε, " you washed yourselves clean ".[1]

Here we must revert to a question already discussed in regard to the rite of John : Ought we to regard baptism

---

[1] The translation is that of Moffatt, and it is in harmony with his interpretation of i. 14, in which he suggests that Paul's action in baptizing a few people was a departure from the usual custom of self-baptism (*I Corinthians*, p. 11).

as mediating forgiveness, assuming that the necessary faith and repentance are present, or does the act merely express the fact that this forgiveness has already taken place ? The tense of the verb in Romans vi. 2 gives the suggestion that the break with sin came in the actual baptism : " We who died (ἀπεθάνομεν) to sin, how shall we any longer live therein ? Or are ye ignorant that all we who were baptized into Christ Jesus were baptized into His death ? " Whatever the earlier view, it is certain that very soon a tremendous importance began to be attached to the rite as a means of deliverance from the guilt of sin. This is shown by the growth of the custom of postponing the baptismal act until late in life, and still more by the desire for a repetition of baptism which quite early revealed itself, and which the Church had to combat.[1] Yet, despite later belief, we may assume that primitive Christianity interpreted the relation of baptism to forgiveness in terms which made the rite a visible expression of something already accomplished. There is nothing in the New Testament to conflict with this assumption. Also it brings the thought more into harmony with the Gospel teaching on forgiveness, and explains the lack of evidence of any conflict in the New Testament over the question by showing that there was no cause for such a conflict.[2]

[1] Hebrews vi. 4–8 ; Hermas, *Mand.*, iv, 3. A later development is perhaps to be seen in I John v. 16, where a distinction is drawn between " deadly " and venial sins.

[2] Acts iii. 19 ; Acts xiii. 38 ; I Cor. xv. 17, etc. A better understanding of the problem may be found in considering not merely the New Testament teaching on Christian baptism but the references to baptism and forgiveness in the preaching of John the Baptist. Some allowance must be made for the fact that the descriptions of John's baptism came from men who were more familiar with the Christian rite, but they must have had also earlier sources of information. In the discussion on John's baptism (p. 41) it was suggested that the main purpose of the rite was to give by an outward act the assurance to the candidate for baptism that his repentance had brought forgive-

The negative condition of deliverance from sins was only one side of the work of salvation. There was a new relationship to God. The Old Testament conception of a covenant as the basis of the divine relationship to Israel finds prominence in the New Testament, but it is transferred from the Israel after the flesh to the spiritual Israel and linked with the atoning work of Christ. The words of the Old Testament prophecies are applied to the Christian community. A complete understanding of the thought expressed in the writings of Paul and the epistle to the Hebrews is difficult owing to our inability to determine with any degree of certainty the precise meaning of " diatheke ".[1] There is nevertheless little doubt—whether we translate the term as will or covenant—that the Christians read into it a proof of their claim to be the spiritual heirs of Abraham.[2] Among the Jews circumcision was regarded as the outward sign of membership in Israel and the mark of the covenant (Rom. iv. 11 ff.). While Paul rejected the idea that circumcision was necessary for membership in the new Israel, there is a very significant passage in which he appears to accept baptism as the Christian counterpart of circumcision (Col. ii. 11–13). The aorists used give us every reason to think that the new circumcision should be regarded as

---

ness, although this did not imply a symbolic act in the modern sense of symbol. An illuminating passage is provided by Matthew's Gospel iii. 6 : " and they were baptized of him in the river Jordan, confessing their sins ". Does ἐξομολογούμενοι take the place of ἐξομολογησάμενοι, thus indicating how the baptismal act could come to be understood as including the act of confession and repentance ? (See A. Freiherr v. Stromberg, *Studien zur Theorie und Praxis der Taufe*, 1913, p. 55.) As against this use of the present tense we may observe John's appeal to the Pharisees and Sadducees to bring forth fruits worthy of repentance, which proves that John's demand was for definite signs of repentance before allowing baptism.

[1] *DAC*, I, pp. 261 ff.
[2] Acts iii. 25 ; Gal. iii. 15–17 ; Heb. viii. 6–10, 13 ; ix. 1 ; x. 16, 29 ; xii. 24 ; xiii. 20.

taking place at the moment when the candidate underwent baptism, but this does not mean that Paul thought of the ritual act of baptism after the manner of the rite of circumcision. Not merely does the description " not made with hands " preclude any emphasis on an outward act, but the apostle's well-known attitude to ritual makes such an interpretation impossible.

Yet this passage does encourage the belief that, like circumcision for the Jews, baptism was accepted as the outward sign of admission to a covenant. We may recall also Paul's words in Galatians iii. 29 : " If ye are Christ's, then are ye Abraham's seed, heirs according to promise." The phrase " if ye are Christ's " must be interpreted by the sense of the preceding verses, where we have : " For ye are all sons of God, through faith in Christ Jesus. For as many of you as were baptized into Christ did put on Christ " (26, 27). From this it is clear that " if ye are Christ's " is to be explained as expressing the result of the baptismal experience, and understood in this way there is a fresh meaning in the reference to Abraham's seed and those who are heirs according to the promise. The essential connection of " the promise " with the idea of the covenant is brought out in verses 15–17 (cf. Heb. vi. 17, 18). It is a matter of interest whether in John the Baptist's words to those who came to share his baptism : " Think not to say within yourselves, We have Abraham to our father ; for I say unto you, that God is able of these stones to raise up children unto Abraham " (Matth. iii. 9 ; cf. Luke iii. 8), we have an echo of a Christian doctrine concerning baptism and the new covenant. There is however a difficulty in the figure of the stones.

Leaving aside the idea of the covenant, we find a definite and unmistakable association of baptism with the thought of entrance into the Kingdom of God. In I Corinthians vi. 9, 10, Paul describes the men of sinful character who " will not inherit the Realm of God " and then adds,

" Some of you were once like that ; but you washed yourselves clean " (Moffatt). One may infer from this that
those who had undergone the Christian experience had
part in this Kingdom. We may recall also the words of
the apostle in Colossians i. 13 : " who delivered us out of
the power of darkness, and translated us into the Kingdom of the Son of His love ". A similar idea of transfer-
ence into the divine Kingdom may lie behind the expression in Romans vi. 4, which Moffatt translates : " so that
. . . we too might live and move in the new sphere of
Life ". Moreover the words in Acts x. 47 can be explained
satisfactorily only on the assumption that baptism was
regarded as the sign of entrance into a community. In
the incident it is stated plainly that the men whom it was
proposed to baptize had received already the gift of the
Spirit. This must imply also that they were not only
repentant but had experienced forgiveness, for it is incredible that the gift of the Spirit should have been given
to men in their sinful state. There is only one way of
interpreting Peter's question. It is found in the belief
that baptism was regarded as the way of reception into
the new Israel.[1]

The entry into a new sphere of life by the convert
implied also a new status. The word " regeneration "
is used of baptism only once in the New Testament
(Titus iii. 5), but there can be no doubt that the book
reveals familiarity with the thought. The significance of
the term is set forth clearly in the discussion of Jesus with
Nicodemus, and although Paul does not use the word,
it has been said that everything the idea was held to
include can be found in his teaching on baptism. It was
the conception of regeneration which gave the pagan
religions of redemption their most powerful appeal, and
it is certain that the Christians of the first century, who
lived in close touch with a pagan environment, were not
ignorant of its implications. Most probably the allusion

[1] Cf. I Cor. xii. 13 ; Acts ii. 41.

in I Peter i. 23 (cf. verse 3) should be understood as a reference to baptism under the figure of a new birth : " having been begotten again, not of corruptible seed, but of incorruptible, through the word of God, which liveth and abideth ".

The thought of identification with deity, which in the mystery teaching was closely related to regeneration, is not found in the New Testament. This is not surprising ; since the high spiritual conception of God which Christianity received from Judaism, and the sensuous magical character of the pagan idea, rendered it impossible that such a doctrine could be accepted. Yet in Paul's baptismal doctrine there was something which can be regarded as approximating to this conception, and which certainly answered the longing of man for closer union with deity. On one occasion Paul used the expression : " As many of you as were baptized into Christ did put on Christ " (Gal. iii. 27). What this involved may be gathered from the preceding words : " Ye are all sons of God through faith in Christ Jesus." In later times " adoption ", υἱοθεσία, became a synonym for baptism. The idea of adoption is found in Paul's writings, but its association with baptism is not brought out with any clearness.[1] Indeed, the conception appears at times so confused that one hesitates to claim that Paul linked it with baptism. In Romans viii. 14, 15 we have the words : " For as many as are led by the Spirit of God these are sons of God . . . ye received the Spirit of adoption whereby we cry, Abba, Father." Here adoption is stated to be an act of the Spirit, and it was the Spirit which, in common with all Christians of his day, Paul related closely to baptism. But whereas in Romans viii. 15 and Galatians adoption is treated as a status already experienced—and one may presume that baptism was regarded as the moment of its

[1] See the article " Adoption " by A. J. Maclean, *DAC*, I. The writer calls attention to the aorist form in Romans viii. 15, and compares it with a similar use in Acts xix. 2.

realization—in Romans viii. 23 it appears to belong to the future. Still more perplexing, if it were to be accepted as reflecting the Pauline thought, would be the passage from Ephesians i. 5 which affirms adoption to be an act of eternity.

In Titus iii. 7, those saved " through the washing of regeneration " are said to become " heirs to the hope of life eternal ".[1] This reference brings before us the great conception of eternal life as an experience of the baptized. The idea was very common in the mysteries and there is also plenty of evidence that the Christian Church held a similar belief, although there is no special emphasis on the thought in relation to baptism in the New Testament. In a passage in I Timothy vi. 12, which has an obvious reference to the time of baptism, Timothy is reminded of the need of laying hold " on the life eternal, whereunto thou wast called, and didst confess the good confession in the sight of many witnesses ". Paul and Barnabas declared to the unbelieving Jews in Antioch of Pisidia that they had judged themselves unworthy of eternal life (Acts xiii. 46), and Paul used the custom of baptism for the dead as an argument for the doctrine of immortality. The conception of eternal life is very prominent in the Johannine writings, and in considering the relationship of the idea to baptism it is instructive to compare verses 5 and 15 in the Gospel incident of Nicodemus (John iii.).

The idea of mystical union with Christ in baptism may be regarded as Paul's special contribution to the doctrine of this sacrament. But the most widely held conception was that which associated it with the gift of the Spirit. There were varying ideas relating to the sign of the Spirit's presence and the manner of His coming. More especially does Acts leave us with the impression that although the gift of the Spirit was regarded as most intimately associated with baptism yet there was some confusion of thought and the relationship was difficult to define.

[1] Moffatt's translation.

196

There is a sense in which it may be affirmed that the New Testament teaching on baptism reaches its climax in the Johannine writings. The Fourth Gospel is avowedly theological in aim and tone (xx. 31). In this work there is of necessity a certain recognition of the historical framework, but the author appears deliberately to eschew any great dependence on historical data and to centre his interest in the eternal truth involved. He gives, indeed, a suggestion in the book that the reference to mere earthly facts is apt to obscure the more important meaning, and we have illustrations how the earthly things (τὰ ἐπίγεια, iii. 12) make it difficult for men to comprehend the heavenly truth (τὰ ἐπουράνια).[1]

From this point of view we may regard the writer's selection of events for narration as determined by their symbolical and spiritual value. The important omissions of the Fourth Gospel, compared with the story given in the Synoptic writings, may be explained partly in this way and partly as due to a desire to avoid any undue emphasis on outward facts which might lead to an obscuring of the spiritual content. In all likelihood this attitude was the cause of the omission of the story of the institution of the Eucharist. In place of this narrative we have in chapter vi. a discussion arising from the feeding of the five thousand which brings out the contrast between the material perishable bread and the Bread of Life, and leads up to the dramatic statements of Jesus regarding His flesh and blood. While perhaps one ought not to interpret the words as applying to the Eucharist alone, there is little doubt that the language is more than merely figurative expression. It must be read against a sacramental background, for the Eucharist was a familiar experience for all

[1] We have many illustrations of misunderstandings which arise through crassly material interpretations, among them are the conversations of Jesus with Nicodemus and the woman at the well, and also the criticism of the words of Jesus by the Jews (vi. 41, 42 ; vi. 52).

the readers of the Gospel. The whole chapter is an illustration of how the author sought to lead his readers away from the outward ritual to the inward spiritual truth.

The case is similar for the sacrament of baptism. Despite the absence of any reference to the baptism of Jesus, familiarity with the incident is attested by the fact that the book records its most important detail—the descent of the Spirit on Jesus (i. 32, 33). A possible explanation of the omission is that the author may have been influenced to adopt his attitude through a docetic attempt to attach too much importance to the baptism.[1] The writer is familiar with the rite of John and actually gives fresh and valuable information concerning it which supplements the Synoptic accounts. Moreover, he alone makes mention of the work of Jesus and His disciples in baptizing. He never connects John's baptismal act with the idea of forgiveness, as do the Synoptic writers, but he reports the Baptist as calling attention to " the Lamb of God which taketh away the sin of the world ". It is almost certain that the sacrament of Christian baptism was a very common feature of the period in which the Fourth Evangelist lived and was believed to be based on Dominical sanction, yet there is no statement similar to that of Matthew affirming that Jesus commanded His disciples to baptize. Two conceptions very closely associated with baptism were forgiveness of sins and the gift of the Spirit. It is significant that in xx. 22, 23 the two are brought together, and the risen Christ, who, according to Matthew xxviii., gave His disciples the injunction to baptize, here gives them the gift of the Spirit followed by the power to forgive sins.

In view of the prevalence of baptism throughout the Church in the days when the Gospel of John is supposed to have been written, we are justified in assuming that such a verbal form as the author employs in chapter 5,

[1] J. C. Lambert, *The Sacraments in the N.T.*, p. 119.

verse 24 : " he has already passed from death across to life "—should be interpreted as a definite reference to Christian baptism, and that it was in this act that the change from death to life was experienced.[1]

The most important passage for our purpose is that contained in the third chapter, where we have the discussion of Jesus with Nicodemus, who is described as a ruler of the Jews and the teacher of Israel. In this the sacramental position of the Church at the close of the first century is set forth as a declaration of our Lord ; and the rite is shown to be essential to the full Christian life. Much controversy has arisen over the reference to water in verse 5.[2] The greatest incentive to regarding it as an interpolation is perhaps the fact that it occurs nowhere else in the discussion, and could be omitted with little detriment to the argument. Yet it is probable that the omission of any further mention is deliberate. The conversation centres in the operations of the Spirit and any prominence given to the accompanying ritual would have tended to obscure the main truth.

The words in chapter iii. 5 are a witness to the tremendous importance attached to baptism, but they do not contain the whole of the teaching of the Gospel of John concerning the first sacrament. Equally significant is the sacramental atmosphere of the book, which must be felt by those who read it rather than pointed out in many details. If in the Gospel of Mark it is possible to find a certain polarity of Gospel story with the two sacraments as its centres of interest,[3] one can be even more sure that in the Gospel of John we are in a sacramental atmosphere. Unfortunately this very condition has its dangers for those who seek to enter it. Too much scope

[1] H. J. Holtzmann, *Lehrbuch der N.T. Theologie*, II, p. 555. The quotation given is from Moffatt's translation ; cf. I John iii. 14.
[2] See note, p. 113.
[3] B. W. Bacon, *The Story of Jesus*, p. 147.

is given to the play of the imagination. Many allusions to sacramental ideas have been found in the book, although the discovery brings no real proof but depends entirely on the predilections of the exegetes. At the same time it is generally admitted that there are references. One cannot doubt that incidents like those of the blind man at the Pool of Siloam, the washing of the disciples' feet, and the piercing of the Saviour's side carry a significance beyond the mere recording of the story. They convey a real sacramental message.

To sum up the teaching of the Fourth Gospel on baptism—it may be said that the author holds an advanced sacramental position, perhaps similar to that of Ignatius, but he does seek to direct attention away from the material form to the deeper spiritual truth. It is probable that the attitude of the writer has been modified by the influence of conflicts which had arisen at the close of the first century.

There has been much discussion whether the author of the Fourth Gospel is the same as that of the First Epistle of John, but there is little doubt that the tone and attitude of both are similar. It has been suggested that the Gospel may be regarded as the background of the Epistle, for the impression received from a reading of the latter is that the writer is not seeking to impart any new knowledge to his readers but is endeavouring—to quote one scholar—" to recall to mind and to supplement what has long ago been fully given, but not adequately grasped ".[1] The readers are referred to that which had been theirs " from the beginning " (ii. 24). This phrase most naturally indicates the commencement of the Christian life, or, more precisely, the baptismal experience. In several places those whom he addresses are termed " little children ", and much of the language might be understood as a recall to their early teaching of those who were formerly little children in the Lord—" filioli, quia bap-

[1] A. E. Brooke, *The Johannine Epistles*, I.C.C., 1912, p. xxvii.

tismo neonati sunt ", to borrow the words of Augustine
in defining the use of the phrase in ii. 12.

It is interesting to trace the writer's expansion of his
phrase " from the beginning ". This is followed immediately by a promise that if this experience " from the
beginning " is retained " ye also shall abide in the Son,
and in the Father ", after which comes a reminder of the
promise of eternal life. In verse 27 the reference to " the
anointing which ye received " points to the definite occasion when the Spirit was received, that is, the day of
baptism.[1] The use of $\chi\varrho\tilde{\iota}\sigma\mu\alpha$ and the form of the verb
are both significant, as is also the succeeding phrase " his
anointing teacheth you concerning all things ", these
words being explanatory of the previous sentence " ye
need not that any one teach you ". The language recalls
the Gospel (xvi. 13) ; but it suggests also that favourite
baptismal conception of enlightenment, of which not
many years later Justin Martyr wrote " this washing
($\lambda o \upsilon \tau \varrho \grave{o} \nu$) is called enlightening ($\varphi\omega\tau\iota\sigma\mu\acute{o}\varsigma$) since those
who have learned these things are enlightened in the
mind " ($\varphi\omega\tau\iota\zeta\omega\mu\acute{\epsilon}\nu\omega\nu$ $\tau\grave{\eta}\nu$ $\delta\iota\acute{\alpha}\nu o\iota\alpha\nu$).

These statements of chapter ii. 24–7 with their close
association of such ideas as anointing with the Spirit,
union with Christ and the promise of eternal life remind
us of other references to baptism in New Testament
writings and may be accepted as witness to the doctrine
held by the writer. Perhaps the clearest evidence of the
writer's interest in baptismal doctrine is afforded by his
discussion of the distinction between " sin unto death "
and " sin not unto death ". We may be fairly certain
that he has in mind the doctrine of the sacrament of baptism.[2] Much discussion has arisen over the obscure

[1] The " anointing " should be understood most probably as
a metaphorical description of baptism and not as implying that
the act had become so early a part of the baptismal rite.

[2] " This passage is intelligible only in light of the discussion
as to the possibility of forgiveness for sin after baptism " (K.
Lake, *ERE*, II, p. 384).

passage of I John v. 8 : " For there are three who bear witness, the Spirit, and the water, and the blood ; and the three agree in one." We may ignore the interpolation concerning the Three Heavenly Witnesses which the Revisers of the Authorised Version rejected. The water and the blood must be explained by the use of the same words in verse 6, where it seems fairly obvious that the baptism and death of Jesus are indicated. While this witness of His baptism to the Messiahship of Jesus has significance the passage offers little help in ascertaining the baptismal teaching of the epistle.[1]

A consideration of the message of this epistle leads one to the conclusion that, without putting any strained interpretation on the book, it was designed for those who were near enough to the beginning of their Christian experience to be able to feel still the impression and solemn significance of their baptism. There is the difficulty created by such passages as ii. 7 and ii. 12–14 ; yet an appeal to those whose state was that of " little children " in the faith seems to be the best way of understanding the purpose of the writer. It was these " little children " who would appreciate most keenly what the passing of darkness from their lives had meant (ii. 8), and it was they who would feel the full force of the words which reminded them that their lack of love for the brethren (iv. 20)—a love which had been symbolized by the baptismal kiss of fellowship—was also a failure of their professed love of God.

A study of the New Testament teaching on baptism leaves us in no doubt that it is impossible to deduce therefrom a uniform doctrine. But this recognition of variety should not be taken as implying that the ideas of baptism at this stage were chaotic. It was rather the inevitable result of the fact that baptism was in its earliest form an

[1] The utmost that can be said of it is that probably there is a symbolical allusion to the two sacraments (W. F. Howard, *The Fourth Gospel in Recent Criticism and Interpretation*, p. 206).

experience symbolized by the performance of a rite and
not a rite which conveyed a fixed interpretation. Despite
outward appearances, its origin must be associated with
the prophetic and not the priestly side of religion. The
hypothesis which was put forward at the beginning of
this study fits most satisfactorily the facts with which it has
to deal. John the Baptist may have been the son of a
priest, as Luke would have us believe, but he belonged in
his outlook to the order of the prophets. Jesus gave all
ritual its true significance by making the inward condition
of the recipient the determining factor in its value. The
apostles accepted John's rite and introduced it into the
Church in the form of the predicted Spirit baptism, but
their teaching leaves us under no misapprehension and
proves that it was the spiritual experience, not the act,
which was of supreme importance. Perhaps no better
illustration of this can be found than in Paul's contrast of
circumcision with baptism where it is the physical nature
of the former which is placed in contrast with the spiritual
quality of the latter : " In Him you have been circumcised with no material circumcision that cuts flesh from
the body, but with Christ's own circumcision, when you
were buried with Him in your baptism and thereby
raised with Him as you believed in the power of the God
who raised Him from the dead. "[1] The tremendous
change which these words describe points to an experience whose efficacy can be explained only in one of two
ways : it was either intensely magical or it was intensely
spiritual. The first suggestion is ruled out by a consideration of the context itself, and the whole New Testament
teaching on the subject. Baptism which brought to the
candidate an experience of our Lord's resurrection was no
act ex opere operato. Faith is supreme : " as you
believed in the power of God ", διὰ τῆς πίστεως τῆς
ἐνεργείας τοῦ θεοῦ, or to quote the words of St. Chry-
sostom, to which Lightfoot calls attention in his discussion

[1] Col. ii. 11–12, Moffatt's translation.

of this passage : [1] πίστεως ὅλον ἐστίν· ἐπιστεύσατε ὅτι δύναται ὁ θεὸς ἐγεῖραι, καὶ οὕτως ἠγέρθητε. This leaves us with the spiritual interpretation as the only valid description of the rite.

In passing to the post-apostolic times we are presented with clear evidence of a development in the direction of laying a greater emphasis on the rite itself. We realize that the spiritual conception is receding into the background and that greater prominence is being given to the material form. There is a sense in which this change can be declared to be inevitable. From the beginning Christianity was under pressure of ideas from a pagan environment. In the post-apostolic period it had become a faith which no longer was predominantly Jewish in character, and the origin of Christian baptism had been obscured by the sacramentalism of the Hellenistic world which had accepted it. If Paulinism had furnished the normal interpretation of Christian thought the result would have been different ; but the spiritual experiences of Paul were not understood by the feeble inheritors of his work. Confronted by the rivalry of pagan initiatory rites they sought to defend their position by claims which blurred the true line of demarcation between Christian and pagan sacramental teaching.

Yet despite these aberrations due to human weakness the real message of the Christian doctrine of baptism was not lost, and throughout the centuries it has remained as a witness to the fact that the kingdom of this world is not the Kingdom of our Lord and of His Christ. As an initiatory act the sacrament proclaims man's spiritual birthright. It is unfortunate that the masses outside the Church have so often failed to realize the full meaning of this truth. This misunderstanding has been fostered by the much debated difference in sacramental interpretation within the Church itself. There have been saints who have stressed the ritual act and have sought and found a

[1] J. B. Lightfoot, *Colossians and Philemon*, p. 185.

full experience of fellowship with God.   But we believe that the true New Testament interpretation is that which finds that the value is not in the act but in the faith in Him through Whom the baptismal experience is achieved. It understands baptism as Paul understood other religious observances in his day : " all that is the mere shadow of what is to be ; the substance belongs to Christ." [1]

[1] Col. ii. 17, Moffatt's translation.

SELECTED BIBLIOGRAPHY

1. REFERRED TO IN THE BOOK UNDER ABBREVIATED TITLES

AP. *Apocrypha and Pseudepigrapha of the Old Testament.* R. H. Charles. 1913.

DAC. *Dictionary of the Apostolic Church.* J. Hastings. 1915–18.

DCG. *Dictionary of Christ and the Gospels.* J. Hastings. 5th impress. 1920.

EBi. *Encyclopaedia Biblica.* T. K. Cheyne and J. S. Black. 1914.

ERE. *Encyclopaedia of Religion and Ethics.* J. Hastings. 1908–26.

GJV. *Geschichte des jüdischen Volkes.* E. Schürer. 4th ed. 1901–11.

HDB. *Dictionary of the Bible.* J. Hastings. 5 vols. 1900–4.

ICC. *International Critical Commentary.*

JE. *Jewish Encyclopaedia.* 1904.

JTS. *Journal of Theological Studies.*

JLBC. *The Beginnings of Christianity.* F. J. Foakes-Jackson and K. Lake. 1920–33.

SMP. *The Mysticism of Paul the Apostle.* A. Schweitzer. Eng. trans. 1931.

Studies. *Studies in Pharisaism and the Gospels.* I. Abrahams. 1st series, 1917.

TWNT. *Theologisches Wörterbuch zum neuen Testament.* G. Kittel. Vol. I. 1933.

ZATW. *Zeitschrift für die alttestamentliche Wissenschaft.*

ZNTW. *Zeitschrift für die neutestamentliche Wissenschaft.*

2. OTHER BOOKS

Amicitiae Corolla. Edited by H. G. Wood. 1933.

S. Angus. *The Mystery Religions and Christianity.* 1925.
 The Religious Quests of the Graeco-Roman World. 1929.

B. W. Bacon. *The Story of Jesus.* 1926.

W. Bousset. *Die Religion des Judentums im neutestament-lichen (späthellenistischen,* 3te Auf.) *Zeitalter.* 2te Auf. 1906 ; 3te. Auf. hsgb. von H. Gressman. 1926.

W. Brandt. *Die jüdischen Baptismen.* 1910. *ZATW.*

F. C. Burkitt. *Christian Beginnings.* 1924.

A. Deissmann. *Die neutestamentliche Formel " in Christo Jesu ".* 1892.

E. v. Dobschütz. " Sakrament und Symbol im Urchristentum." *Theologische Studien und Kritiken.* 1905. pp. 1–40.

R. Eisler. *The Messiah Jesus and John the Baptist.* 1931.

F. J. Foakes-Jackson. *Studies in the Life of the Early Church.* 1924.

F. Gavin. *The Jewish Antecedents of the Christian Sacraments.* 1928.

M. Goguel. *Au Seuil de l'Évangile : Jean-Baptiste.* 1928.

C. Guignebert. *The Jewish World in the Time of Jesus* E.T. 1939.

J. E. Hanauer. *Baptism, Jewish and Christian.* 1906.

A. Harnack. *Dogmengeschichte.* 5te Auf. 1914.

W. Heitmüller. *Im Namen Jesu.* 1903.
Taufe und Abendmahl bei Paulus. 1903.
Taufe und Abendmahl im Urchristentum. 1911.

J. W. F. Höfling. *Das. Sakrament der Taufe.* 1846.

P. G. S. Hopwood. *The Religious Experience of the Primitive Church.* 1936.

W. F. Howard. *The Fourth Gospel in Recent Criticism and Interpretation.* 1931.

H. A. A. Kennedy. *St. Paul and the Mystery Religions.* 1913.

K. Lake. *The Earlier Epistles of St. Paul.* 1911. 2nd ed. 1914.

J. C. Lambert. *The Sacraments in the New Testament.* 1903.

J. Leipoldt. *Die urchristliche Taufe im Lichte der Religionsgeschichte.* 1928.

H. Lietzmann. *The Beginnings of the Christian Church.* E.T. 1937.

G. H. Macgregor and A. C. Purdy. *Jew and Greek : Tutors unto Christ.* 1936.

E. Meyer. *Ursprung und Anfänge des Christentums.* 1921–3.

W. Michaelis. *Taufer, Jesus, Urgemeinde.* 1928.

W. Morgan. *The Religion and Theology of Paul.* 1917.

A. D. Nock. " Early Gentile Christianity and its Hellenistic Background ", in *Essays on the Trinity and the Incarnation.* Edited by A. E. J. Rawlinson. 1928.

H. Odeberg. *The Fourth Gospel.* 1929.

R. Otto. *The Kingdom of God and the Son of Man.* E.T. 1938.

R. Reitzenstein. *Die hellenistischen Mysterienreligionen.* 3rd ed. 1927.

Die Vorgeschichte der christlichen Taufe. 1929.

F. M. Rendtorff. *Die Taufe im Urchristentum im Lichte der neueren Forschungen.* 1905.

A. Schweitzer. *Paul and his Interpreters.* E.T. 1912. Ch. vii.

A. Seeberg. *Die Taufe im neuen Testament.* 1913.

Darwell Stone. *Holy Baptism.* 1912.

A. F. v. Stromberg. *Studien zur Theorie und Praxis der Taufe.* 1913.

P. Volz. *Die Eschatologie der jüdischen Gemeinde im neutestamentlichen Zeitalter.* 2te Auf. 1934.

J. Weiss. *The History of Primitive Christianity.* E.T. 1937.

P. Wendland. *Die hellenistisch-römische Kultur in ihren Beziehungen zu Judentum und Christentum.* 1912.

N. P. Williams. " The Origins of the Sacraments ", in *Essays Catholic and Critical.* Edited by E. G. Selwyn. 1926.

H. Windisch. *Taufe und Sünde im ältesten Christentum bis auf Origenes.* 1908.

3. ARTICLES IN JOURNALS

American Journal of Theology. XXIV (1920), pp. 513–18. " Self-Baptism." B. Scott Easton.

Church Quarterly Review. CVIII (1929), pp. 86–119. " The Fourth Gospel and the Sacraments." W. H. Rigg.

The Constructive Quarterly. VII (1919), pp. 98–127. St. Paul and the Sacraments." B. Scott Easton.

Expositor. XII (1916), pp. 353–72. " The Place of the Sacraments in the Teaching of St. Paul." H. T. Andrews.

XIII (1917), pp. 143–4. " Paul not a Sacramentarian." A. T. Robertson.

pp. 193–203. " Thoughts on Infant Baptism." H. R. Mackintosh.

pp. 375–85. 'The Place of the Sacraments in the Teaching of St. Paul." W. H. Griffith Thomas.

Expositor, XIII (1917), pp. 420–31. " The Ministry of John the Baptist." A. C. Deane.

    pp. 446–53. " Baptizing with Fire." D. S. Margoliouth.

    XXI (1921), pp. 321–28. " Jesus and Baptism. The Evidence of the Fourth Gospel." E. W. Winstanley.

    XXIII (1922), pp. 53–68. " The Fourth Gospel and the Sacraments." J. Naish.

    pp. 232–8. " Jesus and Baptism." J. E. Roberts.

Expository Times. XXVII (1915–16), pp. 36 ff., 70 ff., 120 ff. " The Sacrament of Baptism in the New Testament." B. G. Collins.

    XXXVIII (1926–7), pp. 198–202. " The Baptism of Jesus." F. C. Burkitt.

The Interpreter. XIII (1917), pp. 155–60. " The Significance of the Baptism of Christ." F. J. Badcock.

Jewish Quarterly Review. July 1926, pp. 1–81. " The Levitical Impurity of the Gentile before the year 70." A. Büchler.

Journal of Theological Studies. VI (1905), pp. 481–521. " The Lord's Command to Baptize." F. H. Chase.

    XII (1911), pp. 437–45, 609–11 ; XIII (1912), pp. 411–14. Discussion of I. Abrahams and C. F. Rogers on " How did the Jews Baptize ? "

The Modern Churchman. XVI (1926), pp. 296–372.

" Semitic Sacramental Rites." A. Nairne.

" The Pagan Mysteries." P. Gardner.

" Sacraments and the Synoptic Gospels." D. White.

" Sacraments in Acts and the Pauline Epistles." J. S. Bezzant.

" Sacraments in the Fourth Gospel." J. M. Creed.

INDEX OF SUBJECTS AND WRITERS

211

INDEX OF SCRIPTURE REFERENCES

x. 5 f. 71 ; *5–42.* 110 ; *20.* 105 ; *42.* 138
xi. 2 f. 18, 25 ; *3.* 20 ; *3, 6.* 93 ; *7.* 87 ; *10.* 20 ; *12–15.* 92 ; *13.* 10, 20, 92 ; *14.* 93, 96, 97, 99, 100 ; *16–19.* 91 ; *18 ff.* 34 ; *20 ff.* 71
xii. 18–20. 104 ; *28.* 164 ; *34.* 69 ; *41.* 92
xiv. 12. 48
xv. 1–20. 98 ; *2.* 114 ; *28.* 111
xvii. 5. 104 ; *11.* 93 ; *12 f.* 25 ; *13.* 25, 96, 97
xx. 20–27. 110
xxi. 25. 110 ; *26.* 27, 87, 89 ; *31.* 94
xxiii. 15. 59 ; *33.* 69
xxv. 42. 138
xxvii. 40. 21
xxviii. 19. 116, 180, 187 ; *19, 20.* 153

Mark

i. 2, 3. 89 ; *3.* 25 ; *4.* 21, 73 ; *5.* 75, 77 ; *4–8.* 21 f. ; *7.* 23 ; *8.* 28, 62 ; *9.* 75 ; *9–11.* 17, 101 ; *10.* 75 ; *12, 13.* 36 ; *14.* 25, 38, 91 ; *44.* 122
ii. 3–12. 110 ; *5 ff.* 40 ; *7.* 110 ; *18.* 18, 35, 48, 68, 119 ; *18–22.* 98 ; *20.* 36
iii. 21, 31, 35. 18
vi. 7–11. 110 ; *14.* 21, 73 ; *16.* 25 ; *24.* 21, 73
vii. 1–23. 98 ; *2.* 111 ; *4.* 72, 74, 78, 111 ; *8.* 74
viii. 33. 18
ix. 11. 96 ; *12.* 93 ; *13.* 25, 97 ; *38 ff.* 183
x. 14, 15. 175 ; *26.* 18 ; *32.* 18 ; *38.* 18, 123 ; *38, 39.* 53, 72, 110, 142, 165

xi. 28–33. 53 ; *30.* 102, 110 ; *32.* 70, 87
xiii. 11. 105
xvi. 16. 115

Luke

i. 15. 105 ; *17.* 96 ; *35.* 105 ; *77.* 42
ii. 32. 151 ; *49.* 106
iii. 2. 27 ; *2–17.* 21 f. ; *3.* 153 ; *4.* 25 ; *7.* 62, 77, 80, 89, 103 ; *7 ff.* 28, 33, 53 ; *8.* 39, 60, 62, 193 ; *10.* 89 ; *12–14.* 89, 103 ; *15.* 84 ; *16.* 29, 31 ; *21, 22.* 17. 106 ; *22.* 104
iv. 2. 36 ; *19, 21.* 41 ; *27.* 70, 71
v. 14. 122 ; *21.* 110 ; *33.* 18, 35, 48, 68 ; *33–39.* 98
vii. 9. 111 ; *18.* 18, 48 ; *18–35.* 96 ; *19.* 20, 25, 48 ; *19, 23.* 93 ; *24.* 87 ; *27.* 20, 25 ; *29 ff.* 47 ; *30.* 80 ; *31–35.* 91 ; *33 ff.* 34 ; *47–49.* 110
ix. 1–5. 110 ; *57–62.* 125
x. 1–16. 110 ; *13 ff.* 71
xi. 1. 48 ; *20.* 164 ; *38.* 72, 73
xii. 12. 105 ; *50.* 72, 110, 123 f., 142, 165
xiii. 23–30. 71
xvi. 16. 92
xx. 4. 110 ; *6.* 27, 89
xxiv. 47. 42, 43, 115 . *47–49.* 153 . *49.* 109

John

i. 4. 151 ; *6 f.* 18 ; *8.* 20 ; *20.* 100 ; *20, 21.* 99 ; *21 ff.* 95 ; *23.* 23 ; *26 f.* 23 ; *28.* 38 ; *32.* 198 ; *33.* 23, 108, 198 ; *35.* 48, 118 ; *35–37.* 20
ii. 6. 120

Acts

Romans

Printed in Great Britain by
Butler & Tanner Ltd.,
Frome and London